DECENCY&
DEVIANCE

DECENCY& DEVIANCE

Studies in Deviant Behaviour

Jack Haas & Bill Shaffir, editors

McClelland and Stewart Limited

McClelland and Stewart Limited
The Canadian Publishers
25 Hollinger Road, Toronto

Printed and bound in Canada

CONTENTS

PREFACE

This is a book on the sociology of deviance, with emphasis on the Canadian situation. Most of the articles in this reader are based on data collected in Canada, but we have not restricted ourselves to Canadian research. We include those articles which we believe most adequately make a contribution. In addition, we have not restricted ourselves to the professional literature on deviance, but include articles and essays from *Maclean's*, *Saturday Night*, and *Playboy*. We have committed ourselves to selecting the best articles we can find or have contributed for the book. Indeed, we have added and deleted selections up to the very last minute, in the hope of making an interesting and worthwhile book.

The organizing theoretical orientation of this book is referred to as the "labelling perspective." We attempt in the book's introduction and in the introductions to the major sections to present a cogent framework of themes and concepts that we think important to the understanding of deviant behaviour, and, for that matter, "normal" behaviour. The perspective we describe and the introductions which analyze the relationship of this perspective to the articles we have selected, will aid the reader in understanding the deviance process.

In our selection, we have tried to strike a balance between offering the readers substance without boggling their minds with pseudo-sophisticated sociologese. We do this in the hope that people from all walks of life will understand that the making of deviants is an important and everyday matter, affecting all of us, whether we be considered, or consider ourselves, decent or deviant.

J.H.
B.S.

INTRODUCTION

The first problem facing the editors of a book on deviance is defining the topic. What is deviant behaviour? The answer is not as obvious as it might appear. The concept of deviant behaviour can only be understood with reference to normal behaviour. In search of a definition for deviant behaviour, we might ask the reader to define "normal" behaviour. An immediate problem arises: When defining deviant or normal behaviour, whose standards do we apply and what are their criteria? In a complex and heterogeneous society, such as ours, there exist many diverse groups with conflicting opinions about appropriate and inappropriate behaviour.

Any definition of deviant behaviour must therefore take into account the fact that individuals, groups, communities, and societies often disagree as to what constitutes deviant behaviour. In Canadian society we may find considerable consensus that delinquency, criminality, drug addiction, alcoholism, and mental illness indicate deviant behaviour. What consensus do we have that the following activities are deviant: premarital sex, oral-genital sex, masturbation, homosexuality, reading and viewing pornography, cheating in school and on income-tax returns, and gambling? Some people might argue that all of these activities are deviant; others, that none of them are. However, despite what opinions are held, some of these activities are engaged in by substantial numbers of people. While some individuals who engage in such behaviour have feelings of guilt or remorse, other practitioners have no such doubts. Some practise such activities openly; others secretly, fearing detection. In brief, there is a multitude of reactions to the same phenomena.

In preparing this book we have included examples of both behaviour that is conventionally thought of as deviant and that which might be considered deviant but is rarely defined or treated as such. Our position is that deviance is ubiquitous; that much of it is secret, denied, unobserved, and unpunished. The fact that some behaviour receives more attention and a stronger, more negative reaction suggests that in the study of deviance, emphasis should be placed on those who make definitions of deviance and those who have the power to bring deviance to the public's attention.

Our organizing framework for this book owes much to a well-developed theoretical orientation in the sociology of deviance referred to as the "labelling perspective."* This orientation gives primacy to the fact that the definition of deviant behaviour must include an understanding of the values and expectations of those who judge various actions or beliefs to be deviant. Depending on our audiences and their morals and standards, we are all potentially deviant.

There is a variety of audiences, some more fateful than others, who react to our behaviour. In a highly organized and complex society, such as ours, there are official organizations and agents created to make and enforce rules about appropriate and inappropriate behaviour. Less formal and officially sanctioned audiences are part of our everyday lives. They also make judgments about us and affect what happens to us. As a consequence of being socialized, we learn many different sets of values and expectations, some of which we believe and act out. Because we incorporate these values, we are able to approve or disapprove of our own actions. However, from the myriad of real and imagined audiences which surround us there arise conflicting sets of criteria which make the definition of any particular act as deviant a problematic issue.

The process of defining deviance, as Erikson so aptly expresses it, depends, therefore, on the particular audience involved:

> Deviance is not a property *inherent* in certain forms of behaviour; it is a property *conferred upon* these forms by the audiences which directly or indirectly witness them. Sociologically, then, the critical variable is the social *audience* . . . since it is the audience which decides whether or not any given action or actions will become a visible case of deviation (Erikson 1962, p. 308).

Despite the flux, variability, situational and temporal variables that affect the deviance-defining process, there exists within groups, communities, and societies, at any given time, some modicum of consensus about behaviour that is deviant. Group life requires some minimal consensus about right and wrong. Without these shared understandings the groups would not persist. Though these definitions are not permanent, nor necessarily unanimous, the stability of the social group requires some concurrence, explicit or implicit, about appropriate and inappropriate beliefs and behaviour.

The labelling perspective emphasizes the processes of social definition of deviance which have consequences for those designated. "The deviant is one to whom that label has successfully been applied; deviant behav-

---

* The reader who wishes to examine more fully the major tenets and contributions of this approach should see Becker 1963; Cicourel 1968; Erikson 1962, 1966; Kitsuse 1962; Lemert 1951, 1967; Matza 1969; Scheff 1966; and Schur 1965, 1971.

iour is behaviour that people so label" (Becker 1963, p. 9). Although we have emphasized the universality of the process, this book is primarily concerned with those designations that create personal and/or collective problems and identities for those defined as deviant.

The dynamic and ever changing character of the deviance-producing process, and the centrality of the group, or audience, in defining actions as deviant make those who define, create, and sustain conceptions of deviance as important foci of study as are the deviants themselves. They are the object of several sociological concerns: (a) the circumstances or conditions under which a person is set apart and labelled a deviant; (b) how the person is cast into the deviant role; (c) actions that others take toward the redefinition of the person; and (d) values, positive or negative, that others place on the facts of deviance (Rubington and Weinberg 1968, p. 3).

We must caution the reader from assuming a stereotypic and simplistic notion that individuals and groups can be readily categorized as deviant or non-deviant, if we know their actions have been so labelled. Implication of and commitment to a deviant identity are related, but distinct, processes. Lemert (1951) provides a useful distinction between initial acts of deviant behaviour, or primary deviation, in which the individual effectively denies a deviant self-image, and secondary deviation, wherein the individual reorganizes his self-conception around the deviant role. The process or sequence of interactions which lead to secondary deviation is described by Lemert as follow:

(1) primary deviation; (2) social penalties; (3) further primary deviation; (4) stronger penalties and rejections; (5) further deviation, perhaps with hostilities and resentments beginning to focus upon those doing the penalizing; (6) crisis reached in the tolerance quotient, expressed in formal action by the community stigmatizing of the deviant; (7) strengthening of the deviant conduct as a reaction to the stigmatizing and penalties; (8) ultimate acceptance of the deviant social status and efforts at adjustment on the basis of the associated role. (Lemert 1951, p. 77)

The process Lemert outlines signifies the important, intimate relationship that exists between the reactors and the individual's view of himself. The more these important "others" define, react to, and treat the individual as deviant, the more he takes this into account and uses it as a basis for his reactions. If the negative reactions continue, the individual is essentially being reconstituted by others. He is assigned a new status and is thought of in disparaging ways. Associated with the new and undesirable status of deviant are the categorical judgments and conceptions that people have of those who have been labelled deviant. If these sequences of interactions and reactions continue we can refer to the individual as taking on a deviant career.

The assigning of the deviant label, the negative reactions and sanctions, the invidious characterizations – all of these affronts and degradations threaten the individual's conception of himself. The deviant faces the dilemma of living down to others' view of him or, through a variety of mechanisms, protecting his self-image from the hostile reconstitution of others. Typically, the deviant reacts against these damaging interpretations of self and attempts, alone or with other people similarly defined, to reconstruct his identity and self-image. Individually or collectively, deviants engage in a process of normalizing or neutralizing their deviant identity (Sykes and Matza 1957, pp. 664-70; Goffman 1963).

The format of this book follows the themes we have described. We begin by asking the question "What is Deviant?" The selections make clear that the answer is always problematic and requires a close examination of the context in which definitions of deviance take place.

The next section, "Decent Citizen Deviance," contributes to this theme of the relativity of the deviance-defining process by indicating the pervasiveness of deviance in all walks of life. This section points out that some "good" people – decent and respected members of the community – do things that might be considered deviant, and probably would be if others of lower status did them or if they became a matter of public attention. Decent citizens, however, are often able to act deviantly without disruption to their lives and without the burden of stigmatization. It is emphasized that the matter of who is defined and treated as deviant is not so much determined by what people do as by the social distance between agents of control and deviating persons.

The third section, "Creating Deviance and Deviant Identities," describes the typical processes by which individuals, groups, institutions, and societies create deviance and, as a consequence, create problems for those so defined. The labelling and consequent stigmatization of deviants transform the identity of the deviant in the eyes of others, and also produce a dilemma whereby the deviant recasts his self-image.

The final section, "Differential Reactions to Labelling," describes the varied reactions of those who have been labelled deviant. These selections describe the actions – individual and/or collective – that deviants take to deflect, accommodate, or attack the invidious distinction of being thought of and treated as deviant.

References

Becker, H. S. *Outsiders: Studies in the Sociology of Deviance*. New York: The Free Press, 1963.

Cicourel, Aaron V. *The Social Organization of Juvenile Justice*. New York: Wiley, 1968.

Erikson, Kai T. *Wayward Puritans*. New York: Wiley, 1966.

_____ "Notes on the Sociology of Deviance," *Social Problems* 9 (Spring) 1962, pp. 307-14.

Goffman, Erving *Stigma*. Englewood Cliffs, New Jersey: Prentice-Hall, 1963.

Kitsuse, John I. "Societal Reactions to Deviant Behaviour: Problems of Theory and Method," *Social Problems* 9 (Winter) 1962, pp. 247-56.

Lemert, Edwin M. *Human Deviance, Social Problems, and Social Control*. Englewood Cliffs, New Jersey: Prentice-Hall, 1967.

_____. *Social Pathology*. New York: McGraw-Hill, 1951.

Matza, David. *Becoming Deviant*. Englewood Cliffs, New Jersey: Prentice-Hall, 1969.

Rubington, Earl and Weinberg, Martin S. *Deviance: The Interactionist Perspective*. New York: MacMillan, 1968.

Scheff, Thomas J. *Being Mentally Ill*. Chicago: Aldine Press, 1966.

Schur, Edwin M. *Labeling Deviant Behavior*. New York: Harper and Row, 1971.

_____. *Crimes Without Victims: Deviant Behavior and Public Policy*. Englewood Cliffs, New Jersey: Prentice-Hall, 1965.

Sykes G. and Matza D. "Techniques of Neutralization: A Theory of Delinquency," *American Sociological Review* 22 (December) 1957, pp. 664-70.

WHAT IS DEVIANT BEHAVIOUR?

A major problem in the sociology of deviance is understanding why some acts and individuals are defined as deviant, and others are not. While different kinds of answers, couched in various theoretical perspectives, have been advanced, most sociologists and other social scientists have attempted to respond to the layman's question: *why* do individuals engage in deviant behaviour? In so doing they have accepted two common-sense judgments: a) acts that break social rules are inherently different from acts that adhere to social rules, and b) the deviant act occurs as a result of some impairment of the actor's personality which inevitably compels him to commit the deviant act (Becker, 1963:3).

The emergence of the labelling perspective in deviance in the early 1960s, the ideas of which germinated in the writings of Tannenbaum (1938) and Lemert (1951), offer an alternative approach to understanding the nature of deviance. In regard to such matters as who and what are deviant, proponents of this perspective suggest a shift in focus from the traditional concern of what makes social actors engage in deviant acts to the process by which social actors come to be defined and treated as deviant (Filstead, 1972). Thus, the focus of concern shifted to others' *reactions* which were not assumed to be constant but rather were judged as problematic. Such a shift required that the social scientist revise the contention that certain forms of behaviour were *per se* deviant and were so defined by the larger society (Kitsuse, 1962). The notion that certain forms of behaviour were by their very nature deviant was categorically rejected:

> From this point of view, deviance is *not* a quality of an act a person commits, but rather a consequence of the application by others of rules and sanctions to an "offender" (Becker, 1963:9).

> Forms of behaviour *per se* do not differentiate deviants from non-deviants; it is the response of conventional and conforming members of society who identify and interpret behavior as deviant which sociologically transforms people into deviants (Kitsuse, 1962:253).

Social deviants, then, are persons who have been successfully labelled as such. Lemert's (1962) investigation of paranoia and Scott's (1970) analysis of blindness are excellent analyses of how actors are successfully conferred with a deviant label. The successful assignation of a deviant status necessarily involves others' reaction to an event and their subsequent interpretation of appropriate action. It is important to realize, however, that societal reaction to deviant behaviour is not automatic and fixed, but that, instead, the distinction between deviant and non-deviant is both ambiguous and relative. As Becker (1963) has argued, the likelihood that certain behaviour will be identified as deviant varies in accordance with the time at which it occurs, where the behaviour is enacted and what individuals observing the conduct decide to do about it.

This section emphasizes the relativity of the deviance defining process, a process that varies temporally, by community, and by the social status of the accused and accuser. While deviance is a universal phenomenon, consensus as to what constitutes deviance and who is so defined is relative and in constant flux and redefinition. In the first reading in this section, Dexter emphasizes the social nature of the labelling process by considering how people tagged as mentally deficient might, under certain circumstances, evade this invidious label and its consequences. He creates a hypothetical category, the physically graceless or "gawkies," who might in another place and time be considered deviant. The author's speculations as to the probable societal reaction to, and treatment of, "gawkies" is an effective foil for raising questions about our present attitudes and treatment of the mentally deficient. In the next paper, Clairmont shows how communities, under certain circumstances, tolerate and support behaviour ordinarily judged to be deviant. He argues that the transformation of Africville, a black community, into a deviant service centre for whites, must be understood in terms of the minority community's functional relationship to the dominant society. Rosenhan, in the last paper of this section, points out that official designations of sanity or insanity may be in error. The author and his friends, all "normal" and "sane," commit themselves to a variety of mental institutions. Despite the fact they are normal in all respects, save the feigned symptom of having heard voices, they are committed, defined, and treated as mentally ill. Their normality goes unnoticed by the staffs, but is suspected by their fellow inmates. The official diagnosis of the patient as, for example, schizophrenic, strongly influences the staff's perception and treatment of these "normals" as if they were "mentally ill." The personal experiences of the researchers is convincing testimony of the unintentioned but too often corrosive and destructive nature of psychiatric institutions.

References

Becker, H. S. *Outsiders: Studies in the Sociology of Deviance*. New York: The Free Press, 1963.

Filstead, W. F. *An Introduction To Deviance: Readings in the Process of Making Deviants.* Chicago: Markham Publishing Company, 1972.

Kituse, J. I. "Societal reactions to deviant behavior: problems of theory and method," *Social Problems*, 9 (Winter, 1962): 247-56.

Lemert, E. *Social Pathology*. New York: McGraw-Hill, 1951.

_____ "Paranoia and the dynamics of exclusion." *Sociometry* 25, 1962, pp. 2-25.

Scott, R. A. *The Making of Blind Men*. New York: Basic Books, 1970.

Tannenbaum, F. *Crime and the Community*. Boston: Ginn and Company, 1938.

1
On the Politics and Sociology of Stupidity in Our Society*

Lewis Anthony Dexter

Why are the high grade retarded – and more generally the "dull" and stupid, slow learners of all sorts – regarded as one of the great problem groups of our society? Why is a special association devoted to mental deficiency and another set up chiefly for parents of retarded children? This inquiry is part of an effort[1] to determine whether application of a prevailing point of view in the study of social problems may be useful in thinking about stupidity. Our concern here is with what Josiah Royce[2] has described as "regulative principles of research [which may] provide the larger ideas of guidance [to] empirical investigation [but which are not in themselves subject to] precise, empirical tests; which, if they happen to prove coherent and illuminating, may provide the basis for more specific hypotheses which can be empirically tested." This prevailing point of view about social problems is based on the postulate that "social problems" are not properly or adequately defined in terms of the obvious and manifest rationalizations or explanations of them by those who experience them. Thus, Myrdal,[3] for instance, demonstrated that the problem of "race," so-called, could best be understood by analysis of *conflicting* moral values; while Wirth[4] similarly was able to show that the common-sense "explanation" of the housing dilemma in the United States in the 1930s omitted the significant *social* factors; and Davis[5] that the stigma imposed upon illegitimacy in most Western societies is subtly interrelated to neglected social institutions.

Generally, problems, ideas, and institutions are taken as given and their consequences seen as self-evident facts of nature. For decades, as is well known, many people, white *and* Negro, saw the issues of "race relations" as self-evident. Similarly, for a century or more, statesmen and thinkers alike adopted a version of laissez-faire economics which made mass unemployment seem absolutely natural in an industrial society. Ultimately, within the last generation, Keynesian economics clarified the conception that the 1929 type of depression is a consequence of systems and institutions, rather than a necessary product of the nature of man in industrial society. This revision of economic

* Financial aid was provided in the preparation of this paper by the Kate Jackson Anthony Trust of Lewiston, Maine; I also am grateful to Michael Begab (U.S. Children's Bureau), Chairman of the Section of the American Association for Mental Deficiency at which the original version of the paper was read (in 1960).

thought forced those of us whose economic ideas were learned before 1935 to *un*learn a good deal. A similar effort at rethinking the problems of mental deficiency may be worth while.

An Analogy: Gawkiness as a Cardinal Social Defect

An easy way to indicate how we might reinterpret mental deficiency along these lines is by means of an analogy. Let us imagine a society in which the major target group of social discrimination is composed of the clumsy people, the so-called "gawkies." Let us assume that this is because such a society stresses grace and style in movement *as* we stress intellectual skill. Let us assume that people are taught to abhor clumsiness as many people in our society are taught to abhor stupidity. Let us suppose, to put the analogy on all fours, that there has been invented a system of writing in that society which can only be mastered by those who are graceful; and that the technology of the society is such that a high degree of grace and skill are necessary to run its machines. This will be so, *not* because of the inherent necessities of industrial processes, but because the engineers and businessmen of the society arrange to have things done in a way which takes grace as a matter of course.

The schools in such a social system would stress movement, dancing, rhythmics, etc. The psychometric institutes of the society would develop an elaborate vocabulary and even more elaborate testing mechanisms for distinguishing between *manifest* grace and inherent *potentiality* for grace of movement. A considerable literature would develop about the "pseudo-clumsy" – and in many cases, parents and schools would be so embarrassed and bothered by the presence of gawky children that they would send them to special custodial institutions where they would not be a constant reminder of parental or pedagogical inadequacy.

Naturally, under such circumstances, the marginally clumsy, permitted to remain at large in the community, would always be conscious of having two strikes already called against them. They would be liable to be institutionalized if they did anything unusual. Naturally, too, clumsy children would become social rejects and isolates, and instead of the moron jokes, beloved in this country,[6] there would probably develop pantomime jokes, directed against the gawky.

Some academic iconoclast might raise considerable doubts as to his own accuracy and academic probity by reporting that, in fact, once out of school and in those economic activities where grace of movement was not really imperative, many persons with a subnormal grace quotient (G.Q.) could earn their own living and even make an economic contribution. There would be great surprise when it was reported that some superficially or evidently clumsy persons could hunt effectively, walk competently, even play games successfully; those reporting such findings would be under considerable pressure to "explain them away." And a scholar, giving a paper with such findings at the National Association on Clumsiness, would find that the news report on her paper made her the target of many scurrilous letters, much as though she had written a Kinsey-type book.[7]

Nevertheless, under the circumstances just described, clumsiness would be regarded as pathological. And these circumstances are analogous to Western European and American attitudes toward stupidity. In making such an assertion, there is no intention to deny the reality of the social problem created by mental deficiency. In the first place, mental deficiency is a problem, or creates problems, because, in fact, there are many activities in our society which *demand* a substantial degree of verbal intelligence. As our analogy suggests, it is probable that some of these activities could be reorganized so as to lessen the problems attendant upon mental deficiency. Nevertheless, mental deficiency would still remain a problem.

But even more significantly in terms of our hypothesis, and going back to the analogy for the moment, clumsiness in our imaginary society would be a real social problem with real social consequences, for as W. I. Thomas[8] has pointed out, the way situations are defined by the society as a whole is for the people in that society the realest of realitities. The mother of twins in a society which regards twin-bearing as wicked and repulsive, cannot escape from that "reality" (nor can the mother of twins in a society which regards twin-bearing as a noble act escape from that reality either!)[9] In our imaginary society, clumsiness would be a real social problem with real consequences. It is necessary to emphasize this because it sometimes happens that if we raise questions about the one-factor strictly physiological explanation of a social problem, we are interpreted as denying its reality.

But Are the Stupid Really Discriminated Against and Despised?

Articles by Strickland[10] and by Johnson and Kirk[11] and such studies as that by Wolfenstein[12] seem to the writer to demonstrate that indeed they are. There is also the experience which may be observed over and over again of the denial of employment, of legal rights, of a fair hearing, of an opportunity, to the stupid because they are stupid (e.g., have a low IQ or show poor academic performance), *and not because the stupidity is relevant to the task, or claim, or situation.* A comment by one student of social problems[13] suggests that because discrimination against stupidity *per se* rarely comes to the attention of middle-class people, they ordinarily are quite unaware of it.

This objectively demonstrable, gross discrimination is of great significance. Within the actual life of most readers of these pages, however, the more subtle forms of "discrimination" against stupidity are more likely to be experienced; by analogy, few U.S. sociologists are likely to observe the type of crude anti-Semitism which occurred in medieval Europe or modern Germany: but most of them have seen gestures of withdrawal, listened to anti-Semitic jokes, etc. Unfortunately, no systematic, empirical study of attitudes toward cleverness or dullness is known to exist. As hypothesis, it is suggested that many influential people in our society—including particularly classroom teachers (the carriers par excellence of public, middle-class culture)—show more repugnance (e.g., frown and scold more often) toward stupidity than toward anything else except dirtiness.

A change appears to have taken place in these attitudes toward "stupidity" in recent years. At one time, the stupid were simply objects of derision or scorn: "Simple Simon met a pieman. . . . " Then, in the first two decades of the twentieth century, in the United States and Great Britain at least (concurrently with the growth of mass education), the stupid were regarded with genuine fear and apprehension; "moron" became a synonym for rapist. Both attitudes closely resemble feelings which people have displayed toward foreigners: foreigners are either ridiculous *or* frightening and wicked. But nowadays, in the era of foreign aid and Point IV programs, we believe in teaching foreigners "democracy," modern technology, and other aspects of "our way of life." And, just as some of us are willing to spend a good deal of money on foreign aid, we are willing to do so on teaching the stupid *not* to be stupid.

But the one thing we often find it hard to tolerate about the foreigner is his remaining *fundamentally* alien *and wishing to do so;* and so, similarly, many with a deep interest in mental defectives, are concerned *only* to make them less defective, less stupid. This is a truism which is so obvious as to "go without saying," but since hardly anybody says it we do not perhaps fully realize its consequences.

Clearly, the hypotheses just advanced could be better tested by study of verbal expression, of gesture, of manner, than by analyses of overt ideology. The sophisticated modern, familiar with cultural differentiation, may not *express* his distaste for foreign ways of doing things, but he will manifest in withdrawal or frown exactly the distaste he is trying to conceal, and perhaps *is* concealing from himself.[14]

The analogy with reactions to stupidity is apparent. What needs to be determined is the degree to which the stupid are aware of the slights, contempt, and scolding to which they are exposed and how far they are affected by them in developing a self-image. On the basis of available knowledge, the most plausible hypothesis seems to be that intellectual skill – skill at handling abstract conceptions – is not related to ability to perceive that one is the object to contempt; stupid people are quite as likely to suffer psychologically from contempt as are the more intelligent.[15]

The School, the Democratic Dogma, and the Glorification of Intellectual Aptitudes

But, in most societies, the stupid are not victims of the same overt discrimination as in our society. For in other societies, race, clan-membership, ancestry, religion, status, physical prowess, and probably appearance, play more of a part in determining what rewards one gets and what values one is deprived of than in ours. A stupid person with the right ancestry, for instance, can "get by" better than with us. A society which increasingly focuses on "excellence," meaning thereby intellectual excellence,[16] as does ours, tends more and more to discriminate against stupidity. This is not logically defensible. Because intellectual excellence is required of atomic physicists or for students of sociology is no reason to require intellectual prowess from people in most occupations and activities. In athletics, we admire skilled performance; but we do not[17] discriminate much more against the very incompetent athlete than against the merely mediocre performer. It seems probable that the attitude and response toward stupidity, characteristic of our society, is a function of the common school and of two interrelated ideologies which affect that school. These ideologies are: (1) the post-Renaissance emphasis upon achievement in certain lines of activity as a justification of one's righteousness, The Protestant Ethic, and (2) the radical aspect of democratic thought, identified particularly with the French Revolution and, later, with Jacksonian democracy, with its emphasis on the rights and obligations of equality.

For our present purposes, it is needless to recapitulate the extensive literature on The Protestant Ethic, and its secular variants, as expressed for instance in "Poor Richard's Almanac."[18] It is sufficient to point out that the impact of that ethic upon those affected by it was to lead them to regard stupidity as a sin, rather than as a common human failing. For, it led to failure; and failure was a manifestation of Heavenly displeasure.

The French Revolutionary notion of equality, as it spread to the American frontier and, later, to Soviet Russia, involved not only the *opportunity* to be equal, but the *obligation* to take advantage of the opportunity to be equal. Equal opportunity for education tended to result in compulsory education; and this notion of compulsory equality was embedded in the institution of the public or common school. As Sarason and Gladwin[19] make clear, the school and its demands and instruments – the intelligence test, for instance – play a substantial part in making the high-grade retarded a problem to themselves and to society. The public school has become, under the inspiration of egalitarian democracy, the central sacred institution of the community to a good many people in our society – more in the suburbs than in the slums, more among the tepidly religious than among the fundamentalists, more for some occupations and temperaments than others.

The high-grade retarded become, in such an interpretation of the school, heretics – unwilling heretics, heretics despite themselves, but heretics nevertheless. By merely being what they are, they challenge and cast doubt upon the system through which most people have gone. If, as many of them do, they succeed in earning their own living and getting along well in the community, they are even more puzzlingly unorthodox than those who accommodate to the system by cheating their way through. For the cheat, like the medieval penitent, admits the rightness of the system by his short-cut method of conforming to it. But the stupid who get along well cast doubt on the alleged secular justification of the system – that it helps people succeed. It is repulsive for some to believe that mental defectives can support themselves, no matter how much evidence is amassed to this effect, because, if so, how can we justify the discomforts and sacrifices and anguish of schooling? And when a scholar reported that some mental defectives have been more successful than non-defective counterparts, it is not surprising that she received fifty or so scurrilous attacks; she was denying the sacred.[20]

Community Reorganization and the Social Problem Status of the Retarded and Stupid: A Wholesaler's Approach to Vocational Placement of the Retarded

It follows from what has just been said that if "society" were reorganized, the social problem and the individual problems of the retarded would be much less serious. Clearly, "society" taken as a whole, is not going to be reorganized. But it may help to clarify the sociological nature of the problem of retardation by making the following conceivable assumption. Suppose that a community were to be planned on the assumption that approximately 25 per cent of its adults would be "feeble-minded." How should it differ from the towns and cities we actually know?

First: we would underline the point that there is no evidence that such a community would have any great economic difficulty. Verbal intelligence is necessary for administrators, accountants, attorneys, and engineers, for instance; but this intelligence is not necessary for all employees in manufacturing and service occupations *as such*. (It is, of course, necessary for these individuals as citizens, and as consumers, in the *modern* world, but it is precisely these peripheral necessities we wish to reconsider.)

The widespread use of secondary symbols – for purposes of legal contract and for borrowing money, even for such mechanical activities as reading road signs – is the heart of the problem of the stupid in our world. Accordingly, we would attempt to reorganize matters so that such symbols become less significnat.[21]

In such a society, we would, necessarily, abandon our present pattern of education and even compulsory literacy. We would have to change patterns of voting and limit seriously the right to borrow and to lend on credit for consumer purchases. We would probably reorganize certain activities so that they would be conducted more on a group basis and less by individuals than is currently the case; a stupid woman, as one nursemaid among several caring for children, may do an excellent job, but she lacks the adaptability and initiative to care for them *by herself*. In many old-fashioned villages, mothers, aunts, and cousins, on the whole, cared for children as a joint enterprise, so one particularly stupid woman did not necessarily cause too much trouble. Day-care centers could make it possible for our imaginary community to make similar good use of stupid, good-hearted, affectionate women to care for young children.[22]

The proposal is not purely speculative. If constitutional barriers could be overcome,[23] the organization of such a town or city (ideally on some isolatable spot, such as St. Croix or Martha's Vineyard) would permit us to find out how much of a handicap mental retardation really is (and vice versa, where verbal intelligence is essential). But even if the idea remains in the realm of speculation, it would be extremely valuable if specialists on retardation and backwardness worked out in detail what it would involve if put into practice, because this would permit us to "think out" the social meaning of these conditions in a way which has never been done.

Directions of Research

Usually, when research is started on social problems, it is based upon common-sense assumptions. The history of knowledge suggests, however, that common-sense assumptions are frequently inadequate or erroneous. Until fundamental assumptions have been critically examined, and alternatives postulated and explored, much talent and ingenuity may be wasted. The entire argument of the present paper rests on the assertion that perhaps the common-sense assumptions about mental deficiency need more criticism than they have received. One way to criticize them is to suggest alternative ways of looking at the issues as in the examples of the "gawkies" above, or the proposal in the last section for setting up a community with 25 per cent retarded adults. It is very likely that the last approach is unworkable; but this is not the major point. So long as effort is devoted to formulating alternative constructions[24] and alternative formulations of the issues, there is a better prospect of resolving our problems successfully than there is if we simply stick to elementary common-sense.[25] In other words, the greatest current need in mental deficiency research is the search for new, unorthodox perspectives; they can help to test the value and appropriateness of the prevailing doctrines.

Postscript (1963)

The comments on this article indicate that I should have elaborated the reason why I used the words "Politics" in the title. Perhaps I should have instead used the words "Political Ideology ... " In any case, I was suggesting or trying to suggest that the whole set of values focusing upon equality, tracing back or often attributed to the French Revolution, help to make the high-grade retardate a problem. In our society, particularly in the United States and in Russia, but to a considerable degree throughout "modern" nations, emphasis upon education as a means of equality is considerable. But in the case of the high-grade retardate (and probably of other "exceptional" persons) the distinction between an opportunity and a compulsion becomes seriously blurred. This is characteristic of the Rousseauian emphasis upon the general will and universal democracy, and poses one of the traditional dilemmas of political philosophy: To emphasize equality means penalizing individuals (loss of liberty) but to stress liberty (for high-grade retardates, for example) means that they ought not to be compelled to be equal. Empirically it is quite probable (the experiments by Moore, Sarason, and Blatt may modify the statement) that compulsory equality cannot in fact produce the results it is supposed to; which is to say merely that human differences in ability are real.

I stated some other aspects of the relationship of political theory to the problem of retardation elsewhere:

> Research (in this field) demands an initial philosophical willingness to consider the possibility that traditional values are contradictory and dysfunctional; without a willingness to consider the possibility that the fundamental sources of the problem of high-grade retardation lie in the conflict between the insistence upon forcing everybody to be academically equal, or at least to expose themselves to the opportunity for intellectual equality, and the facts of personality difference, we are not going to get any great benefit out of sociological research on high-grade retardation. To be sure, we will get *comfortable* studies labelled "sociological" in the periphery of the problem, or dealing with the treatment of the severely retarded, but they will be largely irrelevant to the central issue of "adaptation" to retardation.
>
> The point is: sociological research is often *by itself* of little use; to solve problems demands, also, a willingness to reconsider deeply-felt values. The reverse may also be true. The willingness to reconsider values may be useless without implementing research. Remembering Immanuel Kant's famous remark: "The percept without the concept is blind: the concept without the percept is empty," let us say: "Research-based knowledge without the flexible-mindedness to realize that it may imply reconsideration of basic values is blind: the flexible-mindedness which would permit the

reconsideration of basic values without any supporting research data is empty."

But following what has just been said, the final point is that in the seemingly practical field of mental retardation, we need to subsidize and underwrite and encourage and listen to political and social philosophy, just as much as we need to develop field research studies. The two should go together; but in view of the greater likelihood that government will finance empirical field studies, it would perhaps be appropriate for private associations and foundations to concentrate on financing the opportunity for political and social reflection – bearing in mind in both cases that the wider the perspective, the broader the framework, the greater the likelihood of valuable results.[26]

Notes

[1] Other articles in the series include: Lewis A. Dexter, "Research on Problems of Mental Subnormality," *American Journal of Mental Deficiency*, 64 (1960), 835-838. Lewis A. Dexter, "A Social Theory of Mental Deficiency," *ibid.*, 62 (1958), 920-928 (bibliog.). Lewis A. Dexter, "Towards a Sociology of Mental Deficiency," *ibid.*, 61 (1956), 10-16. Lewis A. Dexter, "The Sociology of Adjudication: Who Defines Mental Deficiency?" *American Behavioral Scientist*, 4 (October, 1960: 13-15. Lewis A. Dexter, "Heredity and Environment Re-explored," *Eugenics Quarterly*, 3 (1956), 88-93. Lewis A. Dexter, "A Note on Selective Inattention in Social Science," *Social Problems*, 6 (1958), 176-182.

[2] Josiah Royce, "Introduction" to Henri Poincaré, *The Foundations of Science*, New York: Science Press, 1921, pp. xiv-xxi.

[3] G. Myrdal, *American Dilemma*, New York: Harper's, 1944.

[4] L. Wirth, *Contemporary Social Problems*, Second Edition, Chicago: University of Chicago Press, 1940.

[5] K. Davis, "Illegitimacy and the Social Structure," *American Journal of Sociology*, 45 (1939), 215-33.

[6] M. Wolfenstein, *Children's Humor, a Psychological Analysis* (esp. the chapter on the moron joke), New York: The Free Press of Glencoe, 1954.

[7] This actually happened in the field of mental deficiency.

[8] W. I. Thomas and F. Znaniecki, *Polish Peasant in Europe and America*, New York: Knopf, 1927.

[9] W. I. Thomas, *Primitive Behavior*, New York: McGraw-Hill, 1937, 9-18. (The three articles by Dexter, cited in footnote 1, which were published in *American Journal of Mental Deficiency*, expand the relevance of Thomas' theory of "definition of the situation" to the social role of the retarded.)

[10] C. Strickland, "The Social Competence of the Feeble-Minded," *American Journal of Mental Deficiency*, 53 (1949), 504-515.

[11] G. O. Johnson and S. Kirk, "Are Mentally Handicapped Children

Segregated in The Regular Grades?" *Journal of Exceptional Children*, 17 (1950): 65-68.

[12] Wolfenstein, *op. cit.*

[13] On my article dealing with the judicial treatment of alleged mental defectives, *American Behavioral Scientist, op. cit.*

[14] Edward T. Hall, *The Silent Language*, Garden City: Doubleday, 1959, shows how unspoken Latin-American and Anglo-American reactions to the *embrazo*, for instance, and the degree of physical distance it is appropriate to maintain, color many transcultural relationships. The type of analysis which underlies Hall's entire argument could most profitably be applied to the sphere of disapproval.

[15] A particularly perceptive social scientist who has had some contact with retardates, was much surprised at this hypothesis: he had assumed that sensitiveness to slight *and* intelligence go together. No doubt, the definition or recognition of slights depends upon intelligence: a stupid person may notice the praise and not the damnation in being "damned with faint praise," but this and similar facts do not in all probability permit the stupid to live according to the widely accepted stereotype of "the happy moron . . . who does not give a damn."

[16] Many stupid would be better off if we attached more weight to *moral* excellence: "Be good, sweet child, let who will be clever."

[17] Some groups of young males may, in fact, make such a distinction; but it is not a norm for the society as a whole.

[18] M. Weber, *Protestant Ethic and the Spirit of Capitalism*, New York: Scribner's, 1948.

[19] S. Sarason and T. Gladwin, "Psychological and Biological Problems in Mental Subnormality: A Review of Research," *American Journal of Mental Deficiency*, 63 (1958), 1115-1307 (reprinted from *Genetic Psychology Monographs*, 1958, and in S. Sarason, *Psychological Problems of Mental Deficiency*, Third Edition, New York: Harper's, 1959).

[20] Fortunately for the stupid, the eccentric and the unorthodox, we are not consistent in our acceptance of the sacredness of schooling. There are reservations and ambiguities which permit loopholes for escape and accommodation. This is presumably always true of attitudes toward the sacred.

[21] See Lewis A. Dexter, *American Journal of Mental Deficiency*, 1958, *op cit.*

[22] Another example: in the nineteenth century, in a large house with several servants, one *stupid* maid might be very useful. Nowadays, most large houses have only one maid, and she is expected to write down telephone messages, cope with door-to-door salesmen; and otherwise manifest verbal intelligence.

[23] Real barriers *are* constitutional, and for the idea to become practical, a very careful study of constitutional law as it affects proposals of this sort would have to be made. This fact is extremely ironic, because in reality, as I have pointed out in my article in *American Behavioral Scientist, op. cit.* (and as the National Council for Civil Liberties has demonstrated in great detail in Great Britain), under present circumstances, retardates do not receive the benefits of due process. Nevertheless, we can be reasonably certain that a formal proposal of the sort here made would, in the present temper of the Courts and especially of the U.S. Supreme Court,

be regarded as depriving stupid citizens of essential rights (even though these citizens do not, in practice, get the opportunity to exercise many of these rights).

24 The ideas in the present paper were in part stimulated by the theory of postulation, by the theory of naming and by the transactional approach of the late Arthur F. Bentley in his *An Inquiry into Inquiries*, Boston; Beacon Press, 1954, and also *Behavior...Knowledge...Fact*, Bloomington: Principia Press, 1935. Mr. Bentley in correspondence with me indicated that he thought the present effort a satisfactory application of his approach.

25 It may very well be that there is a brain damage affecting all mental defectives, not otherwise physiologically abnormal, and that this will ultimately be ascertained. Even supposing this to be so, the brain damage is not necessarily the important point. To the medieval leper, the sociology of leprosy was often more important than its pathology; to the contemporary homosexual, employed by a Federal agency, the sociology of attitudes toward homosexuality is far more significant than the physiological basis (if any) of his deviation; and so, to the "garden variety" mental defective, attitudes toward his affliction may matter more than its genesis. It might, indeed, also be literally true that the exceptionally clumsy or awkward also suffer from some form of brain damage; but, in our imaginary society, postulated above, the social psychology affecting clumsiness would be far more vital to them than the physiology of their situation.

26 Lewis A. Dexter, "The Sociology of the Exceptional Person," *Indian Journal of Social Research*, IV: 1 (January 1963), 35-36.

2
The Development of a Deviance Service Centre

Donald Clairmont

Significance of Africville

While today (1973) the black population in metropolitan Toronto is perhaps three times as large as the entire black population of Nova Scotia, until the heavy immigration of the past fifteen years Nova Scotia was considered to be the major centre of the black experience in Canada. Black settlement in Nova Scotia goes back to the middle of the eighteenth century, about the same time that Halifax, the foundation city of English-speaking Canada, was established.[1] Of all the black communities in Nova Scotia the most well known – certainly the most notorious – was Africville. A black ghetto, it served as an illustration of how Canada handled the "race problem."[2] Africville was an *enclave* or community, technically within the city of Halifax; but in terms of city services, positive concern shown by officials, and the residents' own perception of the situation, it was "in" but not "of" the city. Tucked away in a corner of the city, relatively invisible, thought of as a "shack town," Africville was a depressed community both in physical and socioeconomic terms.

In 1964 Africville was home for some four hundred persons and eighty families. Their dwellings were located beside the open city dump; railroad tracks cut across the one unpaved dirt road leading into the area. Sewerage and lighting – the usual city amenities and public services – were conspicuously absent. The people had little education, very low incomes and were greatly underemployed. Property claims were in chaos: only a minority of families could establish legal title; others claimed squatters' rights; and still others rented. Africville, long a reproach against the City, had been designated, since the turn of the century, for future industrial and harbour development. Between 1964 and 1968 the Africville residents were relocated, dispersed throughout Halifax and Halifax County.

Africville was not dissimilar from many other black Nova Scotian communities if one considers housing conditions, education, unemployment, and residents' experience of marginality. Even its location beside the open city dump did not mark it off as unique, since several black communities were located on the fringe of white towns and villages and proximate to the latters' open dumps. What did distinguish Africville was its reputation (elaborately exaggerated) as a deviance service centre and as a community of "drifters." Over the years a deviance service centre became established in this off-the-beaten-path and poorly policed area. Africville became identified as a place to go for boot-leg booze and fun. One social scientist observed in 1948:

> Africville has also been the setting for some low level associations; due to its proximity to Halifax [sic] they are probably quite frequent. As one man expressed it, "whenever Whites want to go on a bat they come to Africville."[3]

In terms of its settlement and development, institutions and life style, and its destruction from 1964 to 1968,[4] Africville reflected pointedly the major themes of the black experience in Nova Scotia. A decade ago, this statement would have been denied, perhaps heatedly so, by Nova Scotian blacks living outside Africville. Typically, they did not manifest an identification with its residents and were quick to place some social distance between the latter and themselves. In general, non-Africville blacks shared the larger society's negative conception of the community and its residents. Several black Haligonians recalled that, when younger, they were warned by their parents not to ever go to Africville. Others were quick to point out that they were born and raised in *Halifax proper,* pointedly disassociating themselves from Africville. In the neighbouring black communities, people often echoed the views of a Hammonds Plain lady who reported that "a lot of horrible things were going on down there." A black leader from Preston referred to Africville as "a cancer in the sight of Halifax." The few black Haligonians who dissented from this view of Africville were exceptions that "prove the rule." One man, for instance, noted that he regularly visited Africville and contended that the bad image of the community was, more or less, the creation of the City to obtain the Africville lands; he acknowledged, however, that "there are very few black people in Halifax County who would look upon Africville the way that I do."

Over the past five years there has been a new apperception of Africville, especially among local black leaders.[5] As black awareness and militancy have developed, and as black organizations have sprung up attempting on behalf of blacks to redress past injustices, improve present socio-economic conditions, and effect greater control over black destiny in Nova Scotia, Africville has become central in the new black consciousness. No longer is Africville something to hide, to dissociate oneself from; rather, it is something to understand and appreciate. Africville has become a symbol of how black organization and solidarity is necessary to avoid denigration of community and seizure of black land. One prominent black leader observed that when he enters a new community to organize its residents, he urges them, "Let's pull together, or else we'll be another Africville!" In its death Africville has taken on a new meaning since blacks have come to realize that its historical development is of deep significance for understanding what has happened to black social life elsewhere in Nova

Scotia. In this context it is important to map out how Africville obtained its reputation as a deviance service centre and the relationship between its reputation and the actual community life.

Africville and Transformation

A most significant facet of Africville is its long history. The community was founded before 1850 by descendants of free refugee blacks who fled slavery in the United States during the War of 1812.[6] Government officials settled the refugee blacks on rocky and barren land just beyond the Halifax area. The first Africville settlers, attempting to escape economic hardship, purchased lots in an outlying section of Halifax fronting the Bedford Basin. The land was not significantly more arable, but the location was convenient for fishing and, most important, it was convenient for wage labour in the Halifax area. Removed from the centre of Halifax, the land also was less expensive than the usual town lot. While clearing lots and building shelters in this potentially beautiful residential area, the first residents (Africville had a population of some eighty persons in 1850) were laying concurrently the basis for church and school in the community. A congregation was formed in 1849 and, although few adults could both read and write, residents' recognition of the value of education was evident in a petition they addressed to the Legislative Assembly in 1860, requesting funds to obtain the services of a schoolmaster.[7] Although Africville was not granted school privileges until 1883, as early as 1872 a resident undertook the instruction of children in the community.

It would be a mistake to romanticize about the early beginnings of the Africville community. Economically the first and second generation residents were not particularly well-off. Jobs were scarce and the pattern of race relations channelled the blacks into the low-paying subordinate work roles of maids, waste collectors, and labourers.[8] Educationally, few of the community's children went beyond a rudimentary, formal training.[9] The housing conditions in Africville were beginning to be "sniffed at" by proper Haligonians around the turn of the century.[10] Nevertheless, Africville was clearly a viable community in this period, and the "achievement-gap" between the level of education, occupation, and housing of its residents and that of the majority of Haligonians was not particularly significant. There existed some fine houses, a few small-scale entrepreneurs, plenty of space, and a strong community *esprit de corps* rooted in an encompassing kinship system. Given also the school and the church, there was good cause for hope and optimism. Small wonder, then, that elderly relocatees reminisced happily about their childhood and youth. One woman, who had been a teen-ager in the last quarter of the nineteenth century, observed, "I didn't see no hard life all the time I was comin' up."*

In the last quarter of the nineteenth century Africville was referred to as a "community of intelligent young people, much is expected of them."[11] In 1957 a field representative of a national human rights group visited Nova Scotia's black communities; she referred to Africville as the "worst and most degenerate area I have ever seen." Discounting some overstatement in the 1957 characterization, how did such a dramatic change take place? It is important to place what happened to Africville in the broader context of the black experience in Nova Scotia. In general, blacks throughout Nova Scotia suffered a considerable decline in their well-being vis-à-vis white Nova Scotians during the same period.[12] Winks, while misleading concerning the origin of Africville, aptly refers to this process:

> From the 1870's to the 1930's the condition of the Negro Canadian declined. Nova Scotia Negroes in particular fell into a chronic state of depression, and they were soon trapped in the classic pattern of a vicious cycle: badly educated and often physically ill, they were unable to find steady employment and, unable to find employment, they were in no position to rid themselves of ignorance or disease. Slums developed around Halifax, first in the harbour-hugging self-segregated community of Africville and later in the middle of the city.[13]

Elsewhere we have developed a model of the process whereby black hopes in Nova Scotia were thwarted and deflected.[14] In terms of that path diagram, the basic factors accounting for the marginality and depression of the blacks were three:(1) Nova Scotia has been historically a racist society (slavery was eliminated on a *de facto* basis circa 1800, but "Jim Crow" practices continued and a definition-of-the-situation wherein black deprivation was tolerated and even expected as a natural course of events remained pervasive); (2) the free black immigrants to Nova Scotia were settled, for the most part, on inadequate and barren lands outside the main centres of economic growth; (3) the Nova Scotian economy had been sluggish (if not stagnant) and new economic opportunities that could have channelled the black immigrants and their descendants into the economic mainstream did not develop.[15] These basic factors, in turn, produced educational, social, and occupational opportunity structures that appear to have accounted directly for black marginality in Nova Scotian society. Essentially the same model helps us understand what happened in the

---

* All the personal quotations in this article were obtained in interviews conducted between 1968 and 1971 as part of a study of the Africville relocation co-directed by the author.

case of Africville. It makes predictable the external and internal processes that resulted in Africville becoming a "social problem."

Externally there was a process of encroachment by the various levels
of government and by private economic interests which aborted Africville's possibilities of becoming a fine residential area. Railways, city
disposal yards, and fertilizer plants were situated in and around the
Africville community.[16] One Africville resident, reacting angrily to the
mistaken but widely held idea that Africville residents were mostly
squatters, pointed to these developments and observed, "They said the
people in Africville encroached on the government; but I would say
the government encroached on the people." In general, city officials,
reacting to pressure, placed things in and around Africville which
would not be tolerated by citizens in other neighbourhoods.[17] Thus a
night-soil deposit and an infectious diseases hospital bounded Africville around the turn of the century, and an open dump was placed
within one hundred yards of Africville homes after the Second World
War. Little concern was shown for the health and wishes of the
Africville people.

While government and business encroachment was strangling the
positive prospects of Africville, the City was neglecting to provide
Africville with the usual urban amenities. Residents had to do without
paved roads (or even dust deterrent), convenient public transportation,
water, sewerage, and garbage collection. A deaf ear was turned to
numerous petitions and protests by Africville residents over the years.
The land was zoned for industrial development, and plans were periodically developed for alternative use of it. And so, as one black
leader complained, Africville people became "objects of pity, not
justice."

In discussing the plight of the poor in American society, one sociologist has observed that "they learn that in their communities they can
expect only poor and inferior service and protection from such institutions as the police, the schools, the sanitation department, and the
merchants."[18] Africville residents, in addition to being poor, were
black. The implication of this was succinctly expressed by an Africville
woman:

> The City didn't do anything to improve Africville. All the City
> did was to try and get it, and they did, in the end. They did it,
> too, because we were coloured. If they had been white people
> down there, the City would have been in there assisting them to
> build new homes, putting in water and sewers and building the
> place up.

Associated with poverty and racism is a certain "functional autonomy." Rainwater observes:

> Lower-class groups have a relatively high degree of functional

autonomy vis-à-vis the total social system because the system does little to meet their needs. In general the fewer the rewards a society offers members of a particular group in society, the more autonomous will that group prove to be with reference to the norms of the society. Only by constructing an elaborate repressive machinery, as in concentration camps, can the effect be otherwise.[19]

In the case of Africville, functional autonomy meant that the inhabitants had certain "freedoms" unavailable elsewhere in the city. Building codes could be ignored. People could loiter and make excessive noise. A deviance service centre could be established.

Along with the external process of encroachments described above went another process that "ate away" at Africville's potential from the inside. Economically the Africville situation, relative to that of the broader society, worsened as the twentieth century wore on. A 1962 report stated:

> No matter what one uses as an index of a poor employment situation (low average income, large numbers of weeks unemployed, fewness of people in the more skilled occupations), Africville Negroes rank worse than Halifax as a whole and in general worse than the mid-city Negroes.[20]

Unemployment and underemployment increased; the skilled worker and the small entrepreneur virtually vanished; and the Africville work force became increasingly typified, to use a Marxian concept, as "lumpen-proletariat." The educational gap between Africville residents and other Haligonians widened, and the pattern of stagnation and relative decline, common among blacks throughout Nova Scotia, unfolded.[21]

During the several decades preceding relocation, Africville residents became apathetic, lost confidence in the capacity of indigenous leaders to effect desirable change, and lost hope in the viability of the community itself. Pursuit of redress through standard and legitimate avenues had yielded little fruit. Their petitions and protests had been ignored, and the people had been worn down.

Church elders were unable to translate their ties with city officials and outside voluntary groups into substantial gains for the Africville residents, and thus their status in the community declined. Concomitant with this trend was the diminishing role of the church as a focal point of community consciousness and solidarity. The frequency of single-parent families in the immediate pre-relocation period was in sharp contrast to their rarity in previous generations, an indication perhaps of the decline of community viability.[22]

During the last thirty to forty years of existence, Africville lost much of its close-knit and *gemeinschaft* quality. A relatively mobile, heterogeneous population of blacks and whites began drifting into Africville, primarily because of the housing shortage elsewhere in Halifax and the exploitative freedom possible in Africville by virtue of city policy and practice towards the community and the attendant decline in morale among its inhabitants. Africville became differentiated socially in a manner characteristic of slums elsewhere in North America, accommodating temporary and permanent dwellers, as well as opportunists.[23] Emigration from Africville also appears to have had important social, structural implications. Many of the Africville residents who were relatively higher achievers, especially the young single adults and those possessing special work skills, began to move out of Africville in the several decades before relocation.[24] This emigration sapped the morale of the remaining Africville residents. Potential leaders were lost, and the community, as a collectivity, was transformed.

The two processes, external and internal, were not, of course, unrelated. To a significant degree they underlined the kind of negative exchange which, from the point of view of Africville residents, characterized their relationship with the broader society. City Council did little that was positive for Africville and, on the whole, was unresponsive to petitions and requests from its residents. Expectations of white authorities concerning blacks framed the opportunity context for the latter. Africville residents recognized their marginality and functional autonomy, adjusted their coping behaviour, and reciprocated by not biding certain city rules and directions.

Deviance Service Centre

Minority group members, if oppressed and discriminated against, often find a mode of adjusting to their situation by performing less desirable and sometimes illegitimate services for the majority group. Moreover, the minority group members often acquire under these conditions a certain functional autonomy; that is, not sharing fairly in society's wealth, they are allowed by the authorities a range of behaviour that would not be countenanced elsewhere. Such indulgence by the authorities reflects, not liberality, but a view that the minority people are "different," and a reluctance to expend adequate resources for effective control of the undesirable behaviour in these areas. This model applies aptly to Africville.

It appears that even prior to the First World War it was known in Halifax that Africville, being away from the rest of the city and public surveillance, was a place to go for boot-leg booze and conviviality. One very elderly relocatee observed that his grandfather had kept "quite a bar, well stocked with kegs of rum and the works. The sailors used to come in and buy from him. After a while he drunk himself to death. Put himself on the bum, you know." The proximity of Africville to the dockyards and general port activity facilitated the establishment of Africville as a deviance centre.

It is probematic how extensive and how accepted by Africville residents such boot-legging was prior to the First World War. The war, however, produced a major stimulant to this line of service, and many Africville residents wrote Halifax City Council advising it that the community's well-being and reputation were being destroyed, and requesting police surveillance. The petition, dated June 1919, read:

> We, the undersigned ratepayers, do hereby make application for better police protection at Africville. We base our application on the following grounds: that a police officer seldom or never visits this district, except for a warrant or subpoena; that conditions that now prevail here are worse than at any time before; that these lamentable conditions tend to turn the majority away from the good teaching which they have received; that there is now an utter disregard of the Lord's day by many residents; that there are many persons, strangers in our midst, living openly in a state of debauchery, which must corrupt the minds of youth for we are more or less subject to our environment; that there is nightly confusion, carousel and dissipation which disturb the night; that these carousels have been the centres for speading infection throughout the village; that we believe, if this disgraceful state of affairs continues there will be some grave crime or crimes committed.

> Our earnest desire is that your Honourable Body, in this period of reconstruction, carefully consider our application so that the omission of the past may be rectified and by your assistance the evil influences now at work may be greatly reduced; then shall we be better able to train the young in the way of good citizenship and place the village on a better plane of Social Welfare.[25]

The Africville petitioners were told that "the City Department has no spare men to send such a distance."[26] It was recommended that "the residents of the Africville district form their own police department and anyone they appoint to act as a policeman, the Major would swear in as a Special Constable. . . . In the event of any serious trouble being reported the Chief is always in a position to send a squad to this district."[27]

The petition, and the response of city authorities to it, signalled the end of a particular phase in Africville's history – the phase during which much was expected of community residents and of Africville's potential as a good residential district. In the wake of the First World War, residents themselves detected a qualitative change as a new temporary equilibrium emerged inside the community, and between the community and the rest of Halifax. This equilibrium was based on a greater visibility and relative tolerance of Africville's peculiar service role. As described by a former Africville resident who migrated from the community prior to the relocation:

> There were more white people than there were coloured in the community. This is a fact. They came and stayed to eat and sleep. And they had their drinks. Some who came down were very prominent people. . . . And they had their drinks. Nobody was ever robbed there or anything until the _____ and them came down there. Look, these well-to-do people came down to Africville, they had their drinks, gave us a quarter—a quarter was a lot of money in those days, you know—and moved on. And when they got drunk and tired and fell down on the road and went to sleep, they would be carried into somebody's house and looked after.

As the years went by after the First World War, Africville's deviance service centre continued to grow, but it became less tolerable. The predictions of the petitioners of 1919 were gradually confirmed as boot-legging and conviviality gave way to more raucous and hazardous activity. One black outsider observed that "just before relocation the younger ones [in the Africville community] would rob a man when he drank. But a few years back, Africville used to be a wonderful place to go on a drunk. You could flop your head anywhere." Another black non-Africville Haligonian in referring to the later developments noted that "the people of all sorts used to go to Africville. It had a kind of attraction because it was kind of weird; no law enforcement. One went out there at one's own risk. It really was the other side of the tracks." Most Africville residents who complained of these changes identified the turning point – from acceptable deviance service centre to potentially dangerous place – as being around the time of the Second World War, when Africville received a complement of migrants displaced from the mid-city area. One man observed:

> The war [the Second World War] came along and the scruff from the city, both black and white, descended on Africville to join with the Africville sinners to form an unholy alliance and turn Africville into a no man's land, while the city administration worked on unmindful.

Another relocatee also ascribed Africville's stigma to this immigration:

> The changes were that a lot of people who didn't belong there came and moved in. . . . Something happened at that time that never used to happen in Africville, because men came from the city and all around the place. They would come out there in the summer time and they would drink and get drunk. . . . After the strangers started to move in there, people [who] came out there started to get robbed and all that kind of stuff, and the blame

would go to Africville. But it was not the people from Africville doing those things. . . . It gave Africville a bad name, it gave it a real bad name. Knocking out people, robbing people; Africville never had a stigma, until they came out.

A relocatee who had moved into Africville in the early 1930s echoed this sentiment:

Things were nice in Africville until they started clearing Gerrish and Creighton Streets [during the Second World War] and people came down to Africville. Squatters, boot-leggers and thieves came down, got old boards from the dump and built a shack. Those . . . were the wildest crew you ever seen, dangerous, drinking and fighting all the time.

White authorities with some intimate contact with Africville occasionally reiterated this observation concerning the drastic decline in Africville's life style and also occasionally linked this development with in-migrants during and after the Second World War. One alderman noted that "the class that settled [in Africville] after the war sort of ruined the area."

There is no doubt that the community changed during its last decades; but it is too simplistic to explain this development in terms of the relatively small number of later in-migrants. It would be more realistic to see these people as opportunists who, having virtually nowhere else to go, gravitated toward the rapidly deteriorating Africville because of its cheap housing, relative freedom and autonomy, and because of previously established contacts with its residents. Most of the outsiders who eventually settled in Africville had been coming there for several years to drink and party. Obviously they reinforced the drift of Africville toward a more blatant and hazardous deviance service centre. The pervasiveness of the simplistic mode of change preferred by respectable Africville residents and some white authorities is understandable. Participant models usually are more preservative than explanatory. Respectable Africville residents did not wish to be painted with the same brush as those residents who participated most in "unacceptable behaviour" and, consequently, placed the responsibility for such behaviour primarily with "outsiders." City authorities could find comfort perhaps in a model that interpreted "Africville's problem" in terms of the personality of some of its residents rather than in the historical unfolding of the consequences of city policies, racism, and socio-economic depression. The facts point, however, to the 1919 petitioners' correctness of vision. The relatively small number of in-migrants in the early 1940s neither introduced the deviance service centre nor constituted its sole Africville membership.

With the aftermath of the Second World War, a final pre-relocation equilibrium phase was reached within the community and between it and the broader society. Africville became regarded by outsiders as harbouring a risky deviance service centre and being a model of social disorganization. Blacks elsewhere in Halifax advised their children not to go near the community; middle-class whites advised their friends that Africville was an interesting but dangerous place to visit. Inside the community, according to outsiders and some Africville residents, there was a decline in morale:

> The character of the area had gone down and the character of some of the people who lived there had changed too. Instead of being a good type of citizen as they were prior to the thirties, they seemed to deteriorate to an extent that they just didn't care; certain activities went on there that didn't lend anything to the area.

Yet it would be unwarranted to see the state of affairs in Africville as socially disorganized and to exaggerate the deviance that occurred. The official crime rate over the past forty years was not particularly high, and only a handful of Africville males were sentenced to prison. The director of health services in Halifax reported that, while venereal disease was not uncommon in Africville in the post-Second World War period, usually the same one or two handfuls of persons were the only residents involved. Moreover, outsiders continued, at little risk, to visit Africville for booze and conviviality right up to the time of relocation. One frequent black visitor observed: "Everybody had a good time. More boot-leggers than you could shake a stick at. Girls available for a good time." A white visitor reported that he and his colleagues at the dockyard always went on pay-day to the community for "drinking and carousing" and that "it was rough, but if you weren't looking for trouble, it wasn't bad." Other black and white outsiders frequenting the community underlined this observation, indicating that the risks were no greater than one would expect from drinking and carousing.

Africville residents themselves indicated that they experienced little sense of danger while living in the community. Even those heavily involved in these activities reported that few acts of violence occurred. Adjustment to the higher level of deviance was achieved by segmenting community groups and activities. Although the community did lose its cultural and structural homogeneity, adjustments were made, and Africville did not become an unpredictable social jungle.

To many an oldline resident with a vivid historical consciousness, a justifiable pride, and an acute sense of what his community might have been, Africville was friends and relatives, ancestral property, and rich memories. One such woman, a former leader in the community, whose husband had been a deacon and whose sons were successful migrants in Central Canada, finished her interview with the comment: "I never was ashamed of Africville. I always owned it up as my home and the people as my friends."

THE DEVELOPMENT OF A DEVIANCE SERVICE CENTRE 41

Conclusion

However adequate the above account of the development of a deviance service centre at Africville may be, the reader might well ask why did it occur among this minority group? Unlike some other minority people who could also be classified as marginal, Africville residents were very involved interactionally with the dominant white society. The residents were not physically isolated, nor did they have an autonomous economic base. Moreover, Africville residents, in terms of values and aspirations, were not voluntarily seeking alternatives to the dominant society. Struggling against racism, they sought equal rights and recognition. They played the "mainstream game"; unfortunately the game was fixed, and they were compelled to play it in a way which profoundly and negatively affected their community life.

Notes

1 For further details of black settlement in Nova Scotia, see Donald H. Clairmont and Dennis W. Magill, *Nova Scotia Blacks: An Historical and Structural Overview* (Halifax, N.S.: Institute of Public Affairs, Dalhousie University, 1970).

2 For further details, see Donald H. Clairmont and Dennis W. Magill, *Africville Relocation Report* (Halifax, N.S.: Institute of Public Affairs, Dalhousie University, 1973).

3 C. R. Brookbank, "Afro-Canadian Communities in Halifax County, Nova Scotia," M. A. thesis, University of Toronto, 1949, p. 76.

4 See Clairmont and Magill, *Africville Relocation Report*.

5 Ibid., pp. 650-85.

6 See Clairmont and Magill, *Nova Scotia Blacks*.

7 Educational discrimination against blacks in the Halifax area was such that as late as 1881, Halifax blacks petitioned the Legislative Assembly of Nova Scotia to rescind a decision of the Halifax Council of Public Instruction, to exclude coloured children from the common schools.

8 Clairmont and Magill, *Africville Relocation Report*, pp. 212-228.

9 Ibid., pp. 228-34.

10 Ibid., p. 286.

11 P. E. MacKerrow, *A Brief History of the Coloured Baptists of Nova Scotia, 1832-1895* (Halifax, N.S.: Nova Scotian Printing Company, 1895), p. 65.

12 See Clairmont and Magill, *Nova Scotia Blacks*. See also, Donald H. Clairmont et al., *A Socio-Economic Study and Recommendations: Sunnyville, Lucasville and Upper Big Tracadie, Guysborough County, Nova Scotia* (Halifax, N.S.: Institute of Public Affairs, Dalhousie University, 1965).

13 R. Winks, "The Negro in Canada," p. 465.

14 Clairmont and Magill, *Nova Scotia Blacks*.

15 Ibid.

16 Clairmont and Magill, *Africville Relocation Report*, pp. 197-210.

17 Ibid., pp. 240-50.

[18] L. Rainwater, "Poverty and Deprivation in the Crisis of the American City," Occasional Paper No. 9, mimeographed (St. Louis, Missouri: Washington University, 1966)

[19] L. Rainwater, "Crucible of Identity: the Negro Lower-Class Family," *Daedalus* 95, No. 1 (1966), pp. 172-217.

[20] *The Condition of the Negroes of Halifax City, Nova Scotia,* (Halifax, N.S.: Institute of Public Affairs, Dalhousie University, 1962).

[21] Clairmont and Magill, *Nova Scotia Blacks.*

[22] Ibid., p. 83.

[23] See J. Seeley, "The Slums: Its Nature, Use and Users," *Journal of the American Institute of Planners* 25 (1959): pp. 7-14.

[24] Clairmont and Magill, *Africville Relocation Report,* pp. 212-34.

[25] *Minutes of the Halifax City Council,* June 17, 1919.

[26] Ibid.

[27] Ibid, July 7, 1919.

3
On Being Sane in Insane Places

D. L. Rosenhan

If sanity and insanity exist, how shall we know them?

The question is neither capricious nor itself insane. However much we may be personally convinced that we can tell the normal from the abnormal, the evidence is simply not compelling. It is commonplace, for example, to read about murder trials wherein eminent psychiatrists for the defense are contradicted by equally eminent psychiatrists for the prosecution on the matter of the defendant's sanity. More generally, there are a great deal of conflicting data on the reliability, utility, and meaning of such terms as "sanity," "insanity," "mental illness," and "schizophrenia."[1] Finally, as early as 1934, Benedict suggested that normality and abnormality are not universal.[2] What is viewed as normal in one culture may be seen as quite aberrant in another. Thus, notions of normality and abnormality may not be quite as accurate as people believe they are.

To raise questions regarding normality and abnormality is in no way to question the fact that some behaviors are deviant or odd. Murder is deviant. So, too, are hallucinations. Nor does raising such questions deny the existence of the personal anguish that is often associated with "mental illness." Anxiety and depression exist. Psychological suffering exists. But normality and abnormality, sanity and insanity, and the diagnoses that flow from them may be less substantive than many believe them to be.

As its heart, the question of whether the sane can be distinguished from the insane (and whether degrees of insanity can be distinguished from each other) is a simple matter: do the salient characteristics that lead to diagnoses reside in the patients themselves or in the environments and contexts in which observers find them? From Bleuler, through Kretchmer, through the formulators of the recently revised *Diagnostic and Statistical Manual* of the American Psychiatric Association, the belief has been strong that patients present symptoms, that those symptoms can be categorized, and, implicitly, that the sane are distinguishable from the insane. More recently, however, this belief has been questioned. Based in part on theoretical and anthropological considerations, but also on philosophical, legal, and therapeutic ones, the view has grown that psychological categorization of mental illness is useless at best and downright harmful, misleading, and pejorative at worst. Psychiatric diagnoses, in this view, are in the minds of the observers and are not valid summaries of characteristics displayed by the observed.[3-5]

Gains can be made in deciding which of these is more nearly accurate by getting normal people (that is, people who do not have, and have never suffered, symptoms of serious psychiatric disorders) admitted to psychiatric hospitals and then determining whether they were discovered to be sane and, if so, how. If the sanity of such pseudo-patients were always detected, there would be prima facie evidence that a sane individual can be distinguished from the insane context in which he is found. Normality (and presumably abnormality) is distinct enough that it can be recognized wherever it occurs, for it is carried within the person. If, on the other hand, the sanity of the pseudopatients were never discovered, serious difficulties would arise for those who support traditional modes of psychiatric diagnosis. Given that the hospital staff was not incompetent, that the pseudopatient had been behaving as sanely as he had been outside of the hospital, and that it had never been previously suggested that he belonged in a psychiatric hospital, such an unlikely outcome would support the view that psychiatric diagnosis betrays little about the patient but much about the environment in which an observer finds him.

This article describes such an experiment. Eight sane people gained secret admission to 12 different hospitals.[6] Their diagnostic experiences constitute the data of the first part of this article; the remainder is devoted to a description of their experiences in psychiatric institutions. Too few psychiatrists and psychologists, even those who have worked in such hospitals, know what the experience is like. They rarely talk about it with former patients, perhaps because they distrust information coming from the previously insane. Those who have worked in psychiatric hospitals are likely to have adapted so thoroughly to the settings that they are insensitive to the impact of that experience. And while there have been occasional reports of researchers who submitted themselves to psychiatric hospitalization,[7] these researchers have commonly remained in the hospitals for short periods of time, often with the knowledge of the hospital staff. It is difficult to know the extent to which they were treated like patients or like research colleagues. Nevertheless, their reports about the inside of the psychiatric hospital have been valuable. This article extends those efforts.

Pseudopatients and Their Settings

The eight pseudopatients were a varied group. One was a psychology graduate student in his 20's. The remaining seven were older and "established." Among them were three psychologists, a pediatrician, a psychiatrist, a painter, and a housewife. Three pseudopatients were women, five were men. All of them employed pseudonyms, lest their alleged diagnoses embarrass them later. Those who were in mental health professions alleged another occupation in order to avoid the special attentions that might be accorded by staff, as a matter of courtesy or caution, to ailing colleagues.[8] With the exception of myself (I was the first pseudopatient and my presence was known to the hospital administrator and chief psychologist and, so far as I can tell, to them alone), the presence of pseudopatients and the nature of the research program was not known to the hospital staffs.[9]

The settings were similarly varied. In order to generalize the findings, admission into a variety of hospitals was sought. The 12 hospitals in the sample were located in five different states on the East and West coasts. Some were old and shabby, some were quite new. Some were research-oriented, others not. Some had good staff-patient ratios, others were quite understaffed. Only one was a strictly private hospital. All of the others were supported by state or federal funds or, in one instance, by university funds.

After calling the hospital for an appointment, the pseudopatient arrived at the admissions office complaining that he had been hearing voices. Asked what the voices said, he replied that they were often unclear, but as far as he could tell they said "empty," "hollow," and "thud." The voices were unfamiliar and were of the same sex as the pseudopatient. The choice of these symptoms was occasioned by their apparent similarity to existential symptoms. Such symptoms are alleged to arise from painful concerns about the perceived meaninglessness of one's life. It is as if the hallucinating person were saying, "My life is empty and hollow." The choice of these symptoms was also determined by the *absence* of a single report of existential psychoses in the literature.

Beyond alleging the symptoms and falsifying name, vocation, and employment, no further alterations of person, history, or circumstances were made. The significant events of the pseudopatient's life history were presented as they had actually occurred. Relationships with parents and siblings, with spouse and children, with people at work and in school, consistent with the aforementioned exceptions, were described as they were or had been. Frustrations and upsets were described along with joys and satisfactions. These facts are important to remember. If anything, they strongly biased the subsequent results in favor of detecting sanity, since none of their histories or current behaviors were seriously pathological in any way.

Immediately upon admission to the psychiatric ward, the pseudopatient ceased simulating *any* symptoms of abnormality. In some cases, there was a brief period of mild nervousness and anxiety, since none of the pseudopatients really believed that they would be admitted so easily. Indeed, their shared fear was that they would be immediately exposed as frauds and greatly embarrassed. Moreover, many of them had never visited a psychiatric ward; even those who had, nevertheless had some genuine fears about what might happen to them. Their nervousness, then, was quite appropriate to the novelty of the hospital setting, and it abated rapidly.

Apart from that short-lived nervousness, the pseudopatient behaved on the ward as he "normally" behaved. The pseudopatient spoke to patients and staff as he might ordinarily. Because there is uncommonly little to do on a psychiatric ward, he attempted to engage others in conversation. When asked by staff how he was feeling, he indicated that he was fine, that he no longer experienced symptoms. He responded to instructions from attendants, to calls for medication (which was not swallowed), and to dining-hall instructions. Beyond such activities as were available to him in the admissions ward, he spent his time writing down his observations about the ward, its patients, and the staff. Initially these notes were written "secretly," but as it soon became clear that no one much cared, they were subsequently written on standard tablets of paper in such public places as the dayroom. No secret was made of these activities.

The pseudopatient, very much as a true psychiatric patient, entered a hospital with no foreknowledge of when he would be discharged. Each was told that he would have to get out by his own devices, essentially by convincing the staff that he was sane. The psychological stresses associated with hospitalization were considerable, and all but one of the pseudopatients desired to be discharged almost immediately after being admitted. They were, therefore, motivated not only to behave sanely, but to be paragons of cooperation. That their behavior was in no way disruptive is confirmed by nursing reports, which have been obtained on most of the patients. These reports uniformly indicate that the patients were "friendly," "cooperative," and "exhibited no abnormal indications."

The Normal Are Not Detectably Sane

Despite their public "show" of sanity, the pseudopatients were never detected. Admitted, except in one case, with a diagnosis of schizophrenia,[10] each was discharged with a diagnosis of schizophrenia "in remission." The label "in remission" should in no way be dismissed as formality, for at no time during any hospitalization had any question been raised about any pseudopatient's simulation. Nor are there any indications in the hospital records that the pseudopatient's status was suspect. Rather, the evidence is strong that, once labeled schizophrenic, the pseudopatient was stuck with that label. If the pseudopatient was to be discharged, he must naturally be "in remission"; but he was not sane, nor, in the institution's view, had he ever been sane.

The uniform failure to recognize sanity cannot be attributed to the quality of the hospitals, for, although there were considerable variations among them, several are considered excellent. Nor can it be alleged that there was simply not enough time to observe the pseudopatients. Length of hospitalization ranged from 7 to 52 days, with an average of 19 days. The pseudopatients were not, in fact, carefully observed, but this failure clearly speaks more to traditions within psychiatric hospitals than to lack of opportunity.

Finally, it cannot be said that the failure to recognize the pseudopatients' sanity was due to the fact that they were not behaving sanely. While there was clearly some tension present in all of them, their daily visitors could detect no serious behavioral consequences – nor, indeed, could other patients. It was quite common for the patients to "detect" the pseudopatients' sanity. During the first three hospitalizations, when accurate counts were kept, 35 of a total of 118 patients on the admissions ward voiced their suspicions, some vigorously. "You're not crazy. You're a journalist, or a professor [referring to the continual note-taking]. You're checking up on the hospital." While most of the patients were reassured by the pseudopatient's insistence that he had been sick before he came in but was fine now, some continued to believe that the pseudopatient was sane throughout his hospitalization.[11] The fact that the patients often recognized normality when staff did not raises important questions.

Failure to detect sanity during the course of hospitalization may be due to the fact that physicians operate with a strong bias toward what statisticians call the type 2 error.[5] This is to say that physicians are more inclined to call a healthy person sick (a false positive, type 2) than a sick person healthy (a false negative, type 1). The reasons for this are not hard to find: it is clearly more dangerous to misdiagnose illness than health. Better to err on the side of caution, to suspect illness even among the healthy.

But what holds for medicine does not hold equally well for psychiatry. Medical illnesses, while unfortunate, are not commonly pejorative. Psychiatric diagnoses, on the contrary, carry with them personal, legal, and social stigmas.[12] It was therefore important to see whether the tendency toward diagnosing the sane insane could be reversed. The following experiment was arranged at a research and teaching hospital whose staff had heard these findings but doubted that such an error could occur in their hospital. The staff was informed that at some time during the following 3 months, one or more pseudopatients would attempt to be admitted into the psychiatric hospital. Each staff member was asked to rate each patient who presented himself at admissions or on the ward according to the likelihood that the patient was a pseudopatient. A 10-point scale was used, with a 1 and 2 reflecting high confidence that the patient was a pseudopatient.

Judgments were obtained on 193 patients who were admitted for psychiatric treatment. All staff who had had sustained contact with or primary responsibility for the patient – attendants, nurses, psychiatrists, physicians, and psychologists – were asked to make judgments. Forty-one patients were alleged, with high confidence, to be pseudopatients by at least one member of the staff. Twenty-three were considered suspect by at least one psychiatrist. Nineteen were suspected by one psychiatrist *and* one other staff member. Actually, no genuine pseudopatient (at least from my group) presented himself during this period.

The experiment is instructive. It indicates that the tendency to designate sane people as insane can be reversed when the stakes (in this case, prestige and diagnostic acumen) are high. But what can be said of the 19 people who were suspected of being "sane" by one psychiatrist and another staff member? Were these people truly "sane," or was it rather the case that in the course of avoiding the type 2 error the staff tended to make more errors of the first sort – calling the crazy "sane"? There is no way of knowing. But one thing is certain: any diagnostic process that lends itself so readily to massive errors of this sort cannot be a very reliable one.

The Stickiness of Psychodiagnostic Labels

Beyond the tendency to call the healthy sick – a tendency that accounts better for diagnostic behavior on admission than it does for such behavior after a lengthy period of exposure – the data speak to the massive role of labeling in psychiatric assessment. Having once been labeled schizophrenic, there is nothing the pseudopatient can do to overcome the tag. The tag profoundly colors others' perceptions of him and his behavior.

From one viewpoint, these data are hardly surprising, for it has long been known that elements are given meaning by the context in which they occur. Gestalt psychology made this point vigorously, and Asch[13] demonstrated that there are "central" personality traits (such as "warm" versus "cold") which are so powerful that they markedly color the meaning of other information in forming an impression of a given personality.[14] "Insane," "schizophrenic," "manic-depressive," and "crazy" are probably among the most powerful of such central traits. Once a person is designated abnormal, all of his other behaviors and characteristics are colored by that label. Indeed, that label is so powerful that many of the pseudopatients' normal behaviors were overlooked entirely or profoundly misinterpreted. Some examples may clarify this issue.

Earlier I indicated that there were no changes in the pseudopatient's personal history and current status beyond those of name, employment, and, where necessary, vocation. Otherwise, a veridical description of personal history and circumstances was offered. Those circumstances were not psychotic. How were they made consonant with the diagnosis of psychosis? Or were those diagnoses modified in such a way as to bring them into accord with the circumstances of the pseudopatient's life, as described by him?

As far as I can determine, diagnoses were in no way affected by the relative health of the circumstances of a pseudopatient's life. Rather, the reverse occurred: the perception of his circumstances was shaped entirely by the diagnosis. A clear example of such translation is found in the case of a pseudopatient who had had a close relationship with his mother but was rather remote from his father during his early childhood. During adolescence and beyond, however, his father became a close friend, while his relationship with his mother cooled. His present relationship with his wife was characteristically close and warm. Apart from occasional angry exchanges, friction was minimal. The children had rarely been spanked. Surely there is nothing especially pathological about such a history. Indeed, many readers may see a similar pattern in their own experiences, with no markedly deleterious consequences. Observe, however, how such a history was translated in the psychopathological context, this from the case summary prepared after the patient was discharged.

> This white 39-year-old male . . . manifests a long history of considerable ambivalence in close relationships, which begins in early childhood. A warm relationship with his mother cools during his adolescence. A distant relationship to his father is described as becoming very intense. Affective stability is absent. His attempts to control emotionality with his wife and children are punctuated by angry outbursts and, in the case of the children, spankings. And while he says that he has several good friends, one senses considerable ambivalence embedded in those relationships also. . . .

The facts of the case were unintentionally distorted by the staff to achieve consistency with a popular theory of the dynamics of a schizophrenic reaction.[15] Nothing of an ambivalent nature had been described in relations with parents, spouse, or friends. To the extent that ambivalence could be inferred, it was probably not greater than is found in all human relationships. It is true the pseudopatient's relationships with his parents changed over time, but in the ordinary context that would hardly be remarkable – indeed, it might very well be expected. Clearly, the meaning ascribed to his verbalizations (that is, ambivalence, affective instability) was determined by the diagnosis: schizophrenia. An entirely different meaning would have been ascribed if it were known that the man was "normal."

All pseudopatients took extensive notes publicly. Under ordinary circumstances, such behavior would have raised questions in the minds of observers, as, in fact, it did among patients. Indeed, it seemed so certain that the notes would elicit suspicion that elaborate precautions were taken to remove them from the ward each day. But the precautions proved needless. The closest any staff member came to questioning these notes occurred when one pseudopatient asked his physician what kind of medication he was receiving and began to write down the response. "You needn't write it," he was told gently. "If you have trouble remembering, just ask me again."

If no questions were asked of the pseudopatients, how was their writing interpreted? Nursing records for three patients indicate that the writing was seen as an aspect of their pathological behavior. "Patient engages in writing behavior" was the daily nursing comment on one of the pseudopatients who was never questioned about his writing. Given that the patient is in the hospital, he must be psychologically disturbed. And given that he is disturbed, continuous writing must be a behavioral manifestation of that disturbance, perhaps a subset of the compulsive behaviors that are sometimes correlated with schizophrenia.

One tacit characteristic of psychiatric diagnosis is that it locates the sources of aberration within the individual and only rarely within the complex of stimuli that surrounds him. Consequently, behaviors that are stimulated by the environment are commonly misattributed to the patient's disorder. For example, one kindly nurse found a pseudopatient pacing the long hospital corridors. "Nervous, Mr. X?" she asked. "No, bored," he said.

The notes kept by pseudopatients are full of patient behaviors that were misinterpreted by well-intentioned staff. Often enough, a patient would go "berserk" because he had, wittingly or unwittingly, been mistreated by, say, an attendant. A nurse coming upon the scene would rarely inquire even cursorily into the environmental stimuli of the patient's behavior. Rather, she assumed that his upset derived from his pathology, not from his present interactions with other staff members. Occasionally, the staff might assume that the patient's family (especially when they had recently visited) or other patients had stimulated the outburst. But never were the staff found to assume that one of themselves or the structure of the hospital had anything to do with a patient's behavior. One psychiatrist pointed to a group of patients who were sitting outside the cafeteria entrance half an hour before lunchtime. To a group of young residents he indicated that such behavior was characteristic of the oral-acquisitive nature of the syndrome. It seemed not to occur to him that there were very few things to anticipate in a psychiatric hospital besides eating.

A psychiatric label has a life and an influence of its own. Once the impression has been formed that the patient is schizophrenic, the expectation is that he will continue to be schizophrenic. When a sufficient amount of time has passed, during which the patient has done nothing bizarre, he is considered to be in remission and available for discharge. But the label endures beyond discharge, with the unconfirmed expectation that he will behave as a schizophrenic again. Such labels, conferred by mental health professionals, are as influential on the patient as they are on his relatives and friends, and it should not surprise anyone that the diagnosis acts on all of them, as a self-fulfilling prophecy. Eventually, the patient himself accepts the diagnosis, with all of its surplus meanings and expectations, and behaves accordingly.[5]

The inferences to be made from these matters are quite simple. Much as Zigler and Phillips have demonstrated that there is enormous overlap in the symptoms presented by patients who have been variously diagnosed,[16] so there is enormous overlap in the behaviors of the sane and the insane. The sane are not "sane" all of the time. We lose our tempers "for no good reason." We are occasionally depressed or anxious, again for no good reason. And we may find it difficult to get along with one or another person – again for no reason that we can specify. Similarly, the insane are not always insane. Indeed, it was the impression of the pseudopatients while living with them that they were sane for long periods of time – that the bizarre behaviors upon which their diagnoses were allegedly predicated constituted only a small fraction of their total behavior. If it makes no sense to label ourselves permanently depressed on the basis of an occasional depression, then it takes better evidence than is presently available to label all patients insane or schizophrenic on the basis of bizarre behaviors or cognitions. It seems more useful, as Mischel[17] has pointed out, to limit our discussions to *behaviors*, the stimuli that provoke them, and their correlates.

It is not known why powerful impressions of personality traits, such as "crazy" or "insane," arise. Conceivably, when the origins of and stimuli that give rise to a behavior are remote or unknown, or when the behavior strikes us as immutable, trait labels regarding the *behaver* arise. When, on the other hand, the origins and stimuli are known and available, discourse is limited to the behavior itself. Thus, I may hallucinate because I am sleeping, or I may hallucinate because I have ingested a peculiar drug. These are termed sleep-induced hallucinations, or dreams, and drug-induced hallucinations, respectively. But when the stimuli to my hallucinations are unknown, that is called craziness, or schizophrenia – as if that inference were somehow as illuminating as the others.

The Experience of Psychiatric Hospitalization

The term "mental illness" is of recent origin. It was coined by people who were humane in their inclinations and who wanted very much to raise the station of (and the public's sympathies toward) the psychologically disturbed from that of witches and "crazies" to one that was akin to the physically ill. And they were at least partially successful, for the treatment of the mentally ill *has* improved considerably over the years. But while treatment has improved, it is doubtful that people really regard the mentally ill in the same way that they view the physically ill. A broken leg is something one recovers from, but mental illness, allegedly endures forever.[18] A broken leg does not threaten the observer, but a crazy schizophrenic? There is by now a host of evidence that attitudes toward the mentally ill are characterized by fear, hostility, aloofness, suspicion, and dread.[19] The mentally ill are society's lepers.

That such attitudes infect the general population is perhaps not surprising, only upsetting. But that they affect the professionals – attendants, nurses, physicians, psychologists, and social workers – who treat and deal with the mentally ill is more disconcerting, both because such attitudes are self-evidently pernicious and because they are unwitting. Most mental health professionals would insist that they are sympathetic toward the mentally ill, that they are neither avoidant nor hostile. But is is more liley that an exquisite ambivalence characterizes their relations with psychiatric patients, such that their avowed impulses are only part of their entire attitude. Negative attitudes are there too and can easily be detected. Such attitudes should not surprise us. They are the natural offspring of the labels patients wear and the places in which they are found.

Consider the structure of the typical psychiatric hospital. Staff and patients are strictly segregated. Staff have their own living space, including their dining facilities, bathrooms, and assembly places. The glassed quarters that contain the professional staff, which the pseudo-patients came to call "the cage," sit out on every dayroom. The staff emerge primarily for caretaking purposes – to give medication, to conduct a therapy or group meeting, to instruct or reprimand a patient. Otherwise, staff keep to themselves, almost as if the disorder that afflicts their charges is somehow catching.

So much is patient-staff segregation the rule that, for four public hospitals in which an attempt was made to measure the degree to which staff and patients mingle, it was necessary to use "time out of the staff cage" as the operational measure. While it was not the case that all time spent out of the cage was spent mingling with patients (attendants, for example, would occasionally emerge to watch television in the dayroom), it was the only way in which one could gather reliable data on time for measuring.

The average amount of time spent by attendants outside of the cage was 11.3 percent (range, 3 to 52 percent). This figure does not represent only time spent mingling with patients, but also includes time spent on such chores as folding laundry, supervising patients while they shave, directing ward cleanup, and sending patients to off-ward activities. It was the relatively rare attendant who spent time talking with patients or playing games with them. It proved impossible to obtain a "percent mingling time" for nurses, since the amount of time they spent out of the cage was too brief. Rather, we counted instances of emergence from the cage. On the average, daytime nurses emerged from the cage 11.5 times per shift, including instances when they left the ward entirely (range, 4 to 39 times). Late afternoon and night nurses were even less available, emerging on the average 9.4 times per shift (range, 4 to 41 times). Data on early morning nurses, who arrived usually after midnight and departed at 8 a.m., are not available because patients were asleep during most of this period.

Physicians, especially psychiatrists, were even less available. They were rarely seen on the wards. Quite commonly, they would be seen only when they arrived and departed, with the remaining time being spent in their offices or in the cage. On the average, physicians emerged on the ward 6.7 times per day (range, 1 to 17 times). It proved difficult to make an accurate estimate in this regard, since physicians often maintained hours that allowed them to come and go at different times.

The hierarchical organization of the psychiatric hospital has been commented on before,[20] but the latent meaning of that kind of organization is worth noting again. Those with the most power have least to do with patients, and those with the least power are most involved with them. Recall, however, that the acquisition of role-appropriate behaviors occurs mainly through the observation of others, with the most powerful having the most influence. Consequently, it is understandable that attendants not only spend more time with patients than do any other members of the staff – that is required by their station in the hierarchy – but also, insofar as they learn from their superiors' behavior, spend as little time with patients as they can. Attendants are seen mainly in the cage, which is where the models, the action, and the power are.

I turn now to a different set of studies, these dealing with staff response to patient-initiated contact. It has long been known that the amount of time a person spends with you can be an index of your significance to him. If he initiates and maintains eye contact, there is reason to believe that he is considering your requests and needs. If he pauses to chat or actually stops and talks, there is added reason to infer that he is individuating you. In four hospitals, the pseudopatient approached the staff member with a request which took the following form: "Pardon me, Mr. [or Dr. or Mrs.] X, could you tell me when I will be eligible for grounds privileges?" (or " . . . when I will be presented at the staff meeting?" or " . . . when I am likely to be discharged?"). While the content of the question varied according to the appropriateness of the target and the pseudopatient's (apparent) current needs the form was always a courteous and relevant request for information. Care was taken never to approach a particular member of the staff more than once a day, lest the staff member become suspicious

Table 1. Self-initiated contact by pseudopatient, with psychiatrists and nurses and attendants, compared to contact with other groups.

| Contact | Psychiatric hospitals | | University campus (nonmedical) | University medical center Physicians | | |
	(1) Psychiatrists	(2) Nurses and attendants	(3) Faculty	(4) "Looking for a psychiatrist"	(5) "Looking for an internist"	(6) No additional comment
Responses						
Moves on, head averted (%)	71	88	0	0	0	0
Makes eye contact (%)	23	10	0	11	0	0
Pauses and chats (%)	2	2	0	11	0	10
Stops and talks (%)	4	0.5	100	78	100	90
Mean number of questions answered (out of 6)	*	*	6	3.8	4.8	4.5
Respondents (No.)	13	47	14	18	15	10
Attempts (No.)	185	1283	14	18	15	10

* Not applicable.

or irritated. In examining these data, remember that the behavior of the pseudopatients was neither bizarre nor disruptive. One could indeed engage in good conversation with them.

The data for these experiments are shown in Table 1, separately for physicians (column 1) and for nurses and attendants (column 2). Minor differences between these four institutions were overwhelmed by the degree to which staff avoided continuing contacts that patients had initiated. By far, their most common response consisted of either a brief response to the question, offered while they were "on the move" and with head averted, or no response at all.

The encounter frequently took the following bizarre form: (pseudopatient) "Pardon me, Dr. X. Could you tell me when I am eligible for grounds privileges?" (physician) "Good morning, Dave. How are you today?" (Moves off without waiting for a response.)

It is instructive to compare these data with data recently obtained at Stanford University. It has been alleged that large and eminent universities are characterized by faculty who are so busy that they have no time for students. For this comparison, a young lady approached individual faculty members who seemed to be walking purposefully to some meeting or teaching engagement and asked them the following six questions.

1) "Pardon me, could you direct me to Encina Hall?" (at the medical school: " ... to the Clinical Research Center?").

2) "Do you know where Fish Annex is?" (there is no Fish Annex at Stanford).

3) "Do you teach here?"

4) "How does one apply for admission to the college?" (at the medical school: " ... to the medical school?").

5) "Is it difficult to get in?"

6) "Is there financial aid?"

Without exception, as can be seen in Table 1 (column 3), all of the questions were answered. No matter how rushed they were, all respondents not only maintained eye contact, but stopped to talk. Indeed, many of the respondents went out of their way to direct or take the questioner to the office she was seeking, to try to locate "Fish Annex," or to discuss with her the possibilities of being admitted to the university.

Similar data, also shown in Table 1 (columns 4, 5, and 6), were obtained in the hospital. Here too, the young lady came prepared with six questions. After the first question, however, she remarked to 18 of her respondents (column 4), "I'm looking for a psychiatrist," and to 15 others (column 5), "I'm looking for an internist." Ten other respondents received no inserted comment (column 6). The general degree of cooperative responses is considerably higher for these university groups than it was for pseudopatients in psychiatric hospitals. Even so, differences are apparent within the medical school setting.

Once having indicated that she was looking for a psychiatrist, the degree of cooperation elicited was less than when she sought an internist.

Powerlessness and Depersonalization

Eye contact and verbal contact reflect concern and individuation; their absence, avoidance and depersonalization. The data I have presented do not do justice to the rich daily encounters that grew up around matters of depersonalization and avoidance. I have records of patients who were beaten by staff for the sin of having initiated verbal contact. During my own experience, for example, one patient was beaten in the presence of other patients for having approached an attendant and told him, "I like you." Occasionally, punishment meted out to patients for misdemeanors seemed so excessive that it could not be justified by the most radical interpretations of psychiatric canon. Nevertheless, they appeared to go unquestioned. Tempers were often short. A patient who had not heard a call for medication would be roundly excoriated, and the morning attendants would often wake patients with, "Come on, you m – f – s, out of bed!"

Neither anecdotal nor "hard" data can convey the overwhelming sense of powerlessness which invades the individual as he is continually exposed to the depersonalization of the psychiatric hospital. It hardly matters *which* psychiatric hospital – the excellent public ones and the very plush private hospital were better than the rural and shabby ones in this regard, but, again, the features that psychiatric hospitals had in common overwhelmed by far their apparent differences.

Powerlessness was evident everywhere. The patient is deprived of many of his legal rights by dint of his psychiatric commitment.[21] He is shorn of credibility by virtue of his psychiatric label. His freedom of movement is restricted. He cannot initiate contact with the staff, but may only respond to such overtures as they make. Personal privacy is minimal. Patient quarters and possessions can be entered and examined by any staff member, for whatever reason. His personal history and anguish is available to any staff member (often including the "grey lady" and "candy striper" volunteer) who chooses to read his folder, regardless of their therapeutic relationship to him. His personal hygiene and waste evacuation are often monitored. The water closets may have no doors.

At times, depersonalization reached such proportions that pseudopatients had the sense that they were invisible, or at least unworthy of account. Upon being admitted, I and other pseudopatients took the initial physical examinations in a semipublic room, where staff members went about their own business as if we were not there.

On the ward, attendants delivered verbal and occasionally serious physical abuse to patients in the presence of other observing patients, some of whom (the pseudopatients) were writing it all down. Abusive behavior, on the other hand, terminated quite abruptly when other staff members were known to be coming. Staff are credible witnesses. Patients are not.

A nurse unbuttoned her uniform to adjust her brassiere in the presence of an entire ward of viewing men. One did not have the sense that she was being seductive. Rather, she didn't notice us. A group of staff persons might point to a patient in the dayroom and discuss him animatedly, as if he were not there.

One illuminating instance of depersonalization and invisibility occurred with regard to medications. All told, the pseudopatients were administered nearly 2100 pills, including Elavil, Stelazine, Compazine, and Thorazine, to name but a few. (That such a variety of medications should have been administered to patients presenting identical symptoms is itself worthy of note.) Only two were swallowed. The rest were either pocketed or deposited in the toilet. The pseudopatients were not alone in this. Although I have no precise records on how many patients rejected their medications, the pseudopatients frequently found the medications of other patients in the toilet before they deposited their own. As long as they were cooperative, their behavior and the pseudopatients' own in this matter, as in other important matters, went unnoticed throughout.

Reactions to such depersonalization among pseudopatients were intense. Although they had come to the hospital as participant observers and were fully aware that they did not "belong," they nevertheless found themselves caught up in and fighting the process of depersonalization. Some examples: a graduate student in psychology asked his wife to bring his textbooks to the hospital so he could "catch up on his homework" – this despite the elaborate precautions taken to conceal his professional association. The same student, who had trained for quite some time to get into the hospital, and who had looked forward to the experience, "remembered" some drag races that he had wanted to see on the weekend and insisted that he be discharged by that time. Another pseudopatient attempted a romance with a nurse. Subsequently, he informed the staff that he was applying for admission to graduate school in psychology and was very likely to be admitted, since a graduate professor was one of his regular hospital visitors. The same person began to engage in psychotherapy with other patients – all of this as a way of becoming a person in an impersonal environment.

The Sources of Depersonalization

What are the origins of depersonalization? I have already mentioned two. First are attitudes held by all of us toward the mentally ill – including those who treat them – attitudes characterized by fear, distrust, and horrible expectations on the one hand, and benevolent intentions on the other. Our ambivalence leads, in this instance as in others, to avoidance.

Second, and not entirely separate, the hierarchical structure of the psychiatric hospital facilitates depersonalization. Those who are at the top have least to do with patients, and their behavior inspires the rest of the staff. Average daily contact with psychiatrists, psychologists, residents, and physicians combined ranged from 3.9 to 25.1 minutes, with an overall mean of 6.8 (six pseudopatients over a total of 129 days of hospitalization). Included in this average are time spent in the admissions interview, ward meetings in the presence of a senior staff member, group and individual psycho-therapy contacts, case presentation conferences, and discharge meetings. Clearly, patients do not spend much time in interpersonal contact with doctoral staff. And doctoral staff serve as models for nurses and attendants.

There are probably other sources. Psychiatric installations are presently in serious financial straits. Staff shortages are pervasive, staff time at a premium. Something has to give, and that something is patient contact. Yet, while financial stresses are realities, too much can be made of them. I have the impression that the psychological forces that result in depersonalization are much stronger than the fiscal ones and that the addition of more staff would not correspondingly improve patient care in this regard. The incidence of staff meetings and the enormous amount of record-keeping on patients, for example, have not been as substantially reduced as has patient contact. Priorities exist, even during hard times. Patient contact is not a significant priority in the traditional psychiatric hospital, and fiscal pressures do not account for this. Avoidance and depersonalization may.

Heavy reliance upon psychotropic medication tacitly contributes to depersonalization by convincing staff that treatment is indeed being conducted and that further patient contact may not be necessary. Even here, however, caution needs to be exercised in understanding the role of psychotropic drugs. If patients were powerful rather than powerless, if they were viewed as interesting individuals rather than diagnostic entities, if they were socially significant rather than social lepers, if their anguish truly and wholly compelled our sympathies and concerns, would we not *seek* contact with them, despite the availability of medications? Perhaps for the pleasure of it all?

The Consequences of Labeling and Depersonalization

Whenever the ratio of what is known to what needs to be known approaches zero, we tend to invent "knowledge" and assume that we understand more than we actually do. We seem unable to acknowledge that we simply don't know. The needs for diagnosis and remediation of behavioral and emotional problems are enormous. But rather than acknowledge that we are just embarking on understanding, we continue to label patients "schizophrenic," "manic-depressive," and "insane," as if in those words we had captured the essence of understanding. The facts of the matter are that we have known for a long time that diagnoses are often not useful or reliable, but we have nevertheless continued to use them. We now know that we cannot distinguish insanity from sanity. It is depressing to consider how that information will be used.

Not merely depressing, but frightening. How many people, one wonders, are sane but not recognized as such in our psychiatric institutions? How many have been needlessly stripped of their privileges of citizenship, from the right to vote and drive to that of handling their own accounts? How many have feigned insanity in order to avoid the criminal consequences of their behavior, and, conversely, how many would rather stand trial than live interminably in a psychiatric hospital – but are wrongly thought to be mentally ill? How many have been stigmatized by well-intentioned, but nevertheless erroneous, diagnoses? On the last point, recall again that a "type 2 error" in psychiatric diagnosis does not have the same consequences it does in medical diagnosis. A diagnosis of cancer that has been found to be in error is cause for celebration. But psychiatric diagnoses are rarely found to be in error. The label sticks, a mark of inadequacy forever.

Finally, how many patients might be "sane" outside the psychiatric hospital but seem insane in it – not because craziness resides in them, as it were, but because they are responding to a bizarre setting, one that may be unique to institutions which harbor nether people? Goffman[4] calls the process of socialization to such institutions "mortification" – an apt metaphor that includes the processes of depersonalization that have been described here. And while it is impossible to know whether the pseudopatients' responses to these processes are characteristic of all inmates – they were, after all, not real patients – it is difficult to believe that these processes of socialization to a psychiatric hospital provide useful attitudes or habits of response for living in the "real world."

Summary and Conclusions

It is clear that we cannot distinguish the sane from the insane in psychiatric hospitals. The hospital itself imposes a special environment in which the meanings of behavior can easily be misunderstood. The consequences to patients hospitalized in such an environment – the powerlessness, depersonalization, segregation, mortification, and self-labeling – seem undoubtedly counter-therapeutic.

I do not, even now, understand this problem well enough to perceive solutions. But two matters seem to have some promise. The first concerns the proliferation of community mental health facilities, of crisis intervention centers, of the human potential movement, and of behavior therapies that, for all of their own problems, tend to avoid psychiatric labels, to focus on specific problems and behaviors, and to retain the individual in a relatively non-pejorative environment. Clearly, to the extent that we refrain from sending the distressed to insane places, our impressions of them are less likely to be distorted. (The risk of distorted perceptions, it seems to me, is always present, since we are much more sensitive to an individual's behaviors and verbalizations than we are to the subtle contextual stimuli that often promote them. At issue here is a matter of magnitude. And, as I have shown, the magnitude of distortion is exceedingly high in the extreme context that is a psychiatric hospital.)

The second matter that might prove promising speaks to the need to increase the sensitivity of mental health workers and researchers to the *Catch 22* position of psychiatric patients. Simply reading materials in this area will be of help to some such workers and researchers. For others, directly experiencing the impact of psychiatric hospitalization will be of enormous use. Clearly, further research into the social psychology of such total institutions will both facilitate treatment and deepen understanding.

I and the other pseudopatients in the psychiatric setting had distinctly negative reactions. We do not pretend to describe the subjective experiences of true patients. Theirs may be different from ours, particularly with the passage of time and the necessary process of adaptation to one's environment. But we can and do speak to the relatively more objective indices of treatment within the hospital. It could be a mistake, and a very unfortunate one, to consider that what happened to us derived from malice or stupidity on the part of the staff. Quite the contrary, our overwhelming impression of them was of people who really cared, who were committed and who were uncommonly intelligent. Where they failed, as they sometimes did painfully, it would be more accurate to attribute those failures to the environment in which they, too, found themselves than to personal callousness. Their perceptions and behavior were controlled by the situation, rather than being motivated by a malicious disposition. In a more benign environment, one that was less attached to global diagnosis, their behaviors and judgments might have been more benign and effective.

Notes

1 P. Ash, *J. Abnorm. Soc. Psychol.* 44, 272 (1949); A. T. Beck, *Amer. J. Psychiat.* 119, 210 (1962); A. T. Boisen, *Psychiatry* 2,233 (1938); N. Kreitman, *J., Ment. Sci.* 107, 876 (1961); N. Kreitman, P. Sainsbury, J. Morrisey, J. Towers, J. Scrivener, *ibid.*, p. 837; H. O. Schmitt and C. P. Fonda, *J. Abnorm. Soc. Psychol.* 52, 262 (1956); W. Seeman, *J. Nerv. Ment. Dis.* 118, 541 (1953). For an analysis of these artifacts and summaries of the disputes, see J. Zubin, *Annu. Rev. Psychol.* 13, 373 (1967); L. Phillips and J. G. Draguns, *ibid.* 22, 447 (1971).

2 R. Benedict, *J. Gen. Psycho.* 10, 59 (1934).

3 See in this regard H. Becker, *Outsiders: Studies in the Sociology of Deviance* (Free Press, New York, 1963); B. M. Braginsky, D. D. Braginsky, K. Ring, *Methods of Madness: The Mental Hospital as a Last Resort,* (Holt, Reinehart & Winston, New York, 1969); G. M. Croccetti and P. V. Lemkau, *Amer. Sociol. Rev.* 30, 577 (1965); E. Goffman *Behavior in Public Places* (Free Press, New York, 1964); R. D. Laing, *The Divided Self: A Study of Sanity and Madness* (Quadrangle, Chicago, 1960); D. L. Phillips, *Amer. Sociol. Rev.* 28, 963 (1963); T. R. Sarbin, *Psychol. Today* 6, 18 (1972); E. Schur, *Amer. J. Sociol.* 75, 309 (1969); T. Szasz, *Law, Liberty and Psychiatry* (Macmillan, New York, 1963); *The Myth of Mental Illness: Foundations of a Theory of Mental Illness* (Hoeber Harper, New York, 1963). For a critique of some of these views, see W. R. Gove, *Amer. Sociol. Rev.* 35, 873 (1970).

4 E. Goffman, *Asylums* (Doubleday, Garden City, N.Y., 1961).

5 T. J. Scheff, *Being Mentally Ill: A Sociological Theory* (Aldine, Chicago, 1966).

6 Data from a ninth pseudopatient are not incorporated in this report because, although his sanity went undetected, he falsified aspects of his personal history, including his marital status and parental relationships. His experimental behaviors therefore were not identical to those of the other pseudopatients.

7 A. Barry, *Bellevue Is a State of Mind* (Harcourt, Brace Jovanovich, New York, 1971); I. Belknap, *Human Problems of a State Mental Hospital* (McGraw Hill, New York, 1956); W. Caudill, F. C. Redlich, H. R. Gilmore, E. B. Brody, *Amer. J. Orthopsychiat.* 22, 314 (1952); A. R. Goldman, R. H. Bohr, T. A. Steinberg, *Prof. Psychol.* 1, 427 (1970); unauthored, *Roche Report* 1 (No. 13), 8 (1971).

8 Beyond the personal difficulties that the pseudopatient is likely to experience in the hospital, there are legal and social ones that, combined, require considerable attention before entry. For example, once admitted to a psychiatric institution, it is difficult, if not impossible, to be discharged on short notice, state law to the contrary notwithstanding. I was not sensitive to these difficulties at the outset of the project, nor to the personal and situational emergencies that can arise, but later a writ of habeas corpus was prepared for each of the entering pseudopatients and an attorney was kept "on call" during every hospitalization. I am grateful to John Kaplan and Robert Bartels for legal advice and assistance in these matters.

⁹ However distasteful such concealment is, it was a necessary first step to examining these questions. Without concealment, there would have been no way to know how valid these experiences were; nor was there any way of knowing whether whatever detections occurred were a tribute to the diagnostic acumen of the staff or to the hospital's rumor network. Obviously, since my concerns are general ones that cut across individual hospitals and staffs, I have respected their anonymity and have eliminated clues that might lead to their identification.

¹⁰ Interestingly, of the 12 admissions, 11 were diagnosed as schizophrenic and one, with the identical symptomatology, as manic-depressive psychosis. This diagnosis has a more favorable prognosis, and it was given by the only private hospital in our sample. On the relations between social class and psychiatric diagnosis, see A. B. Hollingshead and F. C. Redlich, *Social Class and Mental Illness: A Community Study* (Wiley, New York, 1958).

¹¹ It is possible, of course, that patients have quite broad latitudes in diagnosis and therefore are inclined to call many people sane, even those whose behavior is patently aberrant. However, although we have no hard data on this matter, it was our distinct impression that this was not the case. In many instances, patients not only singled us out for attention, but came to imitate our behaviors and styles.

¹² J. Cumming and E. Cumming, *Community Ment. Health* 1, 135 (1965); A. Farina and K. Ring, *J. Abnorm. Psychol.* 70, 47 (1965); H. D. Freeman and O. G. Simmons, *The Mental Patient Comes Home* (Wiley, New York, 1963); W. J. Johannson, *Ment. Hygiene* 53, 218 (1969); A. S. Linsky, *Soc. Psychiat.* 5, 166 (1970).

¹³ S. F. Asch. *J. Abnorm. Soc. Psychol.* 41, 258 (1946); *Social Psychology* (Prentice-Hall, New York, 1952).

¹⁴ See also I. N. Mensh and J. Wishner, *J. Personality* 16, 183 (1947); J. Wishner, *Psychol. Rev.* 67, 96 (1960); J. S. Bruner and R. Tagiuri, in *Handbook of Social Psychology.* G. Lindzey, Ed. (Addison Wesley, Cambridge, Mass., 1954), vol. 2. pp. 634-54; J. S. Bruner, D. Shapiro, R. Tagiuri, in *Person Perception and Interpersonal Behavior.* R. Tagiuri and L. Petrullo, Eds. (Stanford Univ. Press, Stanford, Calif., 1958), pp. 277-88.

¹⁵ For an example of a similar self-fulfilling prophecy, in this instance dealing with the "central" trait of intelligence, see R. Rosenthal and L. Jacobsen, *Pygmalion in the Classroom* (Holt, Rinehart & Winston, New York, 1968).

¹⁶ E. Zigler and L. Phillips, *J. Abnorm. Soc. Psychol.* 68, 69 (1961). See also R. K. Freudenberg and J. P. Robertson, *A.M.A. Arch. Neurol. Psychiatr.* 76, 14 (1956).

¹⁷ W. Mischel, *Personality and Assessment* (Wiley, New York, 1968).

¹⁸ The most recent and unfortunate instance of this tenet is that of Senator Thomas Eagleton.

¹⁹ T. R. Sarbin and J. C. Mancuso, *J. Clin. Consult. Psychol.* 25, 159 (1970); T. R. Sarbin, *Ibid.* 31, 447 (1967); J. C. Nunnally, Jr., *Popular Conceptions of Mental Health* (Holt, Rinehart & Winston, New York, 1961).

²⁰ A. H. Stanton and M. S. Schwartz, *The Mental Hospital: A Study of*

Institutional Participation in Psychiatric Illness and Treatment (Basic, New York, 1954).

[21] D. B. Wexler and S. E. Scoville, *Ariz. Law Rev.* 13, 1 (1971).

[22] I thank W. Mischel, E. Orne, and M. S. Rosenhan for comments on an earlier draft of this manuscript.

DECENT CITIZEN DEVIANCE

Most research in deviance focuses on a restricted set of actions, usually illegal and/or exotic, as areas of interest. This emphasis distorts the actual ubiquity and universality of this phenomen, a phenomenon, that pervades all areas of social life. For many years, for example, crime statistics showed unequivocally that criminal behaviour had a high incidence in the lower class and a low incidence among the upper class (Sutherland, 1949; Shaw and McKay, 1942). The labelling perspective critique of the use of official statistics for understanding criminal and deviant behaviour has, over the last ten years, led to a reformulation of the study of official statistics as part of the study of people-processing institutions and rate production (Kitsuse and Cicourel, 1963). It has become increasingly clear that while there are differences in the officially reported incidences and types of deviant behaviour by social class, the differences are partially understood in terms of differential enforcement and the discretionary authority of control agents. Deviant status and sanctions are more likely to be applied to those who can offer the least reward for nonenforcement of the laws and who can be organizationally processed with the least amount of difficulty (Chambliss, 1969; Hills, 1971).

This section emphasizes the pervasiveness of deviance and focuses especially on its presence among so-called respectable and honest individuals – decent citizens. Recognizing this fact long ago, Sutherland wrote:

> The thesis . . . is that persons of the upper socio-economic class engage in much criminal behavior; that this criminal behavior differs from the criminal behavior of the lower socio-economic class principally in the administrative procedures which are used in dealing with the offenders. . . . (1949:9)

Persons of the upper class, noted Sutherland, "are more powerful politically and financially and escape arrest and conviction to a greater extent than persons who lack such power, even when equally guilty of crimes" (1949:8). Sutherland's focus was on occupational crime which he designated as "white collar crime" – crime committed by respectable persons of high social status in the course of their work (Sutherland, 1949; Clinard, 1968:269-79). Our focus in this section is not restricted to occupationally related crime but, instead, encompasses deviant activities by decent citizens which either go undetected or, if discovered, usually result in less severe consequences for the apprehended. For example, as research on juvenile delinquents has shown, delinquents from middle class areas do not advance as far and as rapidly in the legal process when they are apprehended as do boys from slum areas (Cohen and Short, Jr., 1961; E. Vaz, 1967).

Societal reaction to decent citizen deviance contrasts sharply with its response toward those tagged as undesirable – for example, homosexuals, drug addicts, and prostitutes. The most significant difference lies in the offenders' conception of themselves which is intimately linked to the public's view of them. Simply stated, middle and upper class offenders are not regarded and treated by the larger public as basically different kinds of people who are morally tainted, and hence they are able to maintain their self esteem as morally upright citizens.

What constitutes deviance and who the deviants of a society are, is largely a matter of power. Though decent citizens act in ways that could be defined as deviant, the overwhelming societal reaction bears down on those without the wherewithal, resources, and power to avoid or resist effectively the deviant label. Equally important, however, is the ability of the beholder to make his accusation stick.

The readings in this section describe different forms of decent citizen deviance. In our first selection, Sutherland compares the white collar criminal to the professional thief. His analysis suggests they have much in common. An important difference, however, is that white collar criminals are typically not seen, nor do they see themselves, as criminals. The professional thief, acting in much the same way as the white collar criminal, and sharing similar pecuniary motives, develops a deviant identification. Sutherland artfully points out the reasons for these discrepant reactions to questionable or illegal behaviour. Ruddy, in the next article, describes the use of marijuana by middle class respectables. His interviews reveal, still further, how some in the society are able to willfully engage in illegal behaviour but not develop an abiding deviant self-image. In the final selection, Ramsey attacks the idealization and mythology of the RCMP. He exposes the gap between their public relations image and their actual practices. His article brings into question whether these officially mandated enforcers of law and order are, in fact, beset with concerns for order and discipline to the neglect of the ideals they publicly present.

References

Chambliss, W. J. *Crime and the Legal Process*. New York: McGraw-Hill, 1969.

Clinard, M. B. *Sociology of Deviant Behavior*, New York: Holt, Rinehart and Winston, 1968.

Cohen, A. K. and Short, Jr., J. F. "Juvenile Delinquency." pp. 77-126 in Robert K. Merton and Robert A. Nisbet (eds.) *Contemporary Social Problems*. New York: Harcourt, Brace and World, 1961.

Hills, S. L. *Crime, Power, and Morality: The Criminal-Law Process in the United States*. Scranton: Chandler Publishing Company, 1971.

Kituse, J. I. and Cicourel, A. V. "A note on the use of official statistics." *Social Problems,* 11 (Fall) 1963, pp. 131-39.

Shaw, C. R. and McKay, H. D. *Juvenile Delinquency and Urban Areas*. Chicago: University of Chicago Press, 1942.

Sutherland, E. H. *White Collar Crime*. New York: Holt, Rinehart and Winston, 1949.

Vaz, E. W. (ed.) *Middle-Class Juvenile Delinquency*. New York: Harper and Row, 1967.

4
White Collar Crime Is Organized Crime

E. H. Sutherland

The preceding descriptions of the crimes of corporations have shown that these corporations have committed crimes against one or more of the following classes of victims: consumers, competitors, stockholders and other investors, inventors, and employees, as well as against the State, in the form of tax frauds and bribery of public officials. These crimes are not discreet and inadvertent violations of technical regulations. They are deliberate and have a relatively consistent unity. They are in agreement with the general characterization by Veblen:

> The ideal pecuniary man is like the ideal delinquent in his unscrupulous conversion of goods and persons to his own ends, and in a callous disregard of the feelings and wishes of others and of the remote effects of his actions, but he is unlike him in possessing a keener sense of status and in working more far-sightedly to a remoter end.[1]

The "ideal delinquent" of whom Veblen writes is best represented by the professional thief. The behavior of the "ideal pecuniary man" exemplifies the special culture of the business world, just as the "ideal delinquent" exemplifies the special culture of the underworld. The principal specifications of white collar crime in comparison with professional theft are elaborated below, with certain points of similarity and certain points of difference.

First, the criminality of the corporations, like that of professional thieves, is persistent: a large proportion of the offenders are recidivists. Among the seventy largest industrial and mercantile corporations in the United States, 97.1 percent were found to be recidivists, in the sense of having two or more adverse decisions. None of the official procedures used on businessmen for violations of law has been very effective in rehabilitating them or in deterring other businessmen from similar behavior.

Second, the illegal behavior is much more extensive than the prosecutions and complaints indicate. Samuel Insull is reported to have remarked during his trial that he could not understand why he was being prosecuted since he had only done what all other businessmen were doing. Many types of violations of law are industry-wide in the sense that practically all firms in the industry violate the law. This has been demonstrated by many investigations of the Commissioner of Corporations, the Federal Trade Commission, and various Congressional committees. Lowell B. Mason, a member of the Federal Trade Commission, stated in a recent magazine article that

> about the only thing that keeps a businessman off the wrong end of a federal indictment or administrative agency's complaint is the fact that, under the hit-or-miss methods of prosecution, the law of averages hasn't made him a party to a suit.[2]

President Truman, accepting the conclusion that violations of law are industry-wide, announced in his 1947 message to Congress that thereafter the Federal Trade Commission would attack violations of law through trade conferences aimed at the modification of industry-wide practices. The trade conference policy was used also at the end of the decade of the twenties and was based on the same belief in the industry-wide character of many violations of law.

Third, the businessman who violates the laws which are designed to regulate business does not customarily lose status among his business associates. Although a few members of the industry may think less of him, others admire him. Leonor F. Loree, chairman of the board of the Kansas City Southern Railway, in accordance with instructions of the board, appointed a committee in 1924 to purchase shares of the Missouri, Kansas, and Texas Railway. Prior to this, according to reports of official complaints, and with knowledge of the plan of his corporation, he purchased 14,000 shares of Missouri, Kansas, and Texas for his own account and sold them later at a profit of $144,707. According to this complaint, he thus made a profit at the expense of the corporation which he directed. After he had been requested to explain his action and when a suit was about to be filed, he turned over his private profits to the corporation. After this whole transaction had received considerable public attention, he was elected president of the New York Chamber of Commerce.[3] Important executives of three of the seventy large corporations, according to court decisions, illegally appropriated funds of the corporations to their personal use and continued activities thereafter with no loss of status in the corporation or in the industry; it is reported that one of these executives made his reputation as a shrewd manipulator by this illegal transaction. Such illustrations could be multiplied. They amount to the general principle that a violation of the legal code is not necessarily a violation of the business code. Prestige is lost by violation of the business code but not by violation of the legal code except when the legal code coincides with the business code.

Fourth, businessmen customarily feel and express contempt for law, for government, and for governmental personnel. In this respect, also, they are similar to professional thieves, who feel contempt for law, policemen, prosecutors, and judges. Businessmen customarily regard governmental personnel as politicians and bureaucrats, and the persons authorized to investigate business practices as "snoopers." Businessmen characteristically believe that the least government is the best, at least until they desire special favors from government, and in many cases regard the enactment of a law rather than the violation of the law as the crime. The businessman's contempt for law, like that of the professional thief, grows out of the fact that the law impedes his behavior.

White collar crimes are not only deliberate; they are also organized. Organization for crime may be either formal or informal. Formal organizations for crimes of corporations is found most generally in restraint of trade, as illustrated by gentlemen's agreements, pools, many of the practices of the trade associations, patent agreements, and cartels. Formal organization is found, also, in conferences of representatives of corporations on plans regarding labor relations. Businessmen are organized formally, also, for the control of legislation, selection of administrators, and restriction of appropriations for the enforcement of laws which may affect themselves. While some associations have developed codes of business ethics and many of the representatives have been sincere in their formulations of such codes, the actual effect of the codes is no different from what it would have been if the codes had been written by men with their tongues in their cheeks.

Even when no formal organization has been developed, businessmen have consensus. While businessmen, with consensus, give lip service to free competition and free enterprise, they also, with consensus, practice restraint of trade. They are not willing to bear the burdens of competition or to permit the economic system to regulate itself in accordance with the laws of supply and demand. Rather, they adopt the method of industrial planning and manipulation. While corporations seldom insist that their advertising agencies engage in misrepresentation, they reward the agencies which increase sales with little regard for the honesty of the methods employed. They have a high degree of consensus regarding the patent laws, as restrictions which are to be disregarded or circumvented. The chief executive of a corporation stated confidentially:

> If an inventor has secured a patent on a process in our field and his invention has merit, we buy the patent if he is willing to sell it for a reasonable sum. But if he tries to hold us up, we refuse to buy it and "invent around" his patent, which we can easily do after we have examined the plans which he has submitted to us for sale.

The points of similarity between white collar crime and professional theft, which have been elaborated above, are not a complete statement of the relationship between these two types of crimes. These types of crimes have differences as well as similarities. The most significant point of differences lies in the offenders' conceptions of themselves and in the public's conceptions of them. The professional thief conceives of himself as a criminal and is so conceived by the general public. Since he has no desire for a favorable public reputation, he takes pride in his reputation as a criminal. The businessman, on the other hand, thinks of himself as a respectable citizen and, by and large, is so regarded by the general public. The federal court, when imposing sentences on the members of the firm of H. O. Stone and Company in Chicago in 1933 for fraudulent transactions in real estate, said to the defendants:

> You are men of affairs, of experience, of refinement, and of culture, and of excellent reputation and standing in the business and social world.

This characterization of these white collar criminals would apply to practically all of the men in the corporations which have been described as violating the law. Even when they violate the law, they do not conceive of themselves as criminals.

This problem of the conception of one's self as a criminal is an important problem in criminology. Some criminologists have insisted that the white collar criminal is not "really" a criminal since he does not conceive of himself as a criminal. This contention is based on two fallacies in logic: taking the part for the whole and taking the word for the essence. The general problem of criminology is the explanation of criminal behavior. Some persons who engage in criminal behavior conceive of themselves as criminals and some do not. The origin and development of the conception of one's self as a criminal is an important problem, but it is not the entire problem in criminology. Those criminologists who limit their attention to this problem and draw conclusions regarding all criminal behavior are taking the part for the whole.

One's conception of himself as a criminal is based on a general characterization and on an ideal type. Many persons who have been convicted of crime and committed to prison say: "But I am not really a criminal." Such persons do not identify themselves with the ideal type. Two of the principal factors in the identification of self with the ideal type are official treatment as a criminal and intimate personal association with those who conceive of themselves as criminals. The white collar criminal does not conceive of himself as a criminal because he is not dealt with under the same official procedures as other criminals and because, owing to his class status, he does not engage in intimate personal association with those who define themselves as criminals.

Furthermore, many variations are found in the identification of self with others even among those who conceive of themselves as conforming to the ideal type of criminal. The word "criminal" may be applied to all of them, but the essence varies. Prisoners generally constitute a hierarchy, with high-class confidence men at the top at present and with the "yegg" or safe-breaker at the top in earlier generations. One of these classes of prisoners does not identify itself with the others and those in the upper criminal class look with contempt upon the lower criminal class. They place in the lower class of criminals the small number of businessmen who have been convicted and committed to prisons for offenses such as embezzlement. The failure of a white collar criminal to identify himself with other criminals is in part an instance of the general process of stratification and segregation among criminals.

While white collar criminals do not conceive of themselves as conforming to the stereotype of "criminal," they do customarily think of themselves as "law violators." This is another aspect of a different word for the same essence. In their confidential relations businessmen speak with pride of their violations of law, and regard the enactment of the law rather than its violation as reprehensible. Their consciences do not ordinarily bother them, for they have the support of their associates in the violation of the law. The feeling of shame at their business practices is probably found more frequently among younger businessmen who have not thoroughly assimilated the culture and rationalizations of business. A radio announcer made the following statement of his disgust at the practices in which he participated:

> In order to hold my job I am compelled to make the most extravagant statements regarding cigarettes, tooth paste, toilet paper, cathartics, and other products which are on the program. I have to consider the various appeals and use the one which will produce the largest sales. After I have made my statement, I sometimes feel like going outside and vomiting or getting drunk, because I am so disgusted with the statements I am compelled to make.

The public, likewise, does not think of the businessman as a criminal; that is, the businessman does not fit the stereotype of "criminal." This public conception is sometimes referred to as "status." Although the concept of "status" is not entirely clear, it seems to be based principally upon power. The local community studies at least show that a person may have a high status while being recognized as a profligate. Similarly, the businessman often has a low rating as to honesty, even while he has a high social status. Trade unions, farmers, and organized consumers are certainly not convinced that businessmen have high standards of honesty or that they are meticulous in the observance of law.

In order that businessmen may maintain their status and their conception of themselves as not-criminal, public adherence to the law is necessary. The policy of corporations is general public adherence to the law and secret defections from the law. In this respect the businessman is quite different from the professional thief. In professional theft the fact of crime is a matter of direct observation, and the important problem for the thief is to conceal his identity in order to avoid punishment, but not in order to maintain his status in the general public. In white collar crime, on the other hand, the important problem for the criminal is to conceal the fact of crime, since the identity of the firm which violates the law is generally known.

Secrecy regarding the fact of white collar crime is facilitated by the intricacy of the activities and the wide scattering of effects in time and place. Consumers who are dissatisfied with the price of a commodity may not become aware for many years that the price is being manipulated by agreements among producers. Customers who read the claims presented on a label or in an advertisement may not become aware until scientific tests are made that the claims are fraudulent.

Businessmen develop rationalizations which conceal the fact of crime. Fraud in advertising is rationalized by the statement that every one puffs his wares. Businessmen fight whenever words that tend to break down this rationalization are used. A food manufacturer who had been ordered to desist from misrepresentations in his advertisements employed a chemist as adviser on proposed advertising copy. This chemist described his experience with the firm as follows:

> In my first associations with this firm I referred either by word of mouth or by letter to proposed statements as "dishonest" or "fraudulent." The manager of my department objected to my use of these words and ordered me to phrase my objections in other words, such as "it would not be good policy to make such claims," or "this claim does not agree with the scientific findings."

With the same objective of protecting their reputations the business organizations have worked for a different implementation of the laws which apply to them. They do not want to be arrested by policemen, hauled before the criminal court, and convicted of crimes. Substitutes for these procedures have been found in orders to appear at a hearing, decisions by administrative commissions, and desist orders. The essential similarity between white collar crimes and other crimes has been partially concealed by this variation in procedures.

Secrecy regarding the violators of law is secured also by juggling corporate personalities and brand names. This policy has the same function as the alias of the professional thief, namely, anonymity. The policy appears in at least three forms. First, a subsidiary of a corporation conceals its connection with that corporation. A cooperative plant which was purchased by a large meat-packing corporation continued to represent itself as a cooperative. An independent manufacturer of farm machinery was purchased by a near-monopolistic corporation but continued to represent itself as "independent" and "as fighting the trust." A public utility system employed as an appraiser of its property a firm which was represented to be independent, but in which the manager of the utility system was a silent partner. Many of the large corporations have organized dummy corporations for one or more of three purposes: to conceal transactions which would require payment of large income taxes, to increase the number of firms which may successively take profits, and to avoid laws which prohibit a corporation from owning more than a specified percentage of the stock of a public utility corporation. Second, corporations which are known to be subsidiaries are presented as distinct legal personalities. The objective in this case is to produce obfuscation as to responsibility. One of the utility systems had three sub-holding companies, each of which had the same officers and offices as the parent company; each of the sub-holding companies, in turn, had regional companies subsidiary to it, with control over the operating companies in its region. Third, corporations juggle brand names as occasion requires. During World War II, when price ceilings were imposed on old brands, many corporations through subsidiaries not known to be connected with the parent company produced the old commodities with a new brand name and claimed prices higher than the ceilings for old brands.

With the objective of maintaining status and a conception of themselves as non-criminal, the corporations employ experts in law, public relations, and advertising. These agencies are the corporate equivalent of the professional thief's "mouthpiece." The "mouthpiece" of the professional thief has as his principal function the defense of his client against specific charges. The function of the "mouthpiece" of the white collar criminal is much more inclusive. He has the function of influencing the enactment and administration of the law as it applies to his clients, of advising his clients in advance as to the methods which may be used with relative impunity, as well as defending his client before the courts and before the public when specific charges are made against them. Perhaps most important of all is the effort of the associations of businessmen to build up and maintain their status before the public. It is reported that a business concern, which had acquired a bad reputation through one rather scandalous episode involving its chief executive, paid a public relations firm more than a million dollars for a campaign to restore its good reputation. Cohen makes the following generalization which applies to such activities:

> The efficiency with which a ruling class can secure popular recognition of their claims depends upon the popular stereotypes of that class. If ruling class membership suggests merit and ability entitling one to positions of public trust and authority, this recognition will be forthcoming. The ruling class will, accordingly, promote an ideology which incorporates such a stereotype, and will actually put some pressure on its members to conform, at least publicly, to the stereotype. If single members deviate grossly

and publicly, conducting themselves in a manner "unbecoming a gentleman," such conduct reflects not only on the culprit but on the validity of the stereotype and thus threatens the standing of all who share his status and rule by virtue of the acceptance of that stereotype.[4]

The activities of Insull, Hopson, and others who committed gross violations of law were not so much offensive to the sentiments of businessmen as threats to the generalized and simplified stereotypes in terms of which the public evaluates businessmen as a group. The policy of condemning the gross violators of law, whose offenses become publicly known, enables corporations to carry out a general attitude of public adherence to the law while in fact they are engaged privately in defections from the law.

The characteristics of white collar crime, as described above, depend to some extent on the corporate form of business organization. The statement is frequently made that big business is more legal and more honest than small business. No organized research has demonstrated the truth or falsity of this claim. Research on violations of price ceiling during World War II indicated but did not prove conclusively that no significant difference was found between large and small firms.[5] At any rate, the corporate form of organization which is generally used in big business has two advantages over other forms of organization from the point of view of violations of law: anonymity of persons so that the location of responsibility is impeded, and increased rationality in behavior.

The policies of a business which has corporate form are actions of a corporate unit. Responsibility is divided among executives, directors, subordinates, and stockholders. A director loses his personal identity in this corporate behavior and in this respect, but in no other, corporate behavior is like the behavior of a mob. Persons do not act in these situations as they would act if segregated from each other. This is true even when the corporation is essentially a dictatorship under the control of one person. The difficulty of locating responsibility and the resulting security to individuals is exemplified in the decision against the automobile companies in the six percent case, where the corporations were convicted but all of the directors and executives were acquitted: the corporation was guilty of a crime but no person directing the corporation was guilty of a crime.

The corporate form of business organization also has the advantage of increased rationality. The corporation probably comes closer to the "economic man" and to "pure reason" than any other person or any other organization. The executives and directors not only have explicit and consistent objectives of maximum pecuniary gain but also have research and accounting departments by which precise determination of results is facilitated, and have discussions of policies by directors with diverse abilities and diverse interests, so that the sentiments of one person are canceled by those of another. This general advantage does not deny the disadvantages of corporate organization. Two principal disadvantages have been pointed out in the literature. First, the directors do not necessarily have their attention fixed on the balance sheet of the corporation, but often engage in log-rolling for personal advantages, just as is true in politics. Second, the corporation, like a government, tends to become bureaucratic with all of the limitations of bureaucratic organization.

In the earlier days the corporation aimed at technological efficiency; in the later days it has aimed more than previously at the manipulation of people by advertising, salesmanship, propaganda, and lobbying. With this recent development the corporation has developed a truly Machiavellian ideology and policy. It has reached the conclusion that practically anything is possible if resources, ingenuity, and strenuous efforts are used. It has appropriated the physical and biological sciences and applied them to its objectives of technological efficiency, and in the process has made significant contributions to those sciences. Similarly, it has appropriated the social and psychological sciences and applied them to the objective of manipulating people.

Three aspects of the rationality of the corporation in relation to illegal behavior may be mentioned. First, the corporation selects crimes which involve the smallest danger of detection and identification, and against which victims are least likely to fight. The crimes of corporations are similar in this respect to professional thefts: both are carefully selected and both are similar to taking candy from a baby, in that the victim is a weak antagonist. The advantage of selecting weak victims was stated explicitly by Daniel Drew in the decade of the eighties:

> I began to see that it is poor policy for big men in Wall Street to fight each other. When I am fighting a money-king, even my victories are dangerous. Take the present situation. I had scooped a fine profit out of the Erie deal and it was for the most part in solid cash. But – and here was the trouble – it had all come out of one man – Vanderbilt. Naturally it had left him very sore. And being so powerful, he was able to fight back. As has been seen, he did fight back. He had put me and my party to a lot of inconvenience. That always happens when you take money from a man on your own level. On the other hand, if I had taken these profits from outsiders, it would in the aggregate have amounted to the same sum, but the losers would have been scattered all over the country and so wouldn't have been able to get together and hit back. By making my money from people on the outside, an insider like myself could make just as much in the long run, and not raise up any one enemy powerful enough to cause him discomfort.[6]

...e victims of corporate crimes are seldom in a position to fight against the management of the corporation. Consumers are scattered, unorganized, lacking in objective information as to qualities of commodities, and no one consumer suffers a loss in a particular transaction which would justify him in taking individual action. Stockholders seldom know the complex procedures of the corporation which they own, cannot attend annual meetings, and receive little information regarding the policies or the financial status of the corporation. Even if stockholders suspect illegal behavior by the management, they are scattered, unorganized, and frequently cannot even secure access to the names of the other stockholders. In their conflicts with labor, the corporations have the advantage of a friendly press and of news commentators whose salaries are paid by business corporations, so that their unfair labor practices can be learned generally only by consulting official reports.

The ordinary case of embezzlement is a crime by a single individual in a subordinate position against a strong corporation. It is, therefore, one of the most foolish of white collar crimes. The weakness of the embezzler, in comparison with the corporation, is illustrated in the case of J. W. Harriman. He was indicted for embezzlement in 1933 and later convicted. No criminal complaint was made against the banks which were accessory to this crime, and which were discovered in the course of the investigation. Their crimes included loans to one corporation in excess of the limit set by law, a pool formed by the officers of the bank to trade in the stock of the bank in violation of law, concealment of the embezzlement by officers of the bank and of the clearing house, and refusal by many of the banks to meet the losses of the Harriman bank which they had agreed to do on condition that the embezzlement be concealed.

A second aspect of corporate rationality in relation to crime is the selection of crimes in which proof is difficult. In this respect, also, white collar crime is similar to professional theft. The selection of crimes on this basis is illustrated by advertising: since a little puffing is regarded as justifiable, the proof of unreasonable puffing is difficult. Again, a corporation organizes a company union under its own domination because proof that this is an unfair labor practice is difficult.

Third, the rational corporation adopts a policy of "fixing" cases. This is similar to the professional thief who maintains that if he has money and good standing with the "fixer" he can fix any case anywhere, since it is always possible to find a weak link in the chain of persons necessary for a conviction. A former officer of the Federal Food and Drug Administration has described the pressures on that organization to prevent the execution of the law on particular offenders. These pressures include threats by Senators and Representatives that appropriations for the Food and Drug Administration will be cut unless charges against a constituent are withdrawn. When the Federal

Trade Commission after the First World War was active in the enforcement of the law, representatives of large corporations went to the President of the United States, who replaced some of the commissioners by others more sympathetic with business practices; this resulted in the dismissal of many complaints which had been made against corporations. When minority stockholders bring suit against the management of the corporation, a customary procedure is to make a settlement with the leader of that group. This is similar to the reimbursement by the professional thief of the victim of the theft in order to stop prosecution.

The "fixing" of white collar crimes, however, is much more inclusive than the fixing of professional thefts. The corporation attempts not only to "fix" particular accusations against it, but also to develop general good will before accusations are made, and even to prevent the implementation of the law. An instance of this broader policy is provided by the fire insurance companies of Missouri, which had agreed to pay Pendergast a bribe of $750,000 to intervene in a rate case. Four of these companies which paid shares of this bribe immediately appointed as vice-president a person who had great influence in the national capital. While Pendergast was promptly convicted and committed to prison, almost ten years elapsed before the fire insurance companies were convicted and their penalities were limited to fines.

The preceding analysis justifies the conclusion that the violations of law by corporations are deliberate and organized crime. This does not mean that corporations never violate the law inadvertently and in an unorganized manner. It does mean that a substantial portion of their violations are deliberate and organized.

Notes

[1] Thorstein Veblen, *Theory of the Leisure Class* (New York, 1912), p. 237.

[2] *Nation's Business,* vol. 35, no. 1, p. 38, January, 1947.

[3] *New Republic*, 56:33, August 29, 1928.

[4] Albert K. Cohen, *Differential Implementation of the Criminal Law* (Bloomington, Indiana, 1942), pp. 36-37.

[5] George Katona, *Price Control and Business,* Principia Press, Monog. No. 9, 1945.

[6] Bouck White, *The Book of Daniel Drew* (New York, 1910), pp 270-71.

5
Some of the Best People Smoke Pot

Jon Ruddy

The interviews that follow may shock you or touch you or make you mad or make you laugh. They will make you think. We have all heard that marijuana, once the "noxious," "crippling" and "degrading" preserve of criminals, jazz musicians, delinquents and, latterly, hippies, has shown a tremendous upward mobility in the last few years. This is true. It's no pipe dream – it's here. The virtues and dangers of marijuana are debatable but its wide acceptance is obvious. Many of my acquaintances, in the silly lexicon of this underground revolution, "turn on" and profess to believe that doing so is harmless as well as wonderfully pleasant. I don't know any criminals, jazz musicians, delinquents or hippies. I do know a lawyer who says, "Half the law students in the country smoke pot. It is just a matter of time until our legal institutions are comprised mainly of pot-heads. Do you think it will be illegal then?"

Most marijuana users in the middle and professional classes expect that it will be legalized with solid public support. I had no trouble finding a gallery of them, and I discovered that they were anxious to talk about themselves. They asked for anonymity, of course, but they weren't frightened. The simple fact is, they smoke with impunity. Police, in resolutely confining their investigations to intractable youth, have not only failed to check pot's upward mobility, they have failed to grasp it. "I think we have pretty good control of the problem," says the head of a 20-man RCMP drug section in Toronto. He adds that, of the more than 300 Toronto marijuana arrests up to November of last year, not one involved a member of the professional classes. "No arrests have ever been made, to my knowledge, of professional people."

It's a safe bet that no one is ever going to arrest the Toronto lawyer who likes to take a stroll in Nathan Phillips Square on his lunch hour, puffing pot. (Source: another lawyer, who also indulges.) No one is likely to nab the pusher whose beat is the floor of the Toronto Stock Exchange. (Source: a psychologist at the Ontario Hospital at 999 Queen Street West.) No one is going to bash in the front door of a big house in Vancouver's Shaughnessy Heights where a wealthy hostess offers marijuana from a hand-engraved silver cigarette box. (Source: a 23-year-old student at Simon Fraser University who is the son of a vice-president of a large company. "These cigarettes are machine-rolled and filter-tipped," he says. "You don't get any little bits of grass in your mouth. It's very elegant.")

The biggest enclaves of these newly typical pot smokers are in Vancouver and Toronto, although Montreal, Winnipeg and several other cities have their share. The smokers are mostly in their 20s and 30s, affluent, articulate and prepared to do anything to promote the legalization of marijuana, short of risking the seven-year jail term they could still conceivably get for possession. Most of them are as disparaging of hippies and the quasi-religious implications of pot smoking as they are of the law. "I have no sympathy for the Yorkville hippies who get bust," says a lawyer. "Let them listen to the latest platitude-filled *guru* and squat in doorways. I know I'm not going to find The Way through marijuana. It's good, that's all." If the smokers have anything else in common it seems to be a certain glibness and self-indulgence. An RCMP officer asked me, "How do you know they're not kidding you?" A better question might be, how do they know they're not kidding themselves? But who can really say whether they're right or wrong, deluded cop-outs or the perceptive champions of a better, safer, cheaper and more portentous crutch than alcohol?

THE LAWYER SMOKES POT

"The first time I used it, I realized why marijuana is illegal,' says Paul, a hard-driving 34-year-old Toronto lawyer. "Because it's just so damned good." He had some with a friend about a year ago, then overcame his wife's fears and turned her on. They now share a pipe of marijuana about twice a week.

"The effects are different every time," Paul says. "I usually first notice a mild hallucination. My ankle bones seem to vibrate. There is a similar feeling at the back of the neck. There is a mild and pleasant vertigo. There is some visual distortion. I get a buoyant, youthful feeling. I really feel about 18 when I turn on. Things seem funny and I laugh a lot. Sometimes I get terribly thirsty, but that might be just from the smoking. A friend of mine will often drink two quarts of milk when he turns on. And they have called it the killer drug! Or you can get hungry. One night at 4 a.m. my wife and I made an enormous Swiss fondue and ate it all. We were high as kites. That's the only thing my wife doesn't like about it – she's little and watches her weight. It affects taste in funny ways. Some things like cold, fresh fruit taste fantastic. But a glass of wine might be disgusting. You never know. Music seems clearer. I can follow contrapuntal music like Bach horizontally, whereas straight I'd likely hear it vertically as melody and harmony. Rhythmic responses are much better. I'm a lousy dancer but when I'm high I dance very well. Anyone who says it is a sexual depressant is crazy. It stimulates you in the same way as when you go away on a trip and forget your day-to-day hang-ups."

Paul has evolved a certain self-discipline about how he uses pot. "I would never drive when I'm high or go to work high. I know lawyers who do and I disapprove. On the other hand, I think it's probably better than going to the office, drunk. I know a computer programmer who will sometimes stay high for weeks. He says he can work effectively, but it's hard to believe. I think it's probably possible to become psychologically dependent on the stuff. That's why I only turn on twice a week. Also, you want to have time to appreciate it. I work long hours, sometimes at night. We tend to devote spare time to it, as if we were going to a movie. It seems to be compatible with relaxation. I don't think I'd ever use it to calm tension. It might work, but I just don't think it's the right time. If I'm tense I might have a drink with dinner or a glass or two of wine. The beauty of pot is that it's so different from booze. There seems to be no price you have to pay. It's not poisoned like liquor. I mean, you never get sick. There's never any hangover. I've never felt a single adverse effect from pot physically, nor do I know anybody who has."

He says the use of marijuana is so common among the young middle class "that it can be assumed." He is acquainted with pot-smoking lawyers, architects, writers, photographers, businessmen, musicians, doctors and dentists. He himself buys it in bulk – usually a pound for $200 to $300 – and deals it to his friends at no mark-up, keeping a few ounces for himself. "Two ounces would make 25 pipefuls and last me three months." Paul's pusher is an insurance executive. "I understand he gets it from a guy he went to college with, a really big distributor who brings in 40 or 50 pounds. It's probably from Mexico. I don't ask questions."

THE PROFESSOR SMOKES POT

Should an 11-year-old try pot? Graham, a 46-year-old Vancouver university professor and the father of six, was dubious at first. "The three older children, teenagers, all use it when my wife and I do," he says, reclining in a leather chair at the faculty club. "That's only about once a month – we're a somewhat abstemious family. I wasn't sure about the younger boy. But the other kids talked me into it. I let my kids have a glass of wine with their meals – the liquor laws are crazy – so why not a joint? I don't think the 11 year-old got a real high. I hope I haven't done him any harm."

Graham, who is small and aesthetic-looking, buys his marijuana from contacts his older children have established. He started smoking it after one of his lectures, at the end of 1966. "I was talking about ingrained thought processes limiting the imagination. Four kids who were obviously stoned came in to listen. I could see that they were the only ones who were getting anything out of the lecture."

He says that six out of 10 of his faculty colleagues indulge. "Sometimes I think getting stoned is a state we could learn to flip into," he says. "I think we use pot as a trigger to get there now, but maybe we don't need it. When I use it I resonate more easily to things like music, taste, smells. And once or twice it has made a helluva difference to an evening of love-making. It seems to give me all the advantages of youth to go with the advantages of age that I've already got. A couple of my girls reckon that they have achieved a sort of telepathic communication with pot. One thinks she could taste something the other was eating. I never experience wild things like that, but my wife does. It has made things very good for my wife."

THE DOCTOR SMOKES POT

At Toronto's Central Library a handbook called *Weeds of Canada and the Northern United States* is well-thumbed at page 27. That's where there is a botanist's description of *Cannabis sativa*, the hemp or marijuana plant. A tall, rough annual, native to Asia, with coarsely toothed, finger-shaped leaves and tiny greenish flowers, hemp was once grown in Canada and the U.S. as a source of fibre for rope. It still thrives as a weed in many locations. Author F. H. Montgomery states that plants growing this far north "are probably of no value" as a source of marijuana. But he may be wrong about that. At any rate, some very facile minds have been concerned with finding the hemp plant, with cultivating it in flower pots, gardens and rural lots, and with harvesting its small top leaves, flowers and stems.

Among them is a Toronto general practitioner who shall here be known as Dr. Lefferts. A scholarly bachelor in his mid-30s, he has been smoking pot for seven years. He started at college. He says it is neither habit-forming nor harmful, "an entirely innocent diversion." In his analytic way, Dr. Lefferts has acquired a considerable fund of information about his long-time interest. Sometimes he will drive through the southern Ontario countryside looking for it. He has also taken to growing it at home. The procedure, he says, is simple. "The marijuana you buy contains seeds. About half of them will germinate in warm water. Then you plant them in sandy loam – alkaline, not acidic – and nurse them along with plant food. They should mature in about six months. Meanwhile, they are a rather nice house plant. The root structure seems to be such that you can grow a big plant in a 10-inch pot. When it's ready for harvest you can dry the tops in an oven for 20 minutes at 250 degrees, or in a laundry drier in a cheesecloth bag. I've had home-grown pot with friends and found it less potent than the imported stuff, but quite pleasant. It is my ambition to grow enough for my own use."

This decision stemmed from a recent and frightening experience. Dr. Lefferts attended a convention in New York and came home with several ounces of marijuana in his briefcase. He had a lot to carry off the plane and before going through customs asked a colleague to give him a hand. The colleague took the briefcase. Dr. Lefferts went through first and absent-mindedly headed for the door. He was horrified to hear his friend, who didn't know what he was carrying, make a little joke. "Hey, here's your bag of marijuana," he called, holding up Dr. Lefferts' bag of marijuana. The customs inspector looked up, startled. 'Ho, ho, ho," he said, after a second or two.

THE PSYCHOLOGIST SMOKES POT

Ten years ago Tracey played drums in a college band and smoked pot regularly because it was cheaper than liquor. Free, in fact. The lead guitarist had a friend in Tijuana who sent it up in half-pound tobacco tins. Tracey liked it – when he was high he felt he was as good as Gene Krupa – but he forgot all about it, he says, after the band broke up. A year ago, Tracey, now a Vancouver psychologist of 35, a well-tailored bachelor with grey-flecked sideburns, tried marijuana again at a party at the home of a doctor friend. He loved it.

"More than half my friends use it," he says. "It's ridiculously easy to get. I know maybe six people I can get it from at any time. Friends offer you grass or a drink now, the way Air Canada offers you tea, coffee or milk. I am associated with about a dozen doctors and four of us get stoned more or less regularly. What do I get out of it? It adds another dimension to my thinking that wasn't there before. When I'm stoned it seems as if my mind is working on five or six channels. I know it's just what I believe at the time and maybe isn't really happening. But that's what's important, isn't it? What I believe, I mean."

Last winter Tracey went to a ski resort near Vancouver with a friend. "The first night we met a couple of girls, secretaries, and asked them out for a drink and they said, 'Look, why don't you come up to our hotel room and turn on?' It sounds licentious, but it was very innocent and pleasant. Later that week I met a barmaid and she had some stuff, and we went back to her chalet and smoked it through one of those water pipes, but we used crème de menthe instead of water."

THE PSYCHIATRIST DOESN'T SMOKE POT

Dr. Edwin Lipinski is a Vancouver psychiatrist who does not smoke marijuana. As if that were not odd enough, his views on pot pushers and certain users – but not the drug itself – are distinctly jaundiced. "I take the occasional drink and wine with meals, but I don't use marijuana," he says. "It's just not a part of my life. On the other hand, I don't become outraged when people around me use it."

An internationally renowned expert in forensic psychiatry, Dr. Lipinski is in close daily contact with the consumers of various drugs. He says that, of the teenagers and college students among his patients, 90 per cent use pot "more or less regularly." Among his personal friends, a quarter are users.

"It's quite common for people listening to music and attending social functions of various kinds to smoke pot," he says. "You have this thing where they believe that people become more sincere and open and get closer to one another. Pot is a marked social facilitator for many people. Yes, I suppose that's what alcohol is to other people. Me, for instance. And pot is probably a far more innocuous compound in every respect."

But he feels that the pushers are deluding themselves. "They are usually the bright kids. They become occasional users, then they make a bit of money selling pot. The next stage is that they begin to develop a rationale about the system being wrong and the law an ass that should be flouted. They see themselves as defenders of the people against the system. These marijuana peddlers! It falls down when you ask them to stand up and accept responsibility for their actions the way Martin Luther King accepted responsibility for his advocacy of civil disobedience. Then it becomes a different matter. Before long, these young people are pushing Speed and LSD and then a few of them go over the top, pushing the hard stuff."

Multiple users – people who progress from pot to some of the wilder hallucinogens – are caught up in a similarly dangerous and self-defeating game. And a pathetic one. "There is no end to the areas multiple users will investigate," says Dr. Lipinski. "I understand some have even tried meat tenderizer taken intravenously, just because the word got around. It didn't matter that it was absurd and didn't do anything.

"Here's a little story that tells you something about pot smokers. In Vancouver not long ago a group of hip social workers tried a psychological experiment on some runaway kids. They got them together in a psycho-drama and gave half of them pot and half of them dried parsley. About half the kids smoking pot turned on – and 40 per cent of the parsley smokers turned on, too. You always get about 20 per cent of people who respond to the suggestion more than the stimulus."

6
My Case Against the RCMP

Ex-Corporal Jack Ramsay

The whole world knows the Mountie. He's courageous, fair and square, upright and morally sound as the Bank of Canada. His post-card image draws applicants to the Royal Canadian Mounted Police from among the cream of Canada's young men. And after a month or more of checking for health and honesty, loyalty and discipline, intelligence, knowledge and common sense, ambition, courage and maturity, the personnel officer sends the applicant, now a recruit, to a training centre and tells his mother and father, as he told mine 16 years ago: "We take a boy and give you back a man."

Today, after 14 years' service and a year reflecting back on it, I would ask that officer, "What kind of man?" What kind of man does the force create by its 19th-century power structure, its incredible book of rules known as Commissioner's Standing Orders? Not the man the boy had hoped to be. Certainly not the man the world knows.

As a boy on a farm in Saskatchewan I grew up with the legend of the Mounted Police; to me the force was a living embodiment of justice. A man in RCMP uniform was given tremendous respect and when I was recruited I felt privileged to serve people who would respect me in the same way. The force still has fine policemen, men who serve in the old tradition, but it's fast losing public respect, and in trying to regain it the RCMP is much more concerned with polishing its image than with pursuing its ideal. As a result, morale has fallen so low that alcoholism and suicide have become serious problems. And many of the force's officers only make things worse. Some of them are so inept they can maintain discipline only by fear; they mistreat and pressure the lower ranks who, in turn, often persecute the public. Especially during my last seven years on the force, I watched fellow members lying, falsifying records and ignoring suspects' rights until I came to dislike putting on the famous scarlet tunic, because it made me feel like a hypocrite.

Unless public opinion forces a change, a great tradition will die and the Mounted Police will become no more than window dressing for tourists. But public opinion needs information and that's why I'm writing about my experiences, withholding only the names of men whose careers would be placed in jeopardy by what I *must* say. I want people to know what the Mounted Police have become – instead of being constantly reminded of what they used to be.

When I signed up in 1956, I thought I was joining a disciplined force, not a military apparatus that considers men little more than automatons. As a recruit I accepted a life circumscribed by rules. I couldn't swear or smoke or take a drink in public in uniform, couldn't even stop at the liquor store on my way home. I couldn't lend money to a friend in the force without the permission of my Officer Commanding, couldn't talk of my work to friends outside the force. I couldn't sign a petition, discuss politics, attend a political rally. I had to become "thoroughly acquainted with every detail of the Regulations, CSOs and other instructions," which, numbering in the thousands, are enforced with military stringency. I know of members disciplined for "conduct unbecoming a member of the force" for associating with juvenile delinquents they were trying to help. I even know members who had to quit when the force disapproved of their choice of a wife.

The force demands obedience, first and foremost. As the Commissioner's Standing Orders state: "Obedience to lawful authority is an outstanding quality required of a member of the force, and a member shall receive the lawful command of his superior with deference and respect, executing it promptly . . . without question or comment."

A major aim of "depot" division, Regina – where five to 12 troops of 32 men each are usually in various stages of training – is to implant permanently this habit of obedience. In my first confusing weeks of being shouted at till I was dazed, I learned to look with awe on my all-knowing all-powerful corporal and sergeant. I was then allowed to see how they deferred to a sergeant major, and later the sergeant major's response to an officer. After nine months' training (now six) the appearance of an officer triggered automatic subservience.

This subservience is enforced by the usual military punishments: extra drill and menial chores, confinement to barracks or cells. And when I was in training in depot, recruits were encouraged to punish troop mates in a traditional RCMP rite called horse-troughing.

I witnessed my first horse-troughing one day when our small arms class finished early. Our instructor was describing how he had won his World War II medals and a young trainee asked if he had a medal for bullshitting. This was considered rank insubordination, and after classes that day, with the duty NCO (noncommissioned officer) conveniently absent, our troop doubled the offender off to the stables in his fatigues, submerged him several times in the cold water of the horse trough, took him into the riding school where a hole had been dug, poured bran and molasses over him and buried him in sand and sawdust. Then we pulled him out, doused him with water, took him behind the stables, buried him, head and all, in manure, rinsed him and doubled him back to barracks. Another victim of a horse-troughing I witnessed developed blood poisoning and spent some time in hospital. While I felt at the time that such punishment was out of proportion to the offense, the real implications didn't sink in till much later.

Then we had a riot in depot. In the Mounted Police the member with the lowest regimental number has seniority, which gives him authority over those who join later, and the two senior troops in training had been making life miserable for their juniors: making them wait for washrooms, ordering them about. But when one senior troop graduated the other was left outnumbered and the junior troops joined forces to toss every remaining senior in the horsetrough. Early next morning the senior troop broke into the dormitory of the junior troop they considered the instigators and attacked them with riding crops while they slept. After the ensuing battle several men were hospitalized, two dismissed from the force and horse-troughing banned – not because of concern for its harshness as a punishment. Not because of concern for injuries (in almost every training class there are broken arms, legs and noses, and I've known an instructor to kick a recruit in the testicles). No, the force's concern was the loss of control and the aim of horse-troughing remains: to program fear of disobedience indelibly deep in a member's mind.

The force claims that its militarism instills self-discipline. But it is not uncommon for the Officer Commanding the training depot to confine a graduating class to barracks on the night that training has ended. He will do this on any pretext, in part to remind them of the force's authority, in part for fear their frustrations will erupt. If he were really confident that his trainees had gained self-discipline, would he need to confine them to barracks on this of all nights? I have seen recruits break down and cry because they couldn't meet their parents that night.

Rather than instilling it, the force's militarism inhibits self-discipline. When I was assistant training NCO for Saskatchewan last year, I asked a number of recruits how the sight of the sergeant major affected them. All said they felt fear.

A member learns to hide this fear but, throughout his career, it's there. Once when I was stationed at Estevan, Saskatchewan, I had to visit the Weyburn detachment. I was chatting with the sergeant in charge of the highway patrol, the corporal and a stenographer when the OC of their subdivision unexpectedly drove up. As if a button had been pressed, the NCOs dashed about, hands checking ties and buttons, as they frantically straightened up. I'll never forget the shame and disgust on the face of that young stenographer as she watched the mere sight of an officer causing two senior policemen to panic.

Once the force has conditioned you to mindless obedience it posts you to a detachment that calls for utmost flexibility. The telephone jangles incessantly with minor complaints: thefts, assaults, accidents, drunkenness, juvenile delinquency. To be a good detachment man you have to be a self-starter but you've been trained to do only what you're told. A field man needs concentration but you are so apprehensive that whenever your NCO comes near you jump up and stand at attention. A field man should be decisive but you have been governed by rules that are meant to replace your need to decide for yourself. A common complaint from the field is that rookies have to be retrained as soon as they go on detachment, especially in regard to fear of rank.

The force's rules and regulations are intended to cover every conceivable situation, but you soon learn that no matter how hard you try you cannot live up to them. CSO 1376, for example, states that "members arriving on duty . . . shall report immediately to the Officer Commanding or member in charge . . . " But if you obey this order after a long dusty patrol you can be charged for disobedience of CSO 1151, which states that a member "shall always appear clean, and correctly dressed with boots, badges, buttons and accoutrements polished."

I recall a member who had been working on a case for two days without sleep coming back into headquarters unshaven and rumpled. Instead of having his diligence praised he was chewed out for slovenliness. If a rookie reports as soon as he comes in from a case he'll be worried about his appearance and his nervousness may be misinterpreted as a lack of confidence. If he avoids his NCO he may lose the chance of sitting down with him and discussing a case while it's still fresh in his mind. Either way the result is poor communication.

Take CSO 1399 (2) for example: "A noncommissioned officer will not habitually associate with, or allow undue familiarity on the part of, subordinates." When I was corporal in charge at Pelican Narrows, an Indian reserve near Flin Flon, I shared a trailer, the only available accommodation, with my constable. I was violating that CSO every hour we lived together, just as every small-detachment NCO violates it, because if he doesn't he knows he will not get cooperation. Even so, the caste system within the RCMP is one of the greatest obstacles to communication and teamwork, both absolutely vital to efficient policing.

When I was posted to Pierceland in northwest Saskatchewan in 1967, I became concerned at the number of prosecutions for drunkenness. So I took a look at the causes and found that some local stores were selling large amounts of vanilla extract, which contains alcohol, and that the hotel keepers were violating the Liquor Licensing Act by letting Indians keep on drinking till they ran out of money, and then tossing them out on the street.

I persuaded the store owners to stop selling the Indians vanilla extract, and the hotel keepers to stop serving drunks. I spread the word that the Indians could take their liquor home instead of drinking in abandoned cars, or back alleys, or out in the bush. The incidence of drunkenness, fights and accidents suddenly dropped.

But I was breaking both the law and the rules, not only by allowing Indians on a dry reserve to take liquor home, but by checking the beer parlors now and then in uniform to back up the hotel keepers. When I told my subdivision OC what I was doing he wasn't happy. "You're aware," he said, "that our policy prohibits this?"

I explained that I thought our policy wasn't conducive to good police work. "It forces the Indians to act like animals. We allow them to drink like human beings now. They appreciate it. They cooperate. We ask them who did what and they'll tell us."

"Ramsay," he said, "you're a very persuasive young man." And over the beefs of his senior NCOs he supported me. But he was one of the only two officers I've served under who would have. The others would have played it safe and told me to stay with policy.

As a field man you're always in a bind. If you want to live by the book you risk a complaint of poor police service; if you want to do good police work you risk a charge by the force. Thus the members who care the most often get themselves into the most trouble. When a member on highway patrol in Alberta, whose record had been good enough to win him promotion to corporal, padded his gas account to outfit his police car with special accessories, he was fired after 14 years' service.

The rules are a source of frustration, fear and pervasive anxiety. I know a constable in his mid-twenties who in the summer of 1970 was transferred from the Prince Albert subdivision to the one-man post at Denare Beach. This is a summer resort near Flin Flon that attracts the usual troublemakers, bootleggers and drug peddlers. It's no place to start a junior man on his own. And this constable, whose work under supervision had been above average, told his OC that he didn't think he could handle it.

The OC ignored his objections and the constable was soon in trouble with his inexperienced mishandling of some evidence. He was so afraid of the consequences of violating policy that he tried to cover his error with another. He was caught out, investigated, and when his term of enlistment expired, he was not re-engaged. I saw him then. It had hit him hard. He was depressed and bitter. A month later he was charged with robbing a small Saskatchewan bank.

I know members who have been charged under the RCMP Act and interrogated 17 hours at a stretch when the normal interrogation period is three hours or less. Once an orderly room charge has been laid, the force, unlike any other I know, considers its members guilty till proven innocent. I knew a member who was arraigned in service court for using excessive force on a prisoner. He called two members whose eyewitness testimony established his innocence. The trial officer ignored their evidence and took the unsupported word of the complainant, a man continually in trouble with the police. The member was convicted and recommended for dismissal. He appealed and the force's appeal board acquitted him. But by then he had undergone a long period of stress and anxiety that did nothing to help the performance of his duties.

I don't think anything is so bad for morale as injustice within the force, and I could quote case after case where good men have been unfairly treated. One friend of mine, a constable, was charged with assaulting an Indian who resisted arrest. The constable hired a lawyer and won the case in criminal court. He was then convicted in RCMP service court on the same evidence. A senior NCO with a law degree, who has since left the force, told the trial officer afterward: "Where do you think you get the right to find that man guilty when a competent magistrate found him not guilty and the court of appeal upheld his decision?" It's certainly the force's perogative to discipline its members arbitrarily, but it shouldn't claim, as it does, that service court protects their rights in the same way that a criminal court would.

The rationale of the force is simple, if shortsighted. When anyone questions a misdemeanor by one of its members the force can say, "Oh yes, we had such a member but he was appropriately dealt with." That can be a dangerous rationale, given officers with a penchant for power. When a former OC of the Prince Albert subdivision was transferred to a larger subdivision he remarked to his staff: "With a subdivision this size we should be able to average four orderly room cases a month."

The smart member sees that his safest course is to do as little as possible. He shies away from difficult cases, discourages complaints. To escape disciplinary action for breaking rules, as he must, just to function, he begins to think and act self-protectively. He fictionalizes the daily diary that he hasn't time to keep up, he pads the expenses that the force allots with such niggardliness, he submits investigational reports that show him following policy that would have been ridiculous in his circumstances. Any member with 10 years' service has learned to lie skillfully.

In this past year I've heard high-ranking RCMP officers state on television that "it is not the official policy of the force to put undercover men on university campuses." Yet in 1970, when I was in Ottawa taking a course, an NCO from Security and Intelligence told me that the force not only had men on campus but that at a recent S and I meeting an officer had advised members that any man who refused such duty would be transferred out of the branch. A member then asked the officer how far the force would back them if they were found out, and the officer, an inspector, refused to answer. The question is, was the top brass lying or ignorant of what's going on?

Every year every Mounted Policeman is assessed by his superiors on everything from his work to his appearance. And within that assessment loyalty ranks high. It's defined in Standing Orders as "dedication to the force," and the guidelines are explicit: "How far does the member place the welfare of the force ahead of *any other consideration*?" (Italics mine.) A member, in short, must place the force ahead of truth, justice, and service to the people of Canada.

At the same time, if you cling, as I did, to the RCMP ideal, you have to lie not only to the force but to yourself. You become an unconscious hypocrite or a conscious con man. Time and again I've been in court when an Indian prisoner has pleaded not guilty and heard the magistrate say, "There'll be a short adjournment, constable, while you explain things to this man." And then the Indian, who by tradition looks to the Mounted Police for protection, is conned by the constable into pleading guilty.

You lie, first to survive; then, as fear and guilt blunt conscience, to get ahead. I was told by an ex-member of a drug case in which the officer in charge told his investigating team that they had to make the charge stick. At the trial the accused claimed he hadn't left his car at a certain time. One investigator testified that from where he was at that time he had seen the accused leave the car. The accused was convicted not only on the drug charge but for perjury. The ex-member told me that from his stakeout position he could see both the accused and the place the investigator had claimed to be – and the investigator wasn't there.

Under pressure, you conform. You suppress your doubts. You embrace the system. You can see the change in a member who bounces in two or three years from corporal to staff sergeant. He's no longer a policeman, he's a stern disciplinarian. He no longer serves the ideal, he serves the image.

This was brought home to me sharply in the spring of 1969 when I was corporal in charge at Pelican Narrows, near Flin Flon. I investigated a stabbing at Sandy Bay 30 miles distant and found that 20 cases of malt extract had been bought from the general store that weekend. This was capable of making more than 1,000 gallons of an intoxicant the inhabitants, mainly Indians and Métis, call "molly." Indians and Métis when sober are usually gentle but when drunk are often violent. And there was one constable and myself to patrol Pelican Narrows, the isolated villages of Sandy Bay and Deschambault, and to help out at the summer resort of Denare Beach. I requested another constable until Denare Beach closed. The OC interpreted this as reluctance to serve at Pelican Narrows and sent a staff sergeant to investigate me.

During summer and early fall a young Indian came in by canoe to report fighting and drunken gunfire at Deschambault. No one had been shot yet but people were frightened. Deschambault and Sandy Bay could be reached only by air. And the RCMP aircraft at Prince Albert, 265 miles south-west, was available only once every three weeks – and then only in good weather. I submitted a memo to subdivision for authority to charter in three times a week to stop the brewing of molly and persuade the Indians by personal contact to stop drinking. At $30 a flight it would cost about $360 for the first month, and after that we would only need to fly in once a week. The answer came back that such authority might be abused, which would lead to excessive cost. I could charter in only in cases of emergency – in other words, only *after* a crime was committed. But I was authorized to charter into Sandy Bay at any time. Sandy Bay, a former detachment point, had a resident ex-MLA, and the possibility of a complaint to the Attorney General's department outweighed the record of violence at Deschambault.

Within weeks I was radioed by the Deschambault Co-op store manager that several people had been shot. When I got there I found that after a large-scale drinking bout lasting two or three days a 15-year-old Indian girl had shot herself in the foot, then fired into a shack and hit two men, one of them her father, who later died in hospital. And after I had the investigation completed to my satisfaction the OC threw costs to the winds and flew in men to re-interview every witness I had talked to and conduct a useless search for the cartridge cases.

I'll never forget my feelings as I investigated that killing. I couldn't reconcile the fact that I could charter into one village and not the other. I couldn't understand the breach of Standing Order 1373 which states that "the prevention of crime is of greater importance than bringing criminals before the courts of jutice." I couldn't forgive myself for not ignoring instructions. If I had I knew I would have been charged, but that man, I was sure, would still be alive.

That same fall I attended our annual subdivision ball and learned to my surprise that the RCMP aircraft had flown a highranking officer and his wife in from Regina and had picked up the senior subdivision NCO's son in southern Saskatchewan so that he could pipe in the members at head table. I couldn't help but wonder what the people of Deschambault thought of a force that would spend its money to create a favorable impression among the distinguished guests attending its ball while refusing to protect endangered Indians.

As members move up in rank less time is spent on police work and more on managing and controlling junior members. When I was in the North Battleford subdivision, northwest of Saskatoon, 60% of police-public contact was by members who had four years' service or less. NCOs with the greatest experience thus do the least police work and once they're commissioned they do none at all. They issue directives. They administer. They inspect detachments and discipline members. The system ensures that their experience in police work is lost to the force and, even worse, that they lose touch with reality.

Regulations state that "an officer is expected to familiarize himself with conditions throughout his division." Sounds great, but how does he do it? By CSO 1517, which says that "detachments shall be inspected three times a year," twice by the Officer Commanding the subdivision, once by the Section NCO. And since the purpose is "to ascertain and examine the general conditions and development of personnel," it is required "that detachments should not be forewarned . . . unless so directed by the Officer Commanding."

But in practice it's not quite that way. Every officer knows that the rules are so stringent that any surprise inspection would turn up violations, so unless they're disciplining a detachment man they tell him when they're coming. In fact, inspections are so far from random that cars may be polished days in advance, and I *know* of complaints left unattended until inspection was over to keep the patrol car from getting dirty.

As a result, the OC or the Section NCO sees spick-and-span buildings, natty uniforms and shiny equipment. But neither of them sees how the work is done or how the equipment is cared for. So the OC reports that all is well to the Commanding Officer of his division, who reports to the Commissioner, who then can give the Minister of Justice a report that maintains the image of the force.

The higher the officer rises the less he knows of what's going on. Once a year, when the Commissioner makes his inspection of all RCMP divisions, he steps into a dream world. He walks down a line of men in smart dress uniform. "How are you, constable?"

"Fine, sir."

"Any complaints, corporal?"

"No, sir."

And then he goes back to Ottawa and reports that morale is high. He has seen only what he wants to see and heard only what he wants to hear: that everything is just fine in the finest police force in the world. While I was assistant training NCO for Saskatchewan, we spent many thousands of dollars teaching courses in modern interpersonal communication while retaining archaic procedures that cut officers off from reality.

An officer has a vested interest in the system; it's his source of power. And since no one is promoted who doesn't polish and protect the image, an officer's chief concern becomes a paper picture of the force that always shows how great both he and it are doing. The picture is presented by what are called statistics. Every occurrence, every complaint, every case is a statistic, but the most valued ones are successful prosecutions. For these are used to show the force's success in containing a rising crime rate and to justify the never ending request for more men and equipment.

RCMP members are told they don't need statistics to win the ratings that mean promotion, but if you want to remain in the good graces of your superior you make sure your statistics surpass those of last year. And members who try to be fair are the big losers in the statistics game. For example, members on highway patrol who issue warnings instead of prosecution tickets are soon transferred out of a revenue-producing posting, usually with a lower rating on their A-26, their personnel report. I know one subdivision OC who told his highway patrolmen that he wanted 1.7 prosecutions per member per shift.

Naturally, members become over-zealous. They'll charge drivers doing 65 and say, "I clocked you at 70," which is easy to do; you just push your vehicle up to 70 and ignore the fact that you're overtaking. I know a member on highway patrol who watched for violators from a rooftop, one who hid in the slightly opened trunk of his police car, one who entered fictitious cases in his ledger.

I recall a small detachment member whose attitude toward the town's young people was so aggressive and condescending that they felt challenged. They would lure him with one car to one end of the main street while friends in another car at the other end of the street did power turns or threw beer bottles at the RCMP office. His attitude caused the incidents and every incident was a statistic, so his stats went up and he won promotion. He was replaced by a man with a friendly and understanding attitude. "If your drinking doesn't cause anyone trouble," he would tell the young townspeople, "I won't be too concerned. But if you break the law as a result of drinking you'll be prosecuted." Slowly he gained their confidence. Offenses dropped but so did statistics, and he lost his second man. As his subdivision OC said, there wasn't the work – on paper. From then on he had little time for a good preventive program and the community, as a result, got poorer police service.

In this phony paper picture the force uses to build its image, a field man with a radar set can sit comfortably in his car and chalk up 40 to 50 successful prosecutions in a weekend, while a neighboring detachment man may be working twice as hard on a theft that yields him nothing but the goodwill of a community that knows he's at work. But in the RCMP these days, a statistic is a statistic.

What this means to criminal justice is self-evident. You're supposed to read an accused the traditional RCMP warning: "You need not say anything. You have nothing to hope from any promise or favor and nothing to fear from any threat whether or not you say anything. Anything you do say may be used as evidence." But too often you fail to explain it or you rhyme it off so it's not understood, because when it is understood an accused usually buttons up. I have even known members to swear that the warning was read when it wasn't.

And of course the easiest pinch for statistics is the Indian. When the push is on for statistics members will wait on the dry reserves for the Indians to drive in with liquor. They will walk without knocking into Indian homes to catch them drinking. When the Saskatchewan liquor law was changed in 1968 to prohibit the prosecution of persons intoxicated in a public place, overzealous members thwarted its intent and kept their statistics up by charging Indians under the Criminal Code for causing a disturbance. The fact that the Indian is such an easy mark for statistics is a major reason why about half the prisoners in jail in the west are Indians, who make up less than 10% of the population.

When the pressure of stats is added to the pressure of fear and guilt, it saps zest for the job, that famous RCMP *esprit de corps*. Sagging morale means slackening effort, less alertness, slower responses. I think that this is evident in the case of Wilfred Stanley Robertson, widely reported from every point of view but the truth.

In October of 1970 a farmer came into the Prince Albert detachment to complain that he had been shot at by a friend. He was questioned by Constable Douglas Anson who learned that the friend, Stanley Robertson, had caught the farmer parked in a truck with Mrs. Robertson, and had fired at him as he ran off into the night.

About six o'clock that evening Sergeant Robert Schrader and Anson drove out to Robertson's farmhouse several miles southwest of Macdowall. While Schrader looked around outside Anson knocked on the door. "Is your husband home?" he asked Mrs. Robertson.

"Yes," she said, too frightened to say he was in the bedroom loading his rifle, a highpowered 30:06.

Anson went back to the patrol car, got the file and returned to the house, saying "I'd like to talk to you, Mr. Robertson."

"Yes, I'll talk to you all right," Robertson said, and shot him twice. Robertson then stepped out the front door, stood over Anson's body and yelled at Schrader, "Why don't you come and help your buddy?"

Schrader's gun was in the patrol car. With Robertson firing at him, he ran for the trees surrounding the house and circled around to the back. Robertson stepped inside, reloaded, then stepped out the back door. With Schrader calling to him, trying to calm him down, Robertson knelt, caught a glimpse of the yellow stripe on Schrader's breeches, and shot him in the thigh.

Schrader called for help. Robertson walked toward him. "This is all the help I'll give you," he said, shot him again and left him to bleed to death.

As far as I'm concerned both deaths were largely due to low morale. Schrader had 22 years' service, Anson 11. For experienced men all the warning bells were ringing. They knew that this was a family dispute, an emotional volatile situation. But Anson ignored Mrs. Robertson's nervousness and Schrader wasn't wearing sidearms, a fatal omission in this case. At their best, both men would have been on guard, they would have covered each other. But the OC of the subdivision and the NCO of the detachment had a drive on for statistics at this time. On that same night I was talking to an NCO from that detachment who told me morale was "as low as the Earl of Hell's boots."

When Mrs. Robertson phoned the detachment shortly after the murders the OC was out on an inspection trip. When contacted he ordered that nothing be touched at the scene until he arrived. So instead of starting the investigation and manhunt when minutes counted, the men had to stand around, growing jittery, for several hours.

Roadblocks went up all over the province and a 15-year-old boy who refused to stop his car was chased, shot and killed. But no trace was found of Robertson. I was one of the dozens of men brought in from neighboring subdivisions to conduct the manhunt. We were mustered at the meeting point at seven o'clock in the morning and divided into patrols, each led by a senior NCO. Then, on the OC's orders, we stood around until he arrived – four hours later. He made a few perfunctory remarks ("Do not be concerned that this man will shoot. He would be silly to shoot because it would give away his position") and then allowed us to get on with the job.

According to newspapers this manhunt was "the largest in western Canada in modern times." It involved more than 100 men, six police dogs, a helicopter, two fixed-wing aircraft, and two armored personnel carriers. Backed by a $5,000 reward for information, it continued for 35 days. Yet Stanley Robertson wasn't found until the following spring when an RCMP police dog discovered his dead body. He had evidently committed suicide shortly after the search began.

There were experienced investigators on this manhunt but all those I talked to were disgusted by the inept and unnecessary interference of an officer who seemed to want to be in on every phase of a case covered daily by reporters for press, radio and TV. In contrast, the 1967 hunt for the killer of nine people at Shell Lake, Saskatchewan, turned up the accused in five days – with less evidence to go on: the bullets in the bodies, an empty cartridge case, a partial footprint in blood on the farmhouse floor. The difference was that the officer in charge kept morale high. At the end-of-the-day meetings he invited opinions from all members, even the most junior. He kept all members informed of progress, in and out of the search area. If in the Robertson hunt we had been keyed to that pitch of keenness the patrol I was in might have made an extra swing and found the body, which was only a few hundred yards from where we quit.

Most officers, segregated and insulated as they are, soon turn into bureaucrats. Self-protection becomes second nature, inhibiting leadership and decision. I knew, for example, a young recruit who belonged to the Salvation Army. One Sunday he wore a Salvation Army uniform to a meeting and didn't have time to change to his RCMP uniform for church afterward, so he asked permission from the Chief Superintendent in charge of the Training Division to go to church in Salvation Army uniform. The Chief Superintendent was unable to make this simple decision himself. He had to refer it to Ottawa to the Commissioner who granted it. This trainee, incidentally, had difficulty from then on with his instructors. I remember discussing him with the training NCO who called him an oddball, citing the fact that here was a man who was entitled to wear an RCMP uniform yet chose to wear a Salvation Army uniform to church.

There *are* officers in the force who can motivate men and maintain morale. I had two in 14 years and I would have followed those men to hell and back. But most officers will allow you to break the rules to get the job done, then let you take the rap if it brings a complaint. Indeed they'll likely be the ones to mete out your punishment.

An officer may take little responsibility but he has enormous authority. When I was on tour with the Musical Ride in 1958 it was our custom before a performance to exercise our horses. One night I was picking my horse up – making it rear up on its hind legs by the grip of my thighs and a little light rein pressure – when I saw the OC riding back from his place at the head of the column. I thought he was coming to chew me out for hurting the horse's mouth (which I wasn't), but he stopped in front of a constable three or four horsemen down. Figuring I must be mistaken I went on riding and rearing. Again the OC came riding back. Again he spoke to the same man. And after the ride that night the constable he had been speaking to told me, "You've got me in trouble. The OC thought it was me picking up my horse."

"Well, if you're in trouble," I said, "I'll take the blame."

Next morning our staff sergeant said to this man: "The officer in charge saw you picking up your horse. He warned you. You kept on. You're grounded [replaced in the ride]!"

"Staff, that wasn't me," the constable said. "That was Constable Ramsay."

"The OC saw you," the staff sergeant said. "Am I going to take your word over his?" And when *I* tried to explain, he told me, "Forget it. That man has been acting too smart lately anyway."

If an officer is unfair there is no recourse: he has absolute power. Each year all the officers from the subdivisions come for a few days to divisional headquarters to decide which of their men will be transferred where. Since each posting calls for a certain rank, a transfer means, in effect, promotion. And because seniority pulls the most weight, senior officers out-argue their juniors. After a superintendent in Saskatchewan became the second-ranking officer in the province, he promoted so many of his favorites they were known as "special cases." And when a senior sergeant who expected to make staff sergeant protested, the Commanding Officer advised him that he would be on the next list because "all the special cases are now looked after."

If an officer likes you, you've got it made. If he doesn't, you're in trouble: he has any number of ways of getting rid of you. I well remember a constable in a subdivision near mine who had won big money playing poker with other members. Some wouldn't pay up, so he told one debtor, who happened to be his NCO, what he thought of welchers. The NCO complained to the OC about the constable's work and – without any questions, without any checking, without even hearing the constable's story – the OC had him transferred to a larger detachment run by a sergeant who was a tough disciplinarian. Here the constable, afraid of what could happen, worked so hard that his record was one of the best on detachment. Nevertheless he was charged with several minor complaints shortly afterward and let go.

Such tyranny evokes fear, contempt and hate. It's an RCMP tradition that NCOs show respect for their officers by inviting them to an annual Christmas levy, but significantly it's termed a "parade," for which attendance is mandatory. Otherwise only the bootlickers among the NCOs would show up. I know members who hate their officers so much that under the influence of liquor they've threatened to shoot them.

All the way up and down the line, members fear their superiors. I was lucky. I had good NCOs for five years. And then I was posted to a two-man detachment in Manitoba.

In a two-man detachment the constable does most of the police work and the senior man spends most of his time in the office. It can be a rewarding relationship, but my NCO had a drinking problem. I not only did the police work, I did all the office work possible, and in our busiest month, July, worked alone while he took 10 days' leave. I worked 18- and 20-hour days for three months without a day off. I'd be sitting at my typewriter and he'd send me out for a bottle of whiskey, then insist I join him in killing the bottle. Sober, he was a fine policeman. Drunk, he was unbearable. He'd cross-examine me like a criminal when I came in from a case. He once assaulted me physically and afterward I learned that he had assaulted two other men who served under him, breaking the shoulder of one, confining the other to bed for three days. Neither reported it. Nor did I. It meant risking our careers. For eight months he made my life hell and under him I learned hate.

Until that posting I'd never used force, no matter how necessary, without feeling contrite afterward. I would always remember the first time I had to. I was evicting a troublemaker from a bar. He resisted. I knocked him out, and then seeing him lying there on the floor I felt deep remorse. I carried him out to his car, took him home, and didn't charge him. And although I'd had many fights after that, I had never hit a man in anger, never lost that contrite feeling – until that posting.

The town was rough. I was often in fights. But now I could feel the difference. I wasn't just doing my job, I was punishing the person I hit. Some nights I'd go out and be a holy terror. I'd be short with the kid doing power turns on the street, with the young fellow raising his voice in the café. When a drunk refused to get in the police car I'd grab him and fling him in. I was taking out my anger and frustration on the public and this is all too typical of the force.

The system breeds injustice and makes you swallow it. Every member knows that if he complains he'll be labeled a troublemaker, and his NCO will nail him for violating policy. Policemen in other forces have their associations or unions. The Mounted Policeman has no one. He's alone. I might have made an anonymous complaint against my NCO, except that this is an offense. You are allowed to make a signed complaint because the force can deal with you then, but the anonymous complaint is so feared by the force that to make one can cost you a year in prison.

Looking back I can't blame the NCO. He, too, was a victim of the system. I'm sure our divisional officers were aware of his drinking problem because a fight he had with a neighboring detachment NCO was reported to them. Yet those officers did nothing. And he couldn't ask them for help because it's an offense to drink immoderately "at any time."

The force doesn't admit that it has a problem with alcoholism; according to the image, every Mounted Policeman is perfect. Consequently it has no policy or program for dealing with it. When a teetotaling Commanding Officer took over F Division (Saskatchewan) his intolerant attitude toward drinking forced out a number of senior men who were alcoholics. Before the force accepts a man it investigates him thoroughly, but once a problem develops, usually as a direct result of his work, the force will discard him with ruthless indifference.

I know a corporal whose efficiency was so impaired by drinking that complaints about his work were made to his subdivision OC. The OC must have known about his problem, certainly the staff sergeant did. Yet their answer was to promote him to sergeant and get him out of the way by shipping him up north to Uranium City. Predictably, in this isolated post, he drank more heavily than ever. He was soon charged and demoted, and then no doubt felt even more pressure to drink.

The better the man the force recruits the more stress as the truth sinks in: that for you the Bill of Rights doesn't exist, that you're virtually indentured to men you often despise. You then have two choices: you can quit and forfeit your pension, or shut your mind and your mouth (it's dangerous even to talk your problems out; CSO 1149 induces members to inform on each other). But the knowledge of what's happening to you is always there underneath. You try to escape in drink or overwork. You bully the public and your men. You take out your anger, fear and despair on yourself.

There was Johnny Thachik, 37, a sergeant in Regina who fell out of favor with the subdivision OC. After a long absence from field work he was transferred to Weyburn, Saskatchewan, in charge of a busy highway patrol. He soon had administrative problems – one of his men got a girl friend pregnant, others were slipping home for lunch and submitting expense chits for it – and the OC began to pressure him by memo. Johnny took his service revolver, drove out to a side road and shot himself.

There was Russell Brown, 32, a constable in charge of the detachment at Strasbourg, about 50 miles north of Regina. During an inspection of the detachment a section NCO found there was money missing from the contingency fund and told Brown to come to Regina and make a statement. Brown, who had been having marital problems, was getting ready to leave when fire broke out in his wastebasket. Before he could put it out the wall had been scorched. The Commanding Officer of the division was a martinet about cleanliness. Brown went into the Strasbourg fallout shelter at noon and shot himself.

When I was taking a course in Ottawa in 1970 I conducted a two-part guided discussion on "the causes of poor morale in the force and the effects." During the discussion on the effects, a member related an incident in Alberta where a young constable who shot himself lay on the operating table screaming and cursing his staff sergeant before he died.

The only figures on suicide in the RCMP I have seen are for the 10-year period ending September 1964. Of 123 members who died in service, 14 were suicides – by percentage, a thousand times the national average. Two were drinking heavily, five were depressed, one was schizophrenic. Six of the 14 were undergoing investigation or disciplinary action.

RCMP rules are more appropriate to a penal colony than a police force. They're a throwback to a military age when men were pressed into service. Then as now they serve only one purpose: to enable the force to control its men. And the more incompetent its officers, the more they clamp down to keep control. The system, like all such systems, is self-perpetuating.

The force creates fear and guilt in a man, builds intolerable pressure, then ignores the resulting problem until it blows up and threatens the image.

The image is the reason that members wear stetsons, breeches and spurred boots in an age when the only riding on duty is done in the Musical Ride. I have in front of me a Canadian Press clipping dated March 14, 1972. In it an Alberta judge, J. H. Mackenzie, is quoted as stating that such footgear has no place on the feet of police in an urban area. His comment came after a trial in which a Mounted Policeman from Red Deer said he was hampered by his uniform when chasing two fleeing suspects. A reporter then contacted his subdivision OC, Superintendent Robert Mills, who said he would refer the criticism to headquarters. But the Commissioner's office has long ago been inundated with memos complaining of the impracticability of this attire. In fact, it was discarded as a working uniform in 1965 but was reinstated in a memo of August 12, 1970, because, according to the memo: "It is important that we restore rather than further erode our image." In this memo "the image" is mentioned three times, and many other internal memos refer to it.

But the image is slowly tarnishing. Recently, in northern Saskatchewan, 18 Indians came out of the bush; surrounded an RCMP patrol that was checking for liquor violations and told them to get off the reserve or they'd kill them. And Saskatchewan courts are now jammed with Indians contesting cases. I think many people in the West – where the force is the provincial police and they see it in its day-to-day work – are beginning to doubt the truth of the image. One magistrate, a friend of mine, has told me he now looks with suspicion on the testimony of some Mounted Policemen, and I know that he is not alone in this view. Nothing erodes the respect of the public for a police force more than contact with policemen who have lost their self-respect.

And the less the public respects the force the more the force promotes the image. After her husband was killed by Stanley Robertson, Constable Anson's widow informed the subdivision OC that she wanted him buried in Pierceland, her hometown. But the OC persuaded her to let Anson be buried in the RCMP cemetery in Regina with full military honors, including an archbishop, an honor guard (firing an especially inappropriate volley of rifle shots), loudspeakers carrying the chapel ceremony to the overflow crowd in the drill hall, and full coverage by press, radio and television.

Mrs. Anson was still at home in mourning when two GIS (General Investigation Section) members arrived and said they'd like to check Anson's effects for RCMP property. Before his death Anson had received a memo from his subdivision OC telling him to shape up or be shipped out. After the GIS men left all derogatory memos were missing and Mrs. Anson was asked to conduct herself as the widow of a hero. It was also suggested she not take work for a few months. One can see why. If some reporter discovered her, say, slinging hash, it wouldn't reflect well on the force's image.

Later the families of Constable Anson and Sergeant Schrader were brought to the chapel in Regina for the unveiling of a commemorative plaque. A eulogy was delivered by the Commanding Officer of F Division, which takes in all of Saskatchewan. He referred at the beginning and end to "Constable Anson" and at all times in between to "Constable Anderson." Afterward, as a few of us were having a drink with the Anson family, Anson's mother-in-law said tartly, "This was just a great big show. They brought us all the way down here pretending to honor Doug and they don't even know his name."

For years I ignored the disillusioning facts. Every time I saw a member in the witness stand being evasive, suppressing evidence beneficial to the accused, I would say to myself, "That's not the Mounted Police, that's the weakness of one individual." Even after my experience with the alcoholic NCO I blamed the force's bad communications rather than its system of values. And I still liked police work, although in breaking up a fight in 1968 I hit a man who, in falling, struck his head on the sidewalk and died 10 days later. The cause of death was a brain hemorrhage, according to the coroner's jury that exonerated me.

No, it was a trial in the RCMP's service court that finally brought my feelings into focus. Service court is the ultimate disciplinary instrument of the force. Any member charged with violating the RCMP Act or Commissioner's Standing Orders is prosecuted in the RCMP's version of a court martial. His sentence if convicted can be up to one year in jail but usually it's dismissal or a damaged career. The force claims this is necessary for discipline and efficiency and that service court is patterned on civil judiciary procedure which ensures the accused a fair trial. I had often heard that it was more like a kangaroo court and the greatest single source of low morale. But I had never seen it in operation until a close friend, Corporal Robert Harnett, was charged and brought before it.

Bob called me at home in Regina one night in October 1970 to say that he had been charged with conducting himself "in a disgraceful manner by having an association with a female other than his wife." He had been in charge of a three-man detachment at Loon Lake, in northern Saskatchewan, and in winning the trust of the Indians on the bordering reserve, his chief responsibility, he had inevitably stepped on some white toes. The postmaster, for example, had been putting the Indians' relief cheques in the post office boxes of the storekeepers who gave them credit. The storekeepers cashed them, paid themselves, then gave the Indians their change. One Indian had complained and Harnett had put a stop to the practice. That didn't make him too popular with some whites and when a rumor went round that the corporal, married with five children, was dating a young Indian girl, it was passed along to the subdivision.

Harnett could have denied the charge and explained away the rumor as malicious gossip. Or he could have said, "Sure, I'm seeing this girl, she's the best informant I've got." But Harnett was not only one of the best policemen in the subdivision, a man with 14 years' experience, he's an honest man. He had frankly admitted to the investigating staff sergeant that his marriage had not gone well for years, that he and his wife were on the verge of amicable separation, and that in trying to rehabilitate a 16-year-old Indian girl he had fallen in love and they were having an affair.

Harnett had signed two statements admitting his guilt and these had been forwarded to Ottawa with a recommendation that he be charged with a minor service offense. Back had come a memo from the Commissioner's office ordering "a very aggressive and determined investigation . . . to obtain sufficient evidence to establish charging this man with a major service offense." Harnett was calling me now to see if I would act as his defense lawyer. Members who go before service court are not allowed outside counsel.

I couldn't condone his offense, nor did he expect me to. He would have pleaded guilty, he said, except that the charge had claimed that the association had taken place "at or near Loon Lake" and "at other locations in the Province of Saskatchewan and Alberta . . ." Nothing had taken place in Alberta, Bob said, and he refused to plead guilty to a charge that contained a lie. With misgivings, in view of my inexperience, I agreed to defend him.

The prosecution at that point had had three senior NCOs investigating Bob over a six-month period. I had to take a course in Ottawa, after which I had only three days to prepare my defense. I telephoned the prosecutor, Staff Sergeant William Preston, and asked him for particulars of the charge.

Preston had already denied them to Bob. Now he refused to give them to me. Disturbed, I asked for an interview with the division's administration officer, Inspector Dale Henry. "I feel completely incompetent to defend this man," I told him.

"It's just a matter of thinking on your feet," he assured me. "The trial officer, Inspector [Alex] Hawrys, will give you every opportunity to present your case."

We had only one hope, but a good one. A charge is made up of ingredients, and the prosecution must prove beyond reasonable doubt that each ingredient is true. We had only to disprove the ingredient that Harnett assured me was false – his association with the Indian girl in Alberta – to win the case.

The trial took place in the bleak basement room of the North Battleford sub-division. Standing Orders state that witnesses must be placed to face the accused. Here they faced the prosecution, and though Bob and I turned our heads, we couldn't see their expressions, couldn't sense what they didn't say.

It was a portent of what we could expect. Staff Sergeant Preston asked for permission to lead his first witness because of her inexperience with service court, an absurd contention; nine of 10 witnesses are inexperienced in any court, and no lawyer would think of suggesting to a judge that they be led. Yet Inspector Hawrys allowed it. He also allowed the prosecutor to cross-examine his own witnesses, which he could never have done in a court of law. And though we showed that the only witness to an Alberta association had given what appeared to be contradictory evidence, Hawrys ignored it. He found Harnett "guilty as charged," reduced his rank to First Class Constable, and recommended he be "dismissed from the force forthwith."

We immediately appealed and won a new trial on the grounds that Harnett had been refused particulars of the charge. We then appealed the decision of the appeal board, made up of senior RCMP officers, claiming the charge should have been dismissed. Our appeal was turned down and a new trial was ordered. This was more than Harnett could bear. He asked for a discharge.

"I've had it," he told me. "I'm empty. Emotionally drained." In his desire to stay in the force, he had broken with the Indian girl and had thrown himself so deeply into work that he had won a commendation from his OC, but he knew that a new trial meant that he was finished.

"They've dragged me through the dirt for 10 months. They've lost me the respect of friends. Smashed my career. Turned the Indians against the Mounted Police at Loon Lake and undone everything there we worked for. Turned members against each other. Ruined any chance of reconciliation with my wife. And for what? To turn a rumor into a scandal! To prove that what I told them to start with was true. Why couldn't they just have fired me? Why put me through this farce? If they told me I was forgiven now I'd tell them to go to hell. I just want to get away from anything to do with the RCMP, their orderly rooms, their petty stage productions."

The experience had left *me* deeply troubled, too. To me, service court is a mockery of justice. The prosecutor had run roughshod over the rights of the accused and the trial judge had supported him. As a man facing what amounted to a criminal charge, Harnett should have had a lawyer, but I'm convinced that the force wouldn't want anyone from the legal profession to see how its service court functions. I'm sure that any good trial lawyer would have torn the prosecution's case to shreds. As it was Harnett had to rely on what little legal knowledge I had picked up. What's more, the trial officer had no formal legal training. Most important of all, he was well aware that the Commissioner's office had looked at the evidence, and if they order a man charged they must consider him guilty. And who is he to contradict the Commissioner's office? In a public court the evidence determines guilt. In service court it's the wish of the force.

I felt that my stubborn defense of Bob had put my career in jeopardy but that wasn't what made me decide to leave the force. While brooding on Harnett's case I remembered an Indian constable accused of getting a young white girl pregnant and after investigation the force had hushed the whole thing up, because if an Indian was discharged people might think the force prejudiced. And suddenly I saw clearly that this could mean ony one thing: the force isn't concerned with morals, it isn't concerned with justice or truth, it isn't concerned with the public or its men, it is concerned only with increasing its power by polishing its image.

The reputation of the RCMP is a priceless national asset. It still attracts fine young men eager to serve. But nothing is more frustrating than to hold a high ideal and to see yourself driven further from it daily. I think the force can be great again, but it needs a change in attitude, and this change will have to come from the top and come fast. Because the lower the image sinks the more the force pressures its men, crushing their integrity, widening the gap between the police and the public.

It was the public who made the legend because it felt well served. The force cannot restore its image by serving itself. There's an RCMP saying, "the force exists in spite of itself," which means that if it wasn't for the good men risking their futures every day, standing up under constant physical stress while enduring psychic fear, the standard of police service provided by the RCMP would be intolerable, and the image would go the way of the men who made it.

Someone once said that rules are a guide for the wise man, a law for the fool. When the force tells Canadian parents that they make men of their boys, what kind of a man do they have in mind? A wise man? A brave man? Truthful and morally sound? A man treated so fairly by those he serves under that he will himself be fair? A man so secure in his rights that he will ensure ours? Not as things are now.

CREATING DEVIANCE AND DEVIANT IDENTITIES

This section examines the close relationship between the genesis of deviant identities and the structural arrangements in society which give rise to and sustain deviant self-conceptions. Suggestions regarding this affinity can be found in the early writing of Shaw (1930) and Tannenbaum (1938) and are implied in the sociological argument that points to the tendency of societies to create and sustain deviance to promote solidarity and to distinguish what is moral and worthy of pursuit (Durkheim, 1949; Dentler and Erikson, 1959; Coser, 1962). In recent times, proponents of the labelling perspective have argued that agencies of social control, commonly charged to reduce the magnitude of deviant behaviour, inadvertently maintain and reinforce deviant identities through their imposition of a stigma on those under their authority. While traditional sociology has emphasized the belief that deviance leads to social control, Lemert (1967) has suggested that the notion that social control leads to deviance is a potentially richer premise for the study of deviance.

Students of the labelling perspective have addressed themselves to the processes by which deviant identities and careers are shaped, developed and sustained. Sociological literature conceptualizing people as products of organizational work have examined various aspects of what have come to be called "people-processing institutions" (Bittner, 1967; Cicourel and Kitsuse, 1963; Freidson, 1966). This concept, originating with Erving Goffman's study of a public mental hospital (1961), has been recently defined as follows:

> This term . . . refers to a type of social institution in which human beings constitute both the raw materials and the products of organizational work. Although all social institutions are involved in some degree in people-processing activities, the term is properly restricted to those whose primary goal is the shaping, reshaping, removing, overhauling, retooling, reassembling, and recording the physical, psychological, social, legal, or moral aspects of human objects. (Kitsuse, 1970:163)

A consequence of such organizational processing is that the individual is confronted with a drastic change in his public identity. He comes to be designated as a certain kind of person, a designation that will likely have important consequences for his further social participation and everyday life. The agency personnel's perception of the individual, however faulty, effectively produces a self-fulfilling prophecy whereby the individual comes to be shaped in the image his controllers have of him. Blocked in his access to certain career lines and social groups, he may ultimately drift toward unconventional occupations and friendship circles where his tarnished public identity is of little concern. Forcing the person to accept his deviant label may heighten rather than reduce his pursuit of deviant activity. As Lemert (1967) has suggested, the individual's reaction to his being labelled and stigmatized may strengthen the deviant conduct and ultimately result in the person's acceptance of the deviant social status.

We do not wish to imply that everyone labelled inevitably moves toward increased deviance. Obviously, the self-fulfilling prophecy is often unfulfilled. We do mean to emphasize, however, that the development of deviant identities is defined, affirmed, and re-affirmed in the course of interaction between the individual and those responding officially to his deviantly-defined behaviour (Becker, 1963:35).

The articles in this section point to the different levels at which the process of creating deviance and deviant identities occurs. While self-typing can occur in the absence of physically present others, we consider this route least important as far as the attendant consequences of such labelling is concerned. Instead, we direct the reader's attention to how deviant identities may result from interaction at the group, institutional and community levels. While it may be useful to delineate the processes of control at various levels of social organization, it is important to recognize that this analytic distinction should not obscure the relationship between different levels of organization.

In our first selection, Lemert shows how deliberate attempts at social exclusion contribute to individuals' development of paranoid behaviour. His article warns the reader that paranoia is not to be exclusively understood as a problem within the individual, but is related to the real, but peculiar, structured reactions of others to him. Crespo's article further emphasizes the relationships of social structures to individual behaviour. He describes the processes and contingencies which are part of the career of the "school skipper" in an urban, low-income, French speaking high school. The author gives special emphasis to the importance the school's tracking system has in marginalizing certain students that it was believed to commit to full school participation. In the next section, Marshall and Hughes address themselves to recent "reforms" in Canadian Mental Hospital legislation. They criticize this legislative trend for its real or potential abuse of civil liberties. They also raise questions about the usefulness and validity of the medical model of mental illness and argue for an understanding of mental illness in terms of labelling theory. Cameron examines the set of events surrounding the questionable, involuntary hospitalization of a young man in New Brunswick. His description of the events and circumstances compels the reader to consider whether this incarceration was primarily the result of the patient's danger to himself or others, or of his misunderstood and unconventional lifestyle. Finally, Brown presents his own biography as a mental patient. As a consequence of reading sociological and social psychiatric treatises on mental ilı. he is able to redefine his mental hospital experiences in terms of the pec ple-processing work of institutions rather than as a problem within himself.

References

Becker, H. S. *Outsiders: Studies in the Sociology of Deviance*. New York: The Free Press, 1963.

Bittner, E. "Police discretion in apprehending the mentally ill." *Social Problems* 14 (Winter), 1967, pp. 278-92.

Cicourel, A. V. and J. I. Kitsuse. *The Educational Decision-Makers*. Indianapolis: Bobbs-Merrill, 1963.

Coser, L. "Some function of deviant behavior and normative flexibility," *American Journal of Sociology*, 68 (1962), pp. 172-81.

Dentler, R. A. and K. T. Erikson. "The functions of deviance in groups." *Social Problems*, (Fall), 1959, pp. 98-107.

Durkheim, E. *The Division of Labor in Society*. New York: Free Press of Glencoe, 1949.

Freidson, E. "Disability as social deviance," in M. Sussman (ed.) *Sociology and Rehabilitation*. Washington, D.C.: American Sociological Association, 1966.

Goffman, E. *Asylums*. Garden City, N.Y.: Doubleday Anchor, 1961.

Kituse, J. I. "Editor's preface," *American Behavioral Scientist* 14 (Nov./Dec.), 1970, pp. 163-65.

Lemert, E. *Human Deviance, Social Problems, and Social Control*. Englewood Cliffs, N.J.: Prentice-Hall, 1967.

Shaw, C. R. *The Jack-Roller*. Chicago: University of Chicago Press, 1966.

Tannenbaum, F. *Crime and the Community*. Boston: Ginn and Company, 1938.

7
Paranoia and the Dynamics of Exclusion

E. Lemert

One of the few generalizations about psychotic behavior which sociologists have been able to make with a modicum of agreement and assurance is that such behavior is a result or manifestation of a disorder in communication between the individual and society. The generalization, of course, is a large one, and, while it can be illustrated easily with case history materials, the need for its conceptual refinement and detailing of the process by which disruption of communication occurs in the dynamics of mental disorder has for some time been apparent. Among the more carefully reasoned attacks upon this problem is Cameron's formulation of the paranoid pseudocommunity.[1]

In essence, the conception of the paranoid pseudocommunity can be stated as follows:[2]

Paranoid persons are those whose inadequate social learning leads them in situations of unusual stress to incompetent social reactions. Out of the fragments of the social behavior of others the paranoid person symbolically organizes a pseudocommunity whose functions he perceives as focused on him. His reactions to this *supposed community* of response which he sees loaded with threat to himself bring him into open conflict with the actual community and lead to his temporary or permanent isolation from its affairs. The "real" community, which is unable to share in his attitudes and reactions, takes action through forcible restraint or retaliation *after* the paranoid person "bursts into defensive or vengeful activity."[3]

That the community to which the paranoid reacts is "pseudo" or without existential reality is made unequivocal by Cameron when he says:

> As he (the paranoid person) begins attributing to others the attitudes which he has toward himself, he unintentionally organizes these others into a functional community, a group unified in their supposed reactions, attitudes, and plans with respect to him. He in this way organizes individuals, some of whom are actual persons and some only inferred or imagined, into a whole which satisfies for the time being his immediate need for explanation but which brings no assurance with it, and usually serves to increase his tensions. The community he forms not only fails to correspond to any organization shared by others but actually contradicts this consensus. More than this, the actions ascribed by him to its personnel are not actually performed or maintained by

them; *they are united in no common undertaking against him.*[4] [Italics ours.]

The general insightfulness of Cameron's analysis cannot be gainsaid and the usefulness of some of his concepts is easily granted. Yet a serious question must be raised, based upon empirical inquiry, as to whether in actuality the insidious qualities of the community to which the paranoid reacts are pseudo or a symbolic fabrication. There is an alternative point of view, which is the burden of this paper, namely that, while the paranoid person reacts differentially to his social environment, it is also true that "others" react differentially to him and this reaction commonly if not typically involves covertly organized action and conspiratorial behavior in a very real sense. A further extension of our thesis is that these differential reactions are reciprocals of one another, being interwoven and concatenated at each and all phases of a process of exclusion which arises in a special kind of relationship. Delusions and associated behavior must be understood in a context of exclusion which attenuates this relationship and disrupts communication.

By thus shifting the clinical spotlight away from the individual to a relationship and a process, we make an explicit break with the conception of paranoia as a disease, a state, a condition, or a syndrome of symptoms. Furthermore, we find it unnecessary to postulate trauma of early childhood or arrested psychosexual development to account for the main features of paranoia – although we grant that these and other factors may condition its expression.

This conception of paranoia is neither simple *a priori* theory nor is it a proprietary product of sociology. There is a substantial body of writings and empirical researches in psychiatry and psychology which question the sufficiency of the individual as primary datum for the study of paranoia. Tyhurst, for example, concludes from his survey of this literature that reliance upon intrapsychic mechanisms and the "isolated organism" have been among the chief obstacles to fruitful discoveries about this disorder.[5] Significantly, as Milner points out, the more complete the investigation of the cases the more frequently do unendurable external circumstances make their appearance.[6] More precisely, a number of studies have ended with the conclusions that external circumstances – changes in norms and values, displacement, strange environments, isolation, and linguistic separation – may create a paranoid disposition in the absence of any special character structure.[7] The recognition of paranoid reactions in elderly persons, alcoholics, and the deaf adds to the data generally consistent with our thesis. The finding that displaced persons who withstood a high degree of stress during war and captivity subsequently developed paranoid reactions when they were isolated in a foreign environment commands special attention among data requiring explanation in other than organic or psychodynamic terms.[8]

From what has been said thus far, it should be clear that our formulation and analysis will deal primarily with what Tyhurst[9] calls paranoid patterns of behavior rather than with a clinical entity in the classical Kraepelinian sense. Paranoid reactions, paranoid states, paranoid personality disturbances, as well as the seldom-diagnosed "true paranoia," which are found superimposed or associated with a wide variety of individual behavior or "symptoms," all provide a body of data for study so long as they assume priority over other behavior in meaningful social interaction. The elements of behavior upon which paranoid diagnoses are based – delusions, hostility, aggressiveness, suspicion, envy, stubbornness, jealousy, and ideas of reference – are readily comprehended and to some extent empathized by others as social reactions, in contrast to the bizarre, manneristic behavior of schizophrenia or the tempo and affect changes stressed in manic-depressive diagnoses. It is for this reason that paranoia suggests, more than any other forms of mental disorder, the possibility of fruitful sociological analysis.

Data and Procedure

The first tentative conclusions which are presented here were drawn from a study of factors influencing decisions to commit mentally disordered persons to hospitals, undertaken with the cooperation of the Los Angeles County Department of Health in 1952. This included interviews by means of schedules with members of 44 families in Los Angeles County who were active petitioners in commitment proceedings and the study of 35 case records of public health officer commitments. In 16 of the former cases and in seven of the latter, paranoid symptoms were conspicuously present. In these cases family members and others had plainly accepted or "normalized" paranoid behavior, in some instances longstanding, until other kinds of behavior or exigencies led to critical judgments that "there was something wrong" with the person in question, and, later, that hospitalization was necessary. Furthermore, these critical judgments seemed to signal changes in the family attitudes and behavior toward the affected persons which could be interpreted as contributing in different ways to the form and intensity of the paranoid symptoms.

In 1958 a more refined and hypothesis-directed study was made of eight cases of persons with prominent paranoid characteristics. Four of these had been admitted to the state hospital at Napa, California, where they were diagnosed as paranoid schizophrenic. Two other cases were located and investigated with the assistance of the district attorney in Martinez, California. One of the persons had previously been committed to a California state hospital, and the other had been held on an insanity petition but was freed after a jury trial. Added to these was one so-called "White House case," which had involved threats to a President of the United States, resulting in the person's commitment to St. Elizabeth's Hospital in Washington, D.C. A final case was that of a professional person with a history of chronic job difficulties, who was designated and regarded by his associates as "brash," "queer," "irritating," "hypercritical," and "thoroughly unlikeable."

In a very rough way the cases made up a continuum ranging from one with very elaborate delusions, through those in which fact and misinterpretation were difficult to separate, down to the last case, which comes closer to what some would call paranoid personality disturbance. A requirement for the selection of the cases was that there be no history or evidence of hallucinations and also that the persons be intellectually unimpaired. Seven of the cases were of males, five of whom were over 40 years of age. Three of the persons had been involved in repeated litigations. One man published a small, independent paper devoted to exposures of psychiatry and mental hospitals. Five of the men had been or were associated with organizations, as follows: a smalltown high school, a government research bureau, an association of agricultural producers, a university, and a contracting business.

The investigations of the cases were as exhaustive as it was possible to make them, reaching relatives, work associates, employers, attorneys, police, physicians, public officials, and any others who played significant roles in the lives of the persons involved. As many as 200 hours each were given to collecting data on some of the cases. Written materials, legal documents, publications, and psychiatric histories were studied in addition to the interview data. Our procedure in the large was to adopt an international perspective which sensitized us to sociologically relevant behavior underlying or associated with the more apparent and formal contexts of mental disorder. In particular we were concerned to establish the order in which delusions and social exclusion occur and to determine whether exclusion takes conspiratorial form.

The Relevant Behavior

In another paper[10] we have shown that psychotic symptoms as described in formal psychiatry are not relevant bases for predictions about changes in social status and social participation of persons in whom they appear. Apathy, hallucinations, hyperactivity, mood swings, tics, tremors, functional paralysis, or tachychardias have no intrinsic social meanings. By the same token, neither do such imputed attributes as "lack of insight," "social incompetence," or "defective role-taking ability" favored by some sociologists as generic starting points for the analysis of mental disorders. Rather, it is behavior which puts strain on social relationships that leads to status changes:

informal or formal exclusion from groups, definition as a "crank," or adjudication as insane and commitment to a mental hospital.[11] This is true even where the grandiose and highly bizarre delusions of paranoia are present. Definition of the socially stressful aspects of this disorder is a minimum essential, if we are to account for its frequent occurrence in partially compensated or benign form in society, as well as account for its more familiar presence as an official psychiatric problem in a hospital setting.

It is necessary, however, to go beyond these elementary observations to make it preeminently clear that strain is an emergent product of a relationship in which the behaviors of two or more persons are relevant factors, and in which the strain is felt both by ego and *alter* or *alters*. The paranoid relationship includes reciprocating behaviors with attached emotions and meanings which, to be fully understood, must be described cubistically from at least two of its perspectives. On one hand the behavior of the individual must be seen from the perspective of others or that of a group, and conversely the behavior of others must be seen from the perspective of the involved individual.

From the vantage of others the individual in the paranoid relationship shows:

1. a disregard for the values and norms of the primary group, revealed by giving priority to verbally definable values over those which are implicit, a lack of loyalty in return for confidences, and victimizing and intimidating persons in positions of weakness.
2. a disregard for the implicit structure of groups, revealed by presuming to privileges not accorded him, and the threat or actual resort to formal means for achieving his goals.

The second items have a higher degree of relevancy than the first in an analysis of exclusion. Stated more simply, they mean that, to the group, the individual is an ambiguous figure whose behavior is uncertain, whose loyalty can't be counted on. In short, he is a person who can't be trusted because he threatens to expose informal power structures. This, we believe, is the essential reason for the frequently encountered idea that the paranoid person is "dangerous."[12]

If we adopt the perceptual set of ego and see others or groups through his eyes, the following aspects of their behavior become relevant:

1. The spurious quality of the interaction between others and himself or between others interacting in his presence;
2. The overt avoidance of himself by others;
3. The structured exclusion of himself from interaction.

The items we have described thus far – playing fast and loose with the primary group values by the individual, and his exclusion from interaction – do not alone generate and maintain paranoia. It is additionally necessary that they emerge in an interdependent relationship which requires trust for its fulfillment. The relationship is a type in which the goals of the individual can be reached only through cooperation from particular others, and in which the ends held by others are realizable if cooperation is forthcoming from ego. This is deduced from the general proposition that cooperation rests upon perceived trust, which in turn is a function of communication.[13] When communication is disrupted by exclusion, there is a lack of mutually perceived trust and the relationship becomes dilapidated or paranoid. We will now consider the process of exclusion by which this kind of relationship develops.

The Generic Process of Exclusion

The paranoid process begins with persistent interpersonal difficulties between the individual and his family, or his work associates and superiors, or neighbors, or other persons in the community. These frequently or even typically arise out of bona fide or recognizable issues centering upon some actual or threatened loss of status for the individual. This is related to such things as the death of relatives, loss of a position, loss of professional certification, failure to be promoted, age and physiological life cycle changes, mutilations, and changes in family and marital relationships. The status changes are distinguished by the fact that they leave no alternative acceptable to the individual, from whence comes their "intolerable" or "unendurable" quality. For example: the man trained to be a teacher who loses his certificate, which means he can never teach; or the man of 50 years of age who is faced with loss of a promotion which is a regular order of upward mobility in an organization, who knows that he can't "start over"; or the wife undergoing hysterectomy, which mutilates her image as a woman.

In cases where no dramatic status loss can be discovered, a series of failures often is present, failures which may have been accepted or adjusted to, but with progressive tension as each new status situation is entered. The unendurability of the current status loss, which may appear unimportant to others, is a function of an intensified commitment, in some cases born of an awareness that there is a quota placed on failures in our society. Under some such circumstances, failures have followed the person, and his reputation as a "difficult person" has preceded him. This means that he often has the status of a stranger on trial in each new group he enters, and that the groups or organizations willing to take a chance on him are marginal from the standpoint of their probable tolerance for his actions.

The behavior of the individual – arrogance, insults, presumption of privilege, and exploitation of weaknesses in others – initially has a segmental or checkered pattern in that it is confined to status-committing interactions. Outside of these, the person's behavior may be quite acceptable – courteous, considerate, kind, even indulgent. Likewise, other persons and members of groups vary considerably in their tolerance for the relevant behavior, depending on the extent to which it threatens individual and organizational values, impedes functions, or sets in motion embarrassing sequences of social actions. In the early generic period, tolerance by others for the individual's aggressive behavior generally speaking is broad, and it is very likely to be interpreted as a variation of normal behavior, particularly in the absence of biographical knowledge of the person. At most, people observe that "there is something odd about him," or "he must be upset," or "he is just ornery," or "I don't quite understand him."[14]

At some point in the chain of interactions, a new configuration takes place in perceptions others have of the individual, with shifts in figure-ground relations. The individual, as we have already indicated, is an ambiguous figure, comparable to textbook figures of stairs or outlined cubes which reverse themselves when studied intently. From a normal variant the person becomes "unreliable," "untrustworthy," "dangerous," or someone with whom others "do not wish to be involved." An illustration nicely apropos of this came out in the reaction of the head of a music department in a university when he granted an interview to a man who had worked for years on a theory to compose music mathematically:

> When he asked to be placed on the staff so that he could use the electronic computers of the University I *shifted my ground* . . . when I offered an objection to his theory, he became disturbed, so I changed my reaction to "yes and no."

As is clear from this, once the perceptual reorientation takes place, either as the outcome of continuous interaction or through the receipt of biographical information, interaction changes qualitatively. In our words it becomes *spurious*, distinguished by patronizing, evasion, "humoring," guiding conversation onto selected topics, underreaction, and silence, all calculated either to prevent intense interaction or to protect individual and group values by restricting access to them. When the interaction is between two or more persons in the individual's presence it is cued by a whole repertoire of subtle expressive signs which are meaningful only to them.

The net effects of spurious interaction are to:

1. stop the flow of information to ego;
2. create a discrepancy between expressed ideas and affect among those with whom he interacts;
3. make the situation or the group image an ambiguous one for ego, much as he is for others.

Needless to say this kind of spurious interaction is one of the most difficult for an adult in our society to cope with, because it complicates or makes decisions impossible for him and also because it is morally invidious.[15]

The process from inclusion to exclusion is by no means an even one. Both individuals and members of groups change their perceptions and reactions, and vacillation is common, depending upon the interplay of values, anxieties, and guilt on both sides. Members of an excluding group may decide they have been unfair and seek to bring the individual back into their confidence. This overture may be rejected or used by ego as a means of further attack. We have also found that ego may capitulate, sometimes abjectly, to others and seek group reentry, only to be rejected. In some cases compromises are struck and a partial reintergration of ego into informal social relations is achieved. The direction which informal exclusion takes depends upon ego's reactions, the degree of communication between his interactors, the composition and structure of the informal groups, and the perceptions of "key others" at points of interaction which directly affect ego's status.

Organizational Crisis and Formal Exclusion

Thus far we have discussed exclusion as an informal process. Informal exclusion may take place but leave ego's formal status in an organization intact. So long as this status is preserved and rewards are sufficient to validate it on his terms, an uneasy peace between him and others may prevail. Yet ego's social isolation and his strong commitments make him an unpredictable factor; furthermore the rate of change and internal power struggles, especially in large and complex organizations, means that preconditions of stability may be short lived.

Organizational crises involving a paranoid relationship arise in several ways. The individual may act in ways which arouse intolerable anxieties in others, who demand that "something be done." Again, by going to higher authority or making appeals outside the organization, he may set in motion procedures which leave those in power no other choice than to take action. In some situations ego remains relatively quiescent and does not openly attack the organization. Action against him is set off by growing anxieties or calculated motives of associates – in some cases his immediate superiors. Finally, regular organizational procedures incidental to promotion, retirement, or reassignment may precipitate the crisis.

Assuming a critical situation in which the conflict between the individual and members of the organization leads to action to formally exclude him, several possibilites exist. One is the transfer of ego from one department, branch, or division of the organization to another, a device frequently resorted to in the armed services or in large corporations. This requires that the individual be persuaded to make the change and that some department will accept him. While this may be accomplished in different ways, not infrequently artifice, withholding information, bribery, or thinly disguised threats figure conspicuously among the means by which the transfer is brought about. Needless to say, there is a limit to which transfers can be employed as a solution to the problem, contingent upon the size of the organization and the previous diffusion of knowledge about the transferee.

Solution number two we call encapsulation, which, in brief, is a reorganization and redefinition of ego's status. This has the effect of isolating him from the organization and making him directly responsible to one or two superiors who act as his intermediators. The change is often made palatable to ego by enhancing some of the material rewards of his status. He may be nominally promoted or "kicked upstairs," given a larger office, or a separate secretary, or relieved of onerous duties. Sometimes a special status is created for him.

This type of solution often works because it is a kind of formal recognition by the organization of ego's intense commitment to his status and in part a victory for him over his enemies. It bypasses them and puts him into direct communication with higher authority who may communicate with him in a more direct manner. It also relieves his associates of further need to connive against him. This solution is sometimes used to dispose of troublesome corporation executives, high-ranking military officers, and academic *personae non gratae* in universities.

A third variety of solution to the problem of paranoia in an organization is outright discharge, forced resignation or non-renewal of appointment. Finally, there may be an organized move to have the individual in the paranoid relationship placed on sick leave, or to compel him to take psychiatric treatment. The extreme expression of this pressure (as on the family) or direct action to have the person committed to a mental hospital.

The order of the enumerated solutions to the paranoid problem in a rough way reflects the amount of risk associated with the alternatives, both as to the probabilities of failure and of damaging repercussions to the organization. Generally, organizations seem to show a good deal of resistance to making or carrying out decisions which require expulsion of the individual or forcing hospitalization, regardless of his mental condition. One reason for this is that the person may have power within the organization, based upon his position or monopolized skills and information,[16] and unless there is a strong coalition against him the general conservatism of administrative judgments will run in his favor. Herman Wouk's novel, *The Caine Mutiny*, dramatizes some of the difficulties of cashiering a person from a position of power in an essentially conservative military organization. An extreme of this conservatism is illustrated by one case in which we found a department head retained in his position in an organization even though he was actively hallucinating as well as expressing paranoid delusions.[17] Another factor working on the individual's side is that discharge of a person in a position of power reflects unfavorably upon those who placed him there. In-group solidarity of administrators may be involved, and the methods of the opposition may create sympathy for ego at higher levels.

Even when the person is almost totally excluded and informally isolated within an organization, he may have power outside. This weighs heavily when the external power can be invoked in some way, or when it automatically leads to raising questions as to the internal workings of the organization. This touches upon the more salient reason for reluctance to eject an uncooperative and retaliatory person, even when he is relatively unimportant to the organization. We refer to a kind of negative power derived from the vulnerability of organizations to unfavorable publicity and exposure of their private lives that are likely if the crisis proceeds to formal hearings, case review, or litigation. This is an imminent possibility where paranoia exists. If hospital commitment is attempted, there is a possibility that a jury trial will be demanded, which will force leaders of the organization to defend their actions. If the crisis turns into a legal contest of this sort, it is not easy to prove insanity, and there may be damage suits. Even if the facts heavily support the petitioners, such contests can only throw unfavorable light upon the organization.

The Conspiratorial Nature of Exclusion

A conclusion from the foregoing is that organizational vulnerability as well as anticipations of retaliations from the paranoid person lay a functional basis for conspiracy among those seeking to contain or oust him. Probabilities are strong that a coalition will appear within the organization, integrated by a common commitment to oppose the paranoid person. This, the exlusionist group, demands loyalty, solidarity, and secrecy from its members; it acts in accord with a common scheme and in varying degrees utilizes techniques of manipulation and misrepresentation.

Conspiracy in rudimentary form can be detected in informal exclusion apart from an organizational crisis. This was illustrated in an office research team in which staff members huddled around a water cooler to discuss the unwanted associate. They also used office telephones to arrange coffee breaks without him and employed symbolic cues in his presence, such as humming the Dragnet theme song when he approached the group. An office rule against extraneous conversation was introduced with the collusion of supervisors, ostensibly for everyone, actually to restrict the behavior of the isolated worker. In another case an interview schedule designed by a researcher was changed at a conference arranged without him. When he sought an explanation at a subsequent conference, his associates pretended to have no knowledge of the changes.

Conspiratorial behavior comes into sharpest focus during organizational crises in which the exclusionists who initiate action become an embattled group. There is a concerted effort to gain consensus for this view, to solidify the group and to halt close interaction with those unwilling to join the coalition completely. Efforts are also made to neutralize those who remain uncommitted but who can't be kept ignorant of the plans afoot. Thus an external appearance of unanimity is given even if it doesn't exist.

Much of the behavior of the group at this time is strategic in nature, with determined calculations as to "what we will do if he does this or that." In one of our cases, a member on a board of trustees spoke of the "game being played" with the person in controversy with them. Planned action may be carried to the length of agreeing upon the exact words to be used when confronted or challenged by the paranoid individual. Above all there is continuous, precise communication among exclusionists, exemplified in one case by mutual exchanging of copies of all letters sent and received from ego.

Concern about secrecy in such groups is revealed by such things as carefully closing doors and lowering of voices when ego is brought under discussion. Meeting places and times may be varied from normal procedures; documents may be filed in unusual places and certain telephones may not be used during a paranoid crisis.

The visibility of the individual's behavior is greatly magnified during this period; often he is the main topic of conversation among the exclusionists, while rumors of the difficulties spread to other groups, which in some cases may be drawn into the controversy. At a certain juncture steps are taken to keep the members of the in-group continually informed of the individual's movements and, if possible, of his plans. In effect, if not in form, this amounts to spying. Members of one embattled group, for example, hired an outside person unknown to their accuser to take notes on a speech he delivered to enlist a community organization on his side. In another case, a person having an office opening onto that of a department head was persuaded to act as an informant for the nucleus of persons working to depose the head from his position of authority. This group also seriously debated placing an all-night watch in front of their perceived malefactor's house.

Concomitant with the magnified visibility of the paranoid individual, come distortions of his image, most pronounced in the inner coterie of exclusionists. His size, physical strength, cunning, and anecdotes of his outrages are exaggerated, with a central thematic emphasis on the fact that he is dangerous. Some individuals give cause for such beliefs in that previously they have engaged in violence or threats, others do not. One encounters characteristic contradictions in interviews on this point, such as: "No, he has never struck anyone around here – just fought with the policemen at the State Capitol," or "No, I am not afraid of him, but one of these days he will explode."

It can be said parenthetically that the alleged dangerousness of paranoid persons storied in fiction and drama has never been systematically demonstrated.

As a matter of fact, the only substantial data on this, from a study of delayed admissions, largely paranoid, to a mental hospital in Norway, disclosed that "neither the paranoiacs nor paranoids have been dangerous, and most not particularly troublesome."[18] Our interpretation of this, as suggested earlier, is that the imputed dangerousness of the paranoid individual does not come from physical fear but from the organizational threat he presents and the need to justify collective action against him.[19]

However, this is not entirely tactical behavior – as is demonstrated by anxieties and tensions which mount among those in a coalition during the more critical phases of their interaction. Participants may develop fears quite analogous to those of classic conspirators. One leader in such a group spoke of the period of the paranoid crisis as a "week of terror," during which he was wracked with insomnia and "had to take his stomach pills." Projection was revealed by a trustee who, during a school crisis occasioned by discharge of an aggressive teacher, stated that he "watched his shadows," and "wondered if all would be well when he returned home at night." Such tensional states, working along with a kind of closure of communication within the group, are both a cause and an effect of amplified group interaction which distorts or symbolically rearranges the image of the person against whom they act.

Once the battle is won by exclusionists, their version of the individual as dangerous becomes a crystallized rationale for official action. At this point misrepresentation becomes part of a more deliberate manipulation of ego. Gross misstatements, most frequently called "pretexts," become justifiable ways of getting his cooperation, for example, to get him to submit to psychiatric examination or detention preliminary to hospital commitment. This aspect of the process has been effectively detailed by Goffman, with his concept of a "betrayal funnel" through which a patient enters a hospital.[20] We need not elaborate on this, other than to confirm its occurrence in the exclusion process, complicated in our cases by legal strictures and the ubiquitous risk of litigation.

The Growth of Delusion

The general idea that the paranoid person symbolically fabricates the conspiracy against him is in our estimation incorrect or incomplete. Nor can we agree that he lacks insight, as is so frequently claimed. To the contrary, many paranoid persons properly realize that they are being isolated and excluded by concerted interaction, or that they are being manipulated. However, they are at a loss to estimate accurately or realistically the dimensions and form of the coalition arrayed against them.

As channels of communication are closed to the paranoid person, he has no means of getting feedback or consequences of his behavior, which is essential for correcting his interpretations of the social relationships and organization which he must rely on to define his status and give him identity. He can only read overt behavior without the informal context. Although he may properly infer that people are organized against him, he can only use confrontation or formal inquisitorial procedures to try to prove this. The paranoid person must provoke strong feelings in order to receive any kind of meaningful communication from others – hence his accusations, his bluntness, his insults. Ordinarily this is non-deliberate; nevertheless, in one complex case we found the person consciously provoking discussions to get readings from others on his behavior. This man said of himself: "Some people would describe me as very perceptive, others would describe me as very imperceptive."

The need for communication and the identity which goes with it does a good deal to explain the preference of paranoid persons for formal, legalistic, written communications, and the care with which many of them preserve records of their contracts with others. In some ways the resort to litigation is best interpreted as the effort of the individual to compel selected others to interact directly with him as equals, to engineer a situation in which evasion is impossible. The fact that the person is seldom satisifed with the outcome of his letters, his petitions, complaints, and writs testifies to their function as devices for establishing contact and interaction with others, as well as "setting the record straight." The wide professional tolerance of lawyers for aggressive behavior in court and the nature of Anglo-Saxon legal institutions, which grew out of a revolt against conspiratorial or star-chamber justice, mean that the individual will be heard. Furthermore his charges must be answered; otherwise he wins by default. Sometimes he wins small victories, even if he loses the big ones. He may earn grudging respect as an adversary, and sometimes shares a kind of legal comaraderie with others in the courts. He gains an identity through notoriety.

Reinforcement of Delusion

The accepted psychiatric view is that prognosis for paranoia is poor, that recoveries from "true" paranoia are rare, with the implication that the individual's delusions more or less express an unalterable pathological condition. Granting that the individual's needs and dispositions and his self-imposed isolation are significant factors in perpetuating his delusional reactions, nevertheless there is an important social context of delusions through which they are reinforced or strengthened. This context is readily identifiable in the fixed ideas and institutionalized procedures of protective, custodial, and treatment organizations in our society. They stand out in sharpest relief where paranoid persons have come into contact with law enforcement agencies or have been hospitalized. The cumulative and interlocking impacts of such agencies work strongly to nurture and sustain the massive sense of injustice and need for identity which underlie the delusions and aggressive behavior of the paranoid individual.

Police in most communities have a well-defined concept of cranks, as they call them, although the exact criteria by which persons are so judged are not clear. Their patience is short with such persons: in some cases they investigate their original complaints and if they conclude that the person in question is a crank they tend to ignore him thereafter. His letters may be thrown away unanswered, or phone calls answered with patronizing reassurance or vague promises to take steps which never materialize.

Like the police, offices of district attorneys are frequently forced to deal with persons they refer to as cranks or soreheads. Some offices delegate a special deputy to handle these cases, quaintly referred to in one office as the "insane deputy." Some deputies say they can spot letters of cranks immediately, which means that they are unanswered or discarded. However, family or neighborhood quarrels offer almost insoluble difficulties in this respect, because often it is impossible to determine which of two parties is delusional. In one office some complaints are called "50-50," which is jargon meaning that it is impossible to say whether they are mentally stable. If one person seems to be persistently causing trouble, deputies may threaten to have him investigated, which, however, is seldom if ever done.

Both police and district attorney staffs operate continuously in situations in which their actions can have damaging legal or political repercussions. They tend to be tightly in-grouped and their initial reaction to outsiders or strangers is one of suspicion or distrust until they are proved harmless or friendly. Many of their office procedures and general manner reflect this—such as carefully recording in a log book names, times, and reason for calling of those who seek official interviews. In some instances a complainant is actually investigated before any business will be transacted with him.

When the paranoid person goes beyond local police and courts to seek redress through appeals to state or national authorities, he may meet with polite evasion, perfunctory treatment of his case, or formalized distrust. Letters to administrative people may beget replies up to a certain point, but thereafter they are ignored. If letters to a highly-placed authority carry threats, they may lead to an investigation by security agencies, motivated by the knowledge that assassinations are not unknown in American life. Sometimes redress is sought in legislatures, where private bills may be introduced, bills which by their nature can only be empty gestures.

In general, the contacts which the delusional person makes with formal organizations frequently disclose the same elements of shallow response, evasion, or distrust which played a part in the generic process of exclusion. They become part of a selective or selected pattern of interaction which creates a social environment of uncertainty and ambiguity for the individual. They do little to correct and much to confirm his suspicion, distrust, and delusional interpretations. Moreover, even the environment of treatment agencies may contribute to the furtherance of paranoid delusion, as Stanton and Schwartz have shown in their comments on communication within the mental hospital. They speak pointedly of the "pathology of communication" brought about by staff practices of ignoring explicit meanings in statements or actions of patients and reacting to inferred or imputed meanings, thereby creating a type of environment in which "the paranoid feels quite at home."[21]

Some paranoid or paranoid-like persons become well known locally or even throughout larger areas to some organizations. Persons and groups in the community are found to assume a characteristic stance toward such people—a stance of expectancy and preparedness. In one such case, police continually checked the whereabouts of the man and, when the governor came to speak on the courthouse steps, two officers were assigned the special task of watching the man as he stood in the crowd. Later, whenever he went to the state capitol, a number of state police were delegated to accompany him when he attended committee hearings or sought interviews with state officials.[22] The notoriety this man acquired because of his reputed great strength in tossing officers around like tenpins was an obvious source of pleasure to him, despite the implications of distrust conveyed by their presence.

It is arguable that occupying the role of the mistrusted person becomes a way of life for these paranoids, providing them with an identity not otherwise possible. Their volatile contentions with public officials, their issuance of writings, publications, litigations in *persona propria,* their overriding tendency to contest issues which other people dismiss as unimportant or as "too much bother" become a central theme for their lives, without which they would probably deteriorate.

If paranoia becomes a way of life for some people, it is also true that the difficult person with grandiose and persecutory ideas may fulfill certain marginal functions in organizations and communities. One is his scapegoat function, being made the subject of humorous by-play or conjectural gossip as people "wonder what he will be up to next." In his scapegoat role, the person may help integrate primary groups within larger organizations by directing aggressions and blame toward him and thus strengthening feelings of homogeneity and consensus of group members.

There are also instances in which the broad, grapeshot charges and accusations of the paranoid person function to articulate dissatisfactions of those who fear openly to criticize the leadership of the community, organization, or state, or of the informal power structures within these. Sometimes the paranoid person is the only one who openly espouses values of inarticulate and politically unrepresented segments of the population.[23] The "plots" which attract the paranoid person's attention—dope rings, international communism, monopolistic "interests," popery, Jewry, or "psychopoliticans"—often reflect the vague and ill-formed fears and concerns of peripheral groups, which tend to validate his self-chosen role as a "protector." At times in organization power plays and community conflicts his role may even be put to canny use by more representative groups as a means of embarrassing their opposition.

The Larger Sociocultural Context

Our comments draw to a close on the same polemic note with which they were begun, namely, that members of communities and organizations do unite in common effort against the paranoid person prior to or apart from any vindictive behavior on his part. The paranoid community is real rather than pseudo in that it is composed of reciprocal relationships and processes whose net results are informal and formal exclusion and attenuated communication.

The dynamics of exclusion of the paranoid person are made understandable in larger perspective by recognizing that decision-making in American social organization is carried out in small, informal groups through casual and often subtle male interaction. Entry into such groups is ordinarily treated as a privilege rather than a right, and this privilege tends to be jealously guarded. Crucial decisions, including those to eject persons or to reorganize their status in larger formal organizations, are made secretly. The legal concept of "privileged communication" in part is a formal recognition of the necessity for making secret decisions within organizations.

Added to this is the emphasis placed upon conformity in our organization-oriented society and the growing tendency of organization elites to rely upon direct power for their purposes. This is commonly exercised to isolate and neutralize groups and individuals who oppose their policies both inside and outside of the organization. Formal structures may be manipulated or deliberately reorganized so that resistant groups and individuals are denied or removed from access to power or the available means to promote their deviant goals and values. One of the most readily effective ways of doing this is to interrupt, delay, or stop the flow of information.

It is the necessity to rationalize and justify such procedures on a democratic basis which leads to concealment of certain actions, misrepresentation of their underlying meaning, and even the resort to unethical or illegal means. The difficulty of securing sociological knowledge about these techniques, which we might call the "controls behind the controls," and the denials by those who use them that they exist are logical consequences of the perceived threat such knowledge and admissions become to informal power structures. The epiphenomena of power thus become a kind of shadowy world of our culture, inviting conjecture and condemnation.

Concluding Comment

We have been concerned with a process of social exclusion and with the way in which it contributes to the development of paranoid patterns of behavior. While the data emphasize the organizational forms of exclusion, we nevertheless believe that these are expressions of a generic process whose correlates will emerge from the study of paranoia in the family and other groups. The differential responses of the individual to the exigencies of organized exclusion are significant in the development of paranoid reactions only insofar as they partially determine the "intolerable" or "unendurable" quality of the status changes confronting him. Idiosyncratic life history factors of the sort stressed in more conventional psychiatric analyses may be involved, but equally important in our estimation are those which inhere in the status changes themselves, age being one of the more salient of these. In either case, once situational intolerability appears, the stage is set for the interactional process we have described.

Our cases, it will be noted, were all people who remained undeteriorated, in contact with others, and carrying on militant-activities oriented toward recognizable social values and institutions. Generalized suspiciousness in public places and unprovoked aggression against strangers were absent from their experiences. These facts, plus the relative absence of "true paranoia" among mental-hospital populations, lead us to conclude that the "pseudo-community" associated with random aggression (in Cameron's sense) is a sequel rather than an integral part of paranoid patterns. They are likely products of deterioration and fragmentation of personality appearing, when and if they do, in the paranoid person after long or intense periods of stress and complete social isolation.

Notes

1 Norman Cameron, "The Paranoid Pseudocommunity," *American Journal of Sociology* 46 (1943), pp. 33-38.

2 In a subsequent article Cameron modified his original conception, but not of the social aspects of paranoia, which mainly concern us. Norman Cameron, "The Paranoid Pseudocommunity Revisited," *American Journal of Sociology* 65 (1959), pp. 52-58.

3 Cameron, "The Paranoid Pseudocommunity."

4 Ibid.

5 James S. Tyhurst, "Paranoid Patterns," in *Exploration in Social Psychiatry,* eds. Alexander H. Leighton, John A. Clausen, and Robert N. Wilson (New York: Basic Books, 1957), chap. II.

6 K. O. Milner, "The Environment as a Factor in the Etiology of Criminal Paranoia," *Journal of Mental Science* 95 (1949), pp. 124-32.

7 S. Pederson, "Psychological Reactions to Extreme Social Displacement (Refugee Neuroses)," *Psychoanalytic Review* 36 (1946), pp. 344-54.

8 F. F. Kine, "Aliens' Paranoid Reaction," *Journal of Mental Science* 98 (1951), pp. 589-94; I. Listivan, "Paranoid States: Social and Cultural Aspects," *Medical Journal of Australia* (1956), pp. 776-78.

9 Tyhurst, "Paranoid Patterns."

10 Edwin M. Lemert, "Legal Commitment and Social Control," *Sociology and Social Research* 30 (1946), pp. 370-78.

11 Ibid.

12 Robert A. Dentler and Kai T. Erikson, "The Functions of Deviance in Groups," *Social Problems* 7 (1959), p. 102.

13 James L. Loomis, "Communications, The Development of Trust, and Cooperative Behavior," *Human Relations* 12 (1959), pp. 305-15.

14 Elaine Cumming and John Cumming, *Closed Ranks* (Cambridge: Harvard University Press, 1957), chap. VI.

15 The interaction in some ways is similar to that used with children, particularly the *"enfant terrible."* The function of language in such interaction was studied by Sapir years ago. Edward Sapir, "Abnormal Types of Speech in Nootka," *Geological Survey Memoir* 62, Anthropological Series (Ottawa: Canada Department of Mines, 1915).

16 For a systematic analysis of the organizational difficulties in removing an "unpromotable" person from a position see B. Levenson, "Bureaucratic Succession," in *Complex Organizations,* ed. Amitai Etzioni (New York: Holt, Rinehart & Winston, 1961), pp. 362-95.

17 One of the cases in the first study.

18 O. Odegard, "A Clinical Study of Delayed Admissions to a Mental Hospital," *Mental Hygiene* 42 (1958), pp. 66-77.

19 Supra.

20 Erving Goffman, "The Moral Career of the Mental Patient," *Psychiatry* 22 (1959), pp. 127 ff.

21 Alfred H. Stanton and Morris S. Schwartz, *The Mental Hospital* (New York: Basic Books, 1954), pp. 200-10.

22 This technique in even more systematic form is sometimes used in protecting the President of the United States in "White House cases."

23 Judd Marmor, "Science, Health and Group Opposition," mimeographed paper, 1958, UCLA School of Social Work.

8
The Career of the School Skipper[1]

Manuel Crespo

Studies of school non-attendance, mostly American ones, have adopted a "simultaneous" perspective (Becker, 1963): they seek to establish a relationship between a variable or set of variables and school absenteeism, without any definite concern with the considerations, circumstances, and context involved in the process of becoming a school non-attender. Most of these studies treat what Matza (1969) calls "affinities" – that is, characteristics of the school absentee and his situation, which are treated as propensities or predisposing conditions for the activity. More specifically, they have located these predisposing conditions in areas such as status deprivation (Cloward and Ohlin, 1960); parental attitudes toward their children's school (Brooks et al., 1962); exaggerated dependency on parents (Coolidge et al., 1960); character disorders (Kahn and Nursten, 1962); the features of lower class culture (Cohen, 1955; Miller, 1962); peer influence (Elliott et al., 1966; Friesen, 1967); and organisational constraints (Finlayson, 1971).

Whatever specific assessments might be made of these studies of school non-attendance, they all reveal a rather striking absence of concern with the activity itself. While they stress the importance of the independent variable, the dependent one – the activity – is considered as an outcome which needs no describing and which has no effect of its own. For example, the use of the term *behaviour*, instead of *activity*, to refer to school absenteeism suggests that absenteeism is treated as having no independent importance, and as being essentially symptomatic of the real phenomenon which is described in the independent variable.

This neglect of the activity may stem from the idea that school absenteeism is nothing more than a collection of absences. Tabulated recurrence, however, does not account for the permanence of skipping. It is the notion of process that is essential for an understanding of the phenomenon.

The simultaneous model, however, is not conducive to studying the process by which individuals become skippers. Insistence on relationships between variables dims the mediating actions of those being studied. In other words, it either denies, or at least underestimates, choice and reconsideration.

The model proposed by Matza in *Becoming Deviant* is an attempt for effecting a translation from simultaneous to "sequential" (Becker, 1963) concerns. Although he severely criticizes the deterministic perspective with which these studies are written, he does not consider them totally irrelevant insofar as the affinities they describe are considered as parts of the process of becoming deviant and not as wholly determinant factors.[2]

In becoming deviant, Matza writes, "nothing happens behind the subject's back or despite him" (Matza, 1969, 119). The process of affiliation is not a process of capitulation. Man constructs his deviation; it is not imposed upon him by a group. The potential deviant converts himself while in the association of others. Conversion is "choice" against preordination, hence human activity. The predisposition to deviance and the affiliation or association with deviant others provide the willingness and the recipe for deviance; they do not confirm the potential deviant as an accomplished deviant. The affiliative condition does not reveal to the potential deviant his wrong doing. He discovers it when it is perceived by others, and when, through a somewhat complicated interactive process between the Leviathan, the State, and himself, the potential deviant ordains himself deviant (Matza, 1969: passim). This is the process of signification which essentially consists of two converging lines: one is the societal definition of the individual; the other, the progressive acceptance by the individual of this definition. When the junction is realized, identity becomes actualized.

Matza's model is the specific guideline for this study. It must be noted, however, that some of the elements of his framework have been given an altered emphasis to fit the particular subject matter being considered. The process of signification in particular does not, in the case of school skippers, have to do with the more dramatic confrontations with the law; the issue of getting caught is not so significant in the career of the school skipper. In this study, the process of signification will be handled under the more appropriate (for the purposes of describing skippers) notion of "amplification of deviance" and will involve some consideration of the part played by the academic tracking system in shaping deviant identity for skippers.

Data and Method

The data for this paper were gathered in 1972 during an eight months period of participant observation and interviewing in an urban, French-speaking, comprehensive high school situated in a low-income area. This school had, at the moment of the study, an enrolment of around fourteen hundred students, and was the only comprehensive school in the district.

Forty-five students were interviewed for a period ranging from forty-five minutes to an hour and a half. The interviewees were chosen from those students who had been absent twenty-one days or more during the academic year.[3] Interviews and more informal talks with the teachers, administrative officers, and secretarial personnel were also included data. Finally, information was gathered from the skippers' academic dossiers, as well as from those of non-skippers and dropouts. The non-skipper population consisted of a random sample drawn from the entire population – skippers excluded; the dropouts were those students who had quit school during the 1971 – 72 academic year.

Although the material cited in this paper comes from conversations and observations during the research stage, the insights and my confidence in the adequacy of the material are the result of a rather long period of participant observation prior to the research itself, when I was a secondary-school teacher. At that time I had some ideas concerning the impact of school organization on students' behaviour, and also some knowledge of teachers' motivations and attitudes toward lower track students. Therefore, when the themes appeared in conversation in the actual research, I could easily recognize them in the context of what I already knew.

The Career of the School Skipper

The career of the school skipper begins for all practical purposes with the first time he or she skips school.[4] Once a student has actually skipped school, he is in a position to consider whether or not the activity is worth doing again. This paper specifically elaborates the considerations and processes by which a student may try skipping and then abandon it, may get into skipping in a more systematic way and then change his mind, or may become, in the course of systematic skipping, increasingly marginal to school life.

Skipping school for the first time

It is the purpose of this section to account for two seemingly disparate observations: the accidental character of the initial act of skipping as it is described by students, and the heavy concentration of skipping among students in the lower academic tracks.

When students are asked how they came to skip school for the first time, they mention a variety of circumstances ranging from long-term hospitalization to an early morning headache. Some, but not many, mention more specifically school-related reasons. There is no striking pattern to the circumstances they report; these are simply a variety of contingencies which have produced the same result.

R.: But tell me, how did it happen that suddenly you became a skipper?[5]

S.:   Well, my father beats me often. . . . So I stayed three weeks at the hospital; after that, I started to like skipping.

R.:   When was the first time you missed?
S: It was during the first strike. We'd come and they'd send us home. One morning I came to school and there were classes, but I returned home.

R.:   When do you skip?
S.:   It's when I'm in a bad mood.
R.:   Why are you sometimes in a bad mood?
S.:   It's because I go to bed too late, after looking at the late movie.

S.:   It was in Grade 5; I had my leg in a cast for two months because of an infection, and then I took a taste to missing school.
R.:   After that, did you continue missing?
S.:   Yes.

R.:   When did you start skipping?
S.:   In Grade 7.
R.:   At the beginning of the year, or what?
S.:   Sometime near May, when the nice weather arrived.
R.:   How did it happen?
S.:   A bunch of girls asked me to skip with them and I accepted. After that, I began to like it. I didn't like getting up in the morning . . .

R: How did you start skipping?
S.:   It was because in a math course I didn't understand anything . . . so, I started not coming.

A student account of skipping would therefore not suggest any particular pattern of skipping and would certainly not suggest a casual or prior relationship between experiences in school and skipping. Yet, even making a generous allowance for errors in the reporting system (errors which could not easily be related to the academic tracks of various students,[6] skippers are over represented in the lower tracks.[7] As evidence, 71 per cent of all skippers – as compared with 49 per cent of non-skippers – are located in tracks C and D. In other words, an account of skipping based on student interviews would describe the accidental and contingent origins of skipping, while an account constructed from other data would describe the systematic and school-related origins of skipping.

There are a number of ways in which a discrepancy like this can be accounted for; most of these essentially discount what students say as epiphenomenal. The object here, however, is not to *discount* the affinity between being in a lower track and skipping school, but to account for it in ways which mesh with the students' own descriptions of school and skipping. There are two ways to see this affinity.

First, in what ways does a student's lower track position prepare him for considering skipping? Simply by being in a track in which skipping is concentrated, students are more likely to know others who skip and, in fact, to be invited to skip. More importantly, students who do not find school rewarding are more prepared to consider missing it. In this sense, the tracking system provides the invitational edge to the activity of skipping.

R.: What do skippers dislike about school?

S.: You know, we're always sitting down, we read, we write on the board, it's boring; we're like in a prison. Outside, it's freedom, lots of air, we walk around . . .

S.: I don't get anything from school; it's always the same thing: same teachers, same courses; we don't learn anything. Even when we change class, it's always the same; it's dull, we don't learn anything. Nobody gets anything from school.

These quotes also point to another way in which the affinity between being in a lower track and skipping school can be understood. If being in school offers the lower-track student little satisfaction, the out-of-school skipping experience may only serve to emphasize this fact. The following quote shows in more detail the contrasts between a student's experiences in and out of school, and implies that a student may, in fact, learn more out of school than in it.

R.: What do your friends think of school?

S.: They say they don't learn anything here at school, and that they learn better elsewhere, on the street. Let's say they go and walk around, they talk with the men, and they show them things . . .

R.: How?

S.: They walk around and meet men, let's say a man making a desk; so he shows him how we do it, we take plywood, when they have time on their hands, they'll be able to make a desk; but here at school they don't learn anything. One of my chums is in refrigeration, he shows me something he has learned and it's always interesting. Here at school, we don't learn much; outside we learn a lot.

This interpretation would suggest that many students try skipping, but that lower-track students are more likely to continue skipping. There is evidence that many students have at one time or another skipped school, even fairly systematically. Among the non-skippers in this school (non-skippers at the time of this study are defined in accordance with the school's official criterion – that is, students with fewer than twenty-one absences for the year), for example, 11 per cent of those who had attendance records in their dossiers from previous years had reached the twenty-one absences mark in at least one of their previous years. Presumably, an even greater number of these "non-skippers" have at one time or another skipped school, but not often enough or noticeably enough to hit the twenty-one absences mark. An interesting implication of this observation, particularly in conjunction with qualitative data from students, is that students may try out skipping and then abandon it, either after several experiences or after having skipped over a considerable span of time.

"Getting into" skipping and "getting out of" skipping

Once a student has skipped school for the first time, he is in a position to consider whether or not the activity is worth doing again. Students' considerations have generally to do with three matters: the fear of being caught; the enjoyment derived from skipping; and the assessment of school's relevance for the more long-term future. In relation to each of these matters, students' considerations did not occur individually, but involved the support or lack of support of other skippers.

The first problem a skipping student faces is the fear of getting caught. Interviews reveal that potential skippers are afraid when they start skipping, and that, after a while, they overcome it. This stage is crucial for if they do not overcome this fear, they are unlikely to continue skipping.

R.: How can students keep on skipping in spite of the school's supervision?
S.: Because they're not afraid.
R.: You, why did you become a regular attender?
S.: Because, me, I'm afraid.

R.: Do you skip?
S.: I used to, not much.
R.: Why?
S.: Ah well, it wasn't interesting ... not that, but I was afraid of getting caught. When I came back to school I thought everybody was looking at me ... so, I didn't want to continue. My friends weren't afraid; they told me, "They won't get you, you'll see," ... but I had no confidence.

The company of other skippers serves to reduce this fear. "Experienced" skippers tell the newcomer to take it easy and to control his imagination, for it is not as difficult as he thinks to skip unnoticed: teachers are not at every corner ready to pick him up.

S.: At first, when I started skipping I saw teachers everywhere. I thought I'd get caught at every street corner. My chums used to tell me not to be afraid, but I was afraid just the same.

R.: And that lasted long?

S.: Not really, after a week I wasn't afraid any more.

As part of learning how to cope with their fears of getting caught, skippers learn from one another how to skip with relative safety. Those who skip alone are more easily caught, and they may attribute this to their possible lack of sophistication, a sophistication experienced through the company of other skippers.

S.: This year I skipped. I went to the hospital and I missed biology. Next day, I didn't go, I didn't feel like it, but I got caught.

R.: How did you get caught?

S.: The teacher had noticed that I wasn't present and told Mr.____ (director). He called me through the intercom and told me that if I did it again, that he'd suspend me from school for two weeks.

R.: Do the heavy skippers get caught?

S.: The others, they don't get caught. They come into the classroom as if nothing had happened and they go to their place; the teacher doesn't say anything to them for having skipped.

Skippers must also find the activity enjoyable. It is evident that those who do not overcome the fear of getting caught do not have much "fun" skipping. Also, if being in school is more interesting, more fun than being out of school, or if skipping is "platte,"[8] students are not likely to continue it.

R.: What do you do when you skip?

S.: We walk around, we don't do anything, it's very boring walking around all the time. We're much better off at school.

The company of others is an important feature of whether or not one has fun. The common pattern of skipping involves the presence of at least one friend with whom even the simplest things become really enjoyable.

R.: What do you do when you skip?

S.: O.K., we start off and go toward the park . . . there we sit down . . . .

R.: Even when it's cold?

S.: Yes, we tell jokes, we laugh; after that, we take the metro.

Affiliation with skippers can also make it difficult to say no to a skipping invitation, particularly if one is known to have skipped.

S.: Sometimes we don't feel like going, but we go just the same so that, when we'll want to go, we can ask them to come with us.

R.: How do students skip?

S.: Sometimes, there are some who want to skip and say to others

"Come with us." The others, not to look like cowards, will follow them.

R.: So you think that sometimes the guys just follow?

S.: They want to show off, and that they're not scared.

An analysis of skipping shows that after Grade 9 there is a dramatic drop in its occurrence. How can this be accounted for? To begin with, the drop coincides with the cessation of compulsory education. At fifteen years of age, the student is no longer compelled to attend school. Furthermore, the completion of school life, which in the junior years was so distant, is now in sight; and the element of choice makes it possible to see the future as one's own.

R.: You see on this list that there is a radical change, as far as skipping is concerned, between students in Grades 7, 8, 9, and those in Grades 10 and 11. What has happened to make students of Grades 10 and 11 skip less?

S.: What happens in Grades 10 and 11 is that those who skip, we see them quit school. At the beginning of the year, we see students who start missing school and suddenly we learn that they've found a job. . . . We're not obliged to come to school, so if we do, we're necessarily interested in finishing; before that, we didn't think of what we were going to do. Now we're beginning to see. . . . In Grades 7, 8, 9, we don't know what we're doing in school.

The "reality" of the future – that is, the possibility of shaping it according to one's own will – is facilitated by the school curriculum. Students can at this point take new courses which lead directly to that future.

At the end of Grade 9, each student chooses what particular orientation he or she would like to pursue. These students are registered in what is called the Long Professional Course. It is open to all Grade nines, but the recruitment is particularly high among students from track C.[9]

Starting in Grade 10, students can choose an occupational orientation. They can learn a trade and feel that they are directly preparing themselves to enter the labour market; upon leaving school, girls can obtain a secretarial training.

The experience of work, which for some skippers becomes the decisive element in dropping out, is for others an occasion for a different sort of reflection and a consequent decision to continue.

S.: Me, I worked during the summer, so I became more serious and I saw it was better to be at school.

Their future is now patent in the knowledge that they may have difficulty getting ahead without a school degree. They may compare themselves with other workers in the job situation, and see themselves as they will be in a few years, should they cease going to school.

S.: When I was working last summer, I met people who were pretty ignorant and I told myself, "It's not a place for me." I had what? – a Grade 9, so I went back for studying.

R.: Do you think you'll skip this year?

S.: I haven't skipped yet. During the summer I saw that I was earning $1.25 per hour, and my friend was earning $2.35 and we were doing the same thing ... so I told myself, "If I continue and get my Grade 11 diploma, I will earn the same salary."

R.: That made you think, the fact that you weren't getting the same salary?

S.: That's it. My friend who gave up school, who was skipping with me last year, doesn't realize it because on his floor everybody got $1.25. But I was mixed up with others who earned more than me. Suppose that you and I, we present ourselves to work, they'll pay a bigger salary to the one who has more studies, they'll even take him before one who has less. My chum, they took him; at the beginning he was supposed to have a steady job, but they slacked him two months after. So he finds himself poor jobs of $1.25 and he's happy. Me, if I saw others earn more than me, I wouldn't be happy; suppose I wanted to buy a car, I wouldn't be able to and the others could buy it a good two months before me.

Sheer chronological age may also serve to bring the future closer.

R.: Do the boys of Grades 10 and 11 skip?

S.: They skip less.

R.: Why, according to you?

S.: It's that they want to keep on; there isn't much time left and they want to continue their studies to have a diploma.

R.: And the Grades 7, 8, 9?

S.: They don't think about the future too much. In Grades 10 and 11 we think of what we'll do to be happy later. In Grades 7, 8, 9 we don't care about the future, we don't know what we're going to do.

R.: But you're in Grade 8.

S.: But look, it's like I was in Grade 10. I passed three years in Grade 8. My chum also, last year he skipped and this year he's gone up to Grade 9, and he doesn't skip. It's the same thing, he would be in Grade 10.

R.: So, it's a matter of age?

S.: We pass from child to adolescent. When we're in 7, 8, 9, we don't think of what we're going to be.

This student stopped skipping and although he is not in Grade 10, he would be had he not tripled Grade 8. He now views school as a means for achieving some social success; but when he was younger he did not.

In Grade 10 and 11, although there are two more years of high school, skippers see this time as being compressed; they have wasted so much time that, in order to catch up, they feel they cannot miss school any longer.[10]

S.:   In Grade 10 we tell ourselves that we'll succeed better because I have only one year left and if I raise my marks, perhaps I'll be placed in regular.

S.:   Grade 10 is important because after there's Grade 11, and either we work or we go to college. Those in Grade 7, 8, 9 tell themselves they still have many years to catch up.[10]
R.:   Do you think that or did those in 7, 8, 9 tell you?
S.:   They've told me, and I think so too.

Very often skipping friends abandon skipping at about the same time. Although the interviews do not clearly indicate a joint decision to return to normal attendance, the fact of the common "conversion" suggests that some talk has taken place among them concerning the relation between attendance and obtaining a school degree.

The three considerations described – the fear of being caught; the enjoyment derived, or not; and the assessment of school's importance – may lead a student who has tried skipping to abandon it. However, the first two may also lead the skipper to continue skipping and, in fact, to become a systematic skipper.

The amplification of deviance

The consequences of systematic skipping go beyond that of material missed due to absence from class. While a student's knowledge, and even the relevant matter of his reputation, could be handled effectively during the times he is in fact in class, skippers' strategies for not getting caught tend to amplify the consequences of missing classes. One way that skippers cover the fact of their having skipped is to maintain a very low profile in class. The disinterested and anonymous impression they maintain merely suggests to the teachers that they are just part of that general body of bored and mediocre students. Furthermore, if they should make an active attempt to catch up or to understand what is going on by asking the teacher to explain something, the teacher will often suggest that the best way to understand is to come regularly, that the subject has been explained, and that there is not time. Should the student want an explanation, he must see the teacher after school. Seeing teachers after school hours is not a customary activity for a great number of students, especially for skippers.

They never stay after school hours, unless they are being punished. They see the referral, then, as a polite way of refusing to teach them.

A more radical amplification of the consequences of systematic skipping is provided in the link between the tracking system and skipping. The treatment of lower-track skippers takes on aspects of the teachers' more general treatment of and feelings about lower-track students. Teachers assigned to lower-track students believe that those students are the worst the system contains and that teaching them requires a lot of energy and patience. They do not happily accept an assignment to lower tracks. As one female teacher explained:

> Last year, I was all right. I had regular and enriched students. This year, it's more difficult: I was given two classes in the alleviated track. It's different; when I finish my day, I'm glad. Last year, it wasn't the same. I was glad to come to school. This year, it's a big effort.

The same comment, but from the other side – tracks A and B – was made by a male teacher:

> This year, I've got the cream. They are little boys who want to learn. There are a few frictions, but not serious ones; we get along well together. I give them some work and right away, they start doing it. It's generally very well done. I don't have any difficulties with them.

As assignments are based on seniority – though the administrative officer in charge may deny it – young teachers and newcomers have to teach students from tracks C and D.[11] Lower-track students therefore become in the eyes of these teachers indicators of their own low status.

The treatment of lower-track students – the comments on their performance, the comparisons made with higher-track students, and the aggressive behaviour toward them – does not fail to have an affect on them.

R.: Why do young people become skippers?
S.: They come in and the teacher tells them, "What are you coming here for? To be like that, it's much better that you stay home!" And the student stays home! He's not interested in having these things said to him.

It has been suggested above that the first acts of skipping provide students with comparisons between their experiences being in school – experiences significantly determined by their lower-track status – and their experiences out of school. Skipping can clarify, organize, and thus amplify the experience of being in a lower track. In other words, the combined effect of being in a lower track and skipping escalates the sense that school, and being there, is useless.

S.:   It's strange, sir, we're here like in nothing. . . .
R.:   What do you mean?
S.:   We're apart, . . . the teachers don't ask us questions: when we're
      in the shops, they watch us as if we were going to commit a
      crime . . . the courses are not the same as the others'. . . .

S.:   What's the use, sir, of coming to school? It doesn't lead any-
      where, the alleviated course; and if on top of that we have poor
      results. . . . Do you know what an employer thinks when we go
      see him and show him our report card, and he sees "alleviated"?
      With the alleviated course we're blocked; we can't go far.

Since they play an important part in the process by which a skipper
becomes increasingly marginal to school life, the effects of the school's
attempts to control skipping should be considered. When the director
of students comes to know about the frequent absences of a particular
student, he initiates a set of actions intended to get the student back in
school. Generally, he first tries to talk with the student in order to find
out the real reason for the absences. When the interview fails, as it
often does, he calls the parents to inform them about the student's
behaviour. If there is no change, he has the secretary send a letter to
the parents.

The letter is a special form which notifies the parents that student X
has been absent for a precise number of days and provides a space
allowing the parents to write the reason for the absences. It is rare to
find in the parents' responses an incrimination of the student's behaviour. Generally, parents give sickness and baby-sitting as reasons for
the absences.

When there is no answer to the official form, or when absences
continue to be frequent, the director of students refers the case to the
controller, whose duty is to contact the student's family in order to
find some way of getting the student back to school. Basically, the
controller's activities consist of a series of telephone calls and visits to
homes. The reports to the director frequently state that the student
concerned is willing to return to school. In other cases, the controller
may try to intimidate parents, reminding them that there is a law to
protect children and that family allowances may be suspended if they
do not send their children to school.

The effectiveness of the controller's action is doubtful. The majority
of the skippers visited by the controller continue to skip school as
frequently as before. This is evident when one compares the date of
the controller's report and the absentees' cards.[12]

It is clear, therefore, that although these efforts do not contribute
directly to the marginalization of students, they do not contribute
much in the other direction either; that is, these efforts do not succeed
in integrating students back into the school.

The second line of response to the systematic skipper contributes directly to his marginalization from the school. It is perhaps ironic that the most severe measure a school can take against a student – suspension – enforces skipping while presumably being a measure for controlling it.

R.: O.K., they don't like a teacher, a course or the school. . . . What is it exactly they don't like?

S.: They don't give a damn about the school. There are even students who miss for two days and if they're caught, they're suspended for a month, so they're proud of that. . . . When they come back, they get suspended again by missing again!

The irony of this response is not unobserved by students themselves. As one student, who was suspended for, among other things, skipping and who refused to return to school when his time of exclusion expired, pointed out:

They kicked me out of school: they didn't want me . . . . I found a good job and they came to get me back. They're all crazy in this school!

The third line of response is not one taken directly by the school, but by the police – generally, by its Youth Division. Police activity concerning skippers consists essentially in patrolling the streets of the neighbourhood and asking suspects if they are still students. They sometimes force skippers to return to school at once, by picking them up and bringing them *manu militari* to the school.

The police play an important part in the skipper's universe: some characteristics of skipping, namely the number of participants and the place of the activity, are geared to avoid police vigilance. The reason for this importance lies perhaps in the fact that, although police do not mistreat skippers, being picked up by the police and particularly being brought back to school by them is highly noticeable and generates a more serious impression (for oneself and others) of one's deviant status.

The processes in which school skippers are involved do not end, at least in the school under study, only in skipping. As a consequence of the processes just described, skippers become more and more identified with a version of themselves as marginal to school life. When they become fully identified with this version, dropping out becomes sensible to them.

Among the skippers that dropped out during the year under study, 60 per cent were registered in the lower tracks. If one considers not only the skippers registered in the lower tracks, but also those with at least one subject in a lower-track level, the percentage rises to 82 per cent.[13] Such a high percentage is indicative of the impact of marginalization in the final outcome of the skipper's career.

Many skippers felt that they did not have the qualities required to fit into the school setting. They considered themselves different from other students.

R.:   How do you succeed in your classes?
S.:   Not too well. . . .
R.:   Are there girls who get better marks than you?
S.:   Yes, the teacher's pets, the little squares, they're always study-
       ing. . . .
R.:   Do they skip?
S.:   Never, they're much too scared!
R.:   Do the "squares," as you call them, make fun of you?
S.:   Never! I sure would like to see that! No, they're scared; they're
       always busy working. If we talk to them, they say, "Let me
       work." . . . They're sick!

Much of systematic skipping can be treated as commitment to a certain line of activity. The student becomes committed to skipping through the fun he has doing it; through the contrast it provides with his experiences in school; through the obligations and pleasures he shares with skipping friends; and through the several difficulties skipping generates for the possibility of catching up. These are commitments which may be reversed; but they may also become the material for confirming a view of self as unfit for school. At this point systematic skipping becomes a matter of identification rather than commitment, as students become more and more identified with a version of themselves as marginal to school life. When the skipper finally views himself in the same terms as the school views him, he drops out.

School skipping in this comprehensive school may be understood then in terms of a deviant career. The trajectory of the career moves from an accidental beginning to a final confirmation of marginal identity expressed by dropping out, unless skippers' considerations about the activity lead them to abandon it. Between the beginning and the most logical outcome – dropping out – the potential skipper constructs his deviation within the context of the school.

There is a patent irony in organizational processes: the official ideology claims that the aim of the new comprehensive school, and of the tracking system, is to individualize teaching in order to process most effectively the majority of students through the secondary level of education. This ideology, however, plays an active part in marginalizing and extruding students from school.

The same irony is reflected in the social control system: the effect of actions taken by the director, the controller, and the police produce exactly the opposite of what is officially sought. Skippers see the social control activities as forcing them into a meaningless situation; "They kicked me out of school: they didn't want me. . . . I found a good job and they came to get me back." And the more they experience the compulsory actions of these agencies, the more they become convinced that they must get out of their present situation. At the end, the real meaning of such processes, the ironic significance, clearly appears: the skipper becomes a dropout.

Notes

[1] This paper is a revised version of the fourth chapter of my Master's thesis, *Becoming Deviant: The Career of the School Skipper,* Montreal, McGill University, 1973. I am indebted to Professors Prudence Rains, my thesis advisor, and Malcolm Spector for their highly valuable and continuous help.

[2] School skipping is considered in this study as deviance. Deviance is generally defined as a departure from "common" norms. Therefore, deviance is supposedly a marginal phenomenon, while "normality" is a matter of majorities. It is not the place here to discuss the criteria for determining what is deviant. These criteria are often blurred, and what appears to be deviant in one context is, in another, just "normal." Also, deviant phenomena may become normal at one point in time; or conversely, what is normal may become deviant. For the purpose of this research, school skipping is considered as deviating from the regular behaviour of the majority of students – that is, school attendance; it is reacted to as deviance and it is experienced as deviant by those who consider doing it. To treat skipping under the rubric of deviance is not, however, to make a moral judgment about the worthiness of the activity or its participants.

[3] This is an arbitrary official criterion for defining a chronic absentee. It happened that almost all the students (92 per cent) chosen among those with at least twenty-one days of absence were skippers.

[4] Girls also skip school; they account for 45 per cent of all skippers. From now on, however, for convenience's sake, pronouns will be used in the masculine form.

[5] Since all the quotes have been translated from French to English, the flow and meaning is therefore somewhat altered.

[6] The absence accounting system, even if it did not function well, was applied evenly to all tracks. Bias may be the result either of teacher's choice or of the secretary's choice: the former for not counting as absent some students, the latter for failing to record the absences. Both attitudes, though possible, did not seem to operate differentially with respect to academic track. With the exception of the daily call of skippers' and absentees' parents (which the secretary sometimes omitted), she performed the remaining duties in an accurate manner, as sustained observation revealed. She could not exercise bias because she knew only the names and numbers of 'foyers' (administrative groupings of students), and not the academic tracks of particular students. Teachers had to send the absences slip to the secretary; they either sent it or failed to send it; they did not seem to have preferences in reporting absences for one track or another, or for some particular students rather than others.

[7] The tracking system was devised as a means of individualizing the

learning process. Since individuals differ in intellectual abilities and rhythms of learning, the grouping of students by their abilities was considered the best way for adjusting teaching to individuals. Each grouping constitutes a track, and the system comprises four tracks: enriched, regular, alleviated, and practical. These are arranged in order of the capacities they presumably demand. For purposes of the present research these tracks will be called respectively from top to bottom: A, B. C, and D.

[8] French slang word for boring, tedious.

[9] In 1971-72, according to the division chief, almost 100 per cent of the Long Professional Course was composed of students from track C.

[10] The idea of future recuperation does not appear to have real grounds in the senior section of this comprehensive school. If one considers the future academic orientation of students who graduated in 1971, it is obvious that, in general, the students see the Grade 11 diploma as terminal. A survey done on 93 or the 137 graduates of the 1970-71 academic year shows that only 25 per cent of them orient their future toward a university diploma. For the rest, the high school is terminal. The survey does not give data of future orientation by tracks, but one can reasonably suppose that the greatest proportion of this 25 per cent is composed of tracks A and B students. There are no data for 1972 graduates. Nevertheless, there are no reasonable grounds for suspecting a dramatic change in their future orientation.

[11] The same administrative officer denied that some teachers were assigned exclusively to lower tracks. This assertion was not accurate either. Late transfers from another school were often assigned to what remained, that is, to lower tracks. Only 18 per cent of mathematics teachers, and none of the French teachers (the survey covers 70 per cent of all these teachers) had an even assignment, that is, an assignment with equal numbers of higher and lower tracks.

[12] There is a card for each student. Every day the secretary in charge of absences sorts the absentees' cards and marks the absences in the appropriate place.

[13] It is worth noting that profiles of skippers and dropouts have several traits in common. They have a similar past history of absenteeism; their respective distributions by tracks, although not exactly the same (skipping does not necessarily precede *all* dropping out), bear definite resemblances; in academic performance dropouts are closer to skippers than to non-skippers. However, dropouts are not found exclusively (as skippers) in the lowest economic strata of this school.

Bibliography

Becker, Howard S. *Outsiders.* New York: The Free Press, 1963.

Brooks, E. E. et al. "Socioeconomic Factors, Parental Attitudes, and School Attendance," *Social Work* 7 (1962): 103-8.

Cloward, R. A. & L. E. Ohlin. *Delinquency and Opportunity: A Theory of Delinquent Gangs.* Glencoe: The Free Press, 1960.

Cohen, Albert. *Delinquent Boys: The Culture of the Gang.* Glencoe: The Free Press, 1955.

Coolidge, John et al. "School Phobia in Adolescence: A Manifestation of Severe Character Disturbance." *American Journal of Orthopsychiatry* 30 (1960): 599-607.

Elliott, Delbert S. et al. "Drop-out and the Social Milieu of the High School: A Preliminary Analysis." *American Journal of Orthopsychiatry* 36 (1966): 808-17.

Finlayson, Douglas S. "Parental Aspirations and the Educational Achievement of Children." *Educational Research* 14 (1971): 61-64.

Friesen, David. "Profile of the Potential Drop-out." *Alberta Journal of Educational Research* 13 (1967): 299-309.

Kahn, Jacques and Nursten, Jean P. "School Refusal: A Comprehensive View of School Phobia and Other Failures of School Attendance." *American Journal of Orthopsychiatry* 32 (1962): 707-18.

Matza, David. *Becoming Deviant.* Englewood Cliffs, N.J.: Prentice Hall, 1969.

Mead, George H. *Mind, Self and Society.* Chicago: The University of Chicago Press, 1962.

Miller, W. B. "Lower Class Culture as a Generating Milieu of Gang Delinquency." In *The Sociology of Crime and Delinquency,* edited by M. E. Wolfang et al., pp. 267-76. New York: John Wiley & Sons, 1962.

9
"Nothing Else But Mad"*:
Canadian Legislative Trends in the Light of Models of Mental Illness and Their Implication for Civil Liberties

Victor Marshall and David Hughes

The past decade has, ostensibly, been one of great, exciting, and commendable reform of the legislative means by which persons can be admitted for care and treatment in psychiatric facilities.[1] All the provinces have introduced new mental health acts since British Columbia took the lead in 1964. R. G. Roy (1971a; see also 1971b), comparing these acts, has noted that

> These changes in the law had many common features. Preservation of individual patients' rights and civil liberties was a prime area of concern. Review methods for patients held against their will were streamlined, and the admission and discharge procedures were simplified. Particular attention was paid to the informal method of admission to enable patients to receive treatment without any of the legal formalities normally associated with being admitted to a mental hospital.

Nonetheless, all jurisdictions in Canada provide for the incarceration of persons called mental patients, against their will. In essence, then, people are deprived of their liberty under these acts. To look at this situation from the perspective of civil liberties necessitates a consideration of just how some individuals can, under the law, come to be forcibly detained in psychiatric facilities. Since the justification for their detention is always based on a judgment that they are "mentally disordered," and usually also that their continued freedom would prejudice their own safety or that of others, we will have to look at the utilization of those criteria as well. As Roy notes (1971a), " . . . psychiatric admission to a hospital is now recognized as a medical, rather than a legal prerogative." The sociologically informed witness of this shift to a medical model of mental hospitalization (Goffman 1961) may well wish to ask how such a shift could occur in the face of the increase in the numbers of sociologists (Goffman 1961; Scheff 1966, 1972; Lemert 1967), psychiatrists (Laing 1965, 1969; Cooper 1967; Szasz 1961, 1963, 1970a, 1970b), psychologists (Rosenhan 1973), and others (Wooton 1972) who are challenging

* See note 3, below.

the medical model. The central thesis of this paper is that the utilization of a medical model in Canadian mental hospitalization legislation greatly enhances the ease with which persons can be hospitalized while, at the same time, it mitigates against any provision of accountability of the mental-hospitalization process to the public. For purposes of illustration we will attend in particular to the Ontario legislation, arguing that this has come to serve as a model for other jurisdictions. However, the acts of other provinces will be considered when appropriate. (See Swadron 1973; and Roy 1971a, 1971b for more systematic reviews of the other Canadian legislation.) Throughout, this topic will be considered from an interactionist's view of mental illness as deviance and the mental-hospitalization process as deviance production. However, this paper should perhaps be viewed as sociologically informed rhetoric, rather than sociological analysis.

Mental Hospitalization As Big Business

Mental hospitalization is big business in Canada. Confining ourselves to patients in Canada's forty-six public mental hospitals,[2] we find there were 17,259 males and 13,179 females on the books as of December 31, 1972 (Statistics Canada 1973). Movement through public mental hospitals involves a larger number of people. There were, in 1972, 35,637 admissions to public mental hospitals, and 39,007 "separations" (these include patients who were discharged, who died, and those referred to other psychiatric facilities). Generally speaking, there has been a reduction in the numbers hospitalized in public mental hospitals, largely as a result of the introduction of psychotropic drugs in the early 1950s (McGregor 1964) and the growth of alternative facilities such as residential treatment centres, half-way houses, and home-treatment programs (Henderson 1971).

The varieties of facilities for the mentally ill, together with the mix of types of patients which might be confined in any particular hospital, precludes making any sound comparisons among the provinces of Canada, and also precludes making any summary statements about patient populations. As a consequence, we will have to settle for impressionistic inferences to the broader Canadian scene. One way of doing this is to focus on the province where mental hospitalization is the biggest business of all—Ontario. In Ontario, for example, we find there were 12,476 mental patients in hospital in 1971; but there were also an additional 773 patients in approved homes and 2,255 on leave of absence. Thus, of the total number of patients on the books of the mental health system, just 80.5 per cent were hospitalized in mental hospitals. And while there were 15,504 patients on the books of this system during 1971, there were 17,306 admissions during that year

(Ontario 1971). Ontario is typical of other provinces in that the average length of stay of patients in hospital is decreasing, while the ways in which a patient can be kept in the system are increasing with a step-up in the programs for leaves of absence, residence in approved boarding homes, half-way houses, and the like. All the same, the overall tendency is to reduce the total number of patients in the system (and especially in hospital). Thus, in Ontario the patient population reached a high in 1960 of 25,630, and has decreased fairly regularly at an average of 4.6 per cent a year, to the 1971 level of 15,504 patients on the books (Ontario 1971).

Let me emphasize again that the absolute figures are not as important as the trends, which are generally the same for other provinces, though stronger in some. A leading province in this regard has been Saskatchewan, which has reduced its in-patient population from 3,238 in 1960 to 1,070 in 1969, while increasing the provision of psychiatric alernatives to hospital care (Smith, 1970).

Accompanying the triple revolution in provision of alternative facilities, utilization of drug maintenance, and legislative changes, we see not only an overall reduction of patients in hospital, but a change in their legally defined statuses. Again taking Ontario as an example, whereas in 1960 just over one-fifth of admissions to mental hospitals were informal or voluntary, by 1971, 55.6 per cent of admissions were informal. Thus, in that year there were 10,294 informal patients, 4,949 formal patients, and 261 additional patients under compulsion, such as by judicial remand, lieutenant governor's warrant, or ministerial warrant (Ontario 1971). Again, the different use of facilities in various provinces belies comparison, but Ontario proportions are not greatly out of line with those in other provinces.

Our concern is with formal, or involuntary, hospitalization. Although the proportions of patients involuntarily hospitalized is highly variable throughout Canada, and although this proportion is decreasing, this type of mental hospitalization is important in the numbers of people processed, particularly in the light of the fact that involuntary mental hospitalization represents a major way in which individuals are processed, against their wills, into a highly stigmatized deviant status.

The Legal Route to Involuntary Commitment

Something less than, but close to, one-half of mental patients are sent to mental hospitals against their will. This procedure includes those remanded by the courts and sent under warrant of the lieutenant governor of the province, but consists primarily of what we might call civil commitment. Civil commitment is a process by which a decision is made under a mental health act that a person should be hospitalized because he is mentally disordered and, usually though not always, because his continued freedom would constitute, in the eyes of those committing him, a threat to his own safety or the safety of others.

In what follows we will attend most closely to the legislation governing civil commitment in the province of Ontario. As I have indicated above, just under 5,000 patients were admitted to Ontario hospitals under involuntary admission in 1971. The Ontario legislation which makes this possible was greatly changed with the passage of the Mental Health Act, 1967, with subsequent revisions of a non-substantial nature through 1972. The 1968 Annual Report of the Ontario Department of Health (p. 74) says of the 1967 Act that it " ... has been acclaimed as a model by many other jurisdictions." This does appear to be the case, for the subsequent acts passed by Alberta (1972), Prince Edward Island (1968), New Brunswick (1969), Newfoundland (1971, yet to be proclaimed), and the concurrently passed Nova Scotia legislation (1967) bear strong resemblance to the Ontario Act, frequently to the point of exact duplication of provisions. Legislation is not prepared in a vacuum. When a province such as Ontario comes up with strikingly new legislation, it is not unreasonable to expect a fair degree of modelling based not only on the prestige of Ontario but on the mundane fact that consultation on the preparation of new legislation crosses provincial boundaries. As we address the provisions of the Ontario legislation then, we should bear in mind not only its importance for residents of Ontario, but also for those of other jurisdictions.

One major provision of the recent legislation of most provinces makes it easier to voluntarily, or informally, enter a mental hospital. In a major policy statement concerned with many aspects of mental hospitalization, the Canadian Mental Health Association argues as follows:

> Since the patient who recognizes his need for treatment and actively seeks help early has the greater chance of benefit, no barriers should be placed in the way of treatment. The patient should be admitted "informally" on the recommendation of a physician who states that the patient requires hospital care. (Swadron 1973, p. 14)

All well and good. If a person wants to become a mental patient then why not let him? And the screening by one physician can serve to keep out people who would abuse the health care system. Moreover, the legislation usually includes a provision such as article 6 of the Ontario Act, to the effect that

> ... admission to a psychiatric facility may be refused where the immediate needs in the case of the proposed patient are such that hospitalization is not urgent or necessary.

However, the thinking of the Canadian Mental Health Association continues in a remarkable fashion to characterize even voluntary patients as incompetent. Discussing the customary terminology of "informal/formal" as being more suitable than the terms "voluntary involuntary," this report argues:

> . . . "voluntary" admission had to carry with it the capacity of the patient to be an "active volunteer" – a capacity which many did not have (Swadron 1973, p. 14).

Can this be a hint that those entering a mental hospital informally are really not entering it voluntarily? Reviewing Canadian legislation, Roy (1971a) notes that an important aspect of all provincial mental health legislation in the past twenty years has been its emphasis on facilitating voluntary or informal admission:

> As the term "informal" suggests, such admission should be devoid of legal formalities normally associated with the hospitalization of the mentally disordered (Roy 1971a).

But, Roy continues:

> Even a cursory glance at the Mental Health Acts . . . raises the question in one's mind how voluntary is voluntary admission and how devoid of formalities is informal admission?

The main possibility that can occur under this provision is that a person can be admitted after only one examination. It now becomes possible for a physician, or anyone, to more easily implement a threat on the order of, I think you should sign yourself in informally, and if you don't I will have you committed. If this threat is successful, there is less chance of detection or accountability as to whether adequate grounds for formal or involuntary admission existed. The frequency of use of this threat is an undocumented area which needs research. It does occur, as the following case history shows. Not happy with his work, and not "fitting in" with the requirements of his job, this young man accepted the "suggestion" of his employer that he seek proper medical attention for his problems. In his medical interview he was upset at the prospects of possible psychiatric intervention:

> . . . I was confronted with the facts – I could co-operate and voluntarily commit myself for corrective therapy [electroconvulsive therapy] . . . or allow my condition to deteriorate and face the prospect of involuntary confinement[in a particular hospital] in the future. Since I was totally defeated, a failure as a human being, a menace to society, disoriented, distorted, etc., I agreed. Coercion can be enforced in many ways . . . [account given to the author by a former Ontario mental patient].

Making it easier for patients to informally admit themselves into mental hospital can also make it easier for admission to be coerced through a system that is less public than formal admission, because one signature, and not two, is required. It is important to note that the informal patient is not completely free to leave the hospital. He is required while there to submit to treatment, and in some provinces may be detained when he desires to leave. Thus, while five provinces make no provisions regarding discharge of voluntary patients, following request to be discharged a person can be detained for twenty-four hours in Saskatchewan, and for three days in British Columbia, Alberta, Manitoba, and Nova Scotia. More important, perhaps, is that the voluntary patient places himself in greater risk of being formally committed, because the following clause from the Ontario Act is typical:

12.   An informal patient may, upon completion of the prescribed form, be continued as an involuntary patient. . . .

In such cases the criteria governing formal, or involuntary, commitment must be met. Informal, or voluntary, commitment is thus one way to find oneself in a mental hospital, and it carries the risk of conversion to formal, or involuntary, commitment. We can now look at the more direct legal route into the mental hospital. Again, Ontario will be taken as paradigmatic both of what is now the case in several provinces, and of what seems to be the coming trend.

After outlining the provisions for informal commitment, the Mental Health Act of 1967 goes on to discuss formal commitment:

8-(1)   Any person who,
    (a) suffers from mental disorder of a nature or degree so as to require hospitalization in the interests of his own safety or the safey of others; and
    (b) is not suitable for admission as an informal patient, may be admitted as an involuntary patient to a psychiatric facility upon application therefore in the prescribed form signed by a physician.

This regulation requires close scrutiny. Let us consider first the two criteria of mental disorder and safety. While Nova Scotia and Manitoba do not now require that the person formally committed be a danger to himself or others (the person can be either a danger or in need of treatment), the other provinces do, either by explicitly noting the two criteria in their acts, or (as with British Columbia), defining mental disorder so as to include the criteria of safety. None of the acts define safety or danger to self or others. How is "mental disorder" defined? This varies by province, and some examples are –

lack of reason or lack of control of behaviour (Alberta)

"mental disorder" means mental illness, mental retardation, psychopathic disorder, or any other disorder or disability of mind . . . [and]

"mental illness" means a disorder of mind other than psychopathic disorder or mental retardation, that results in a disturbance in a person's behaviour or feelings or thought and conversation and that results in mental distress or impaired ability to associate with others or results in a person's inability to react appropriately or efficiently to his environment and in respect of which medical treatment is advisable . . . (Saskatchewan; Manitoba's is very similar.)

any disease or disability of the mind (Ontario, New Brunswick, Newfoundland)

any disease or disability of the mind . . . and includes the disease or disability of the mind caused by the use of alcohol or other chemical substance (Prince Edward Island)

In view of the circular, tautological nature of these definitions,[3] the fact that Quebec and Nova Scotia have no definitions in their acts does not place these provinces far behind in the clarity of their legislation. The operational definition of both "mental disorder" and the danger or safety provision is provided, of course, by those with the power to commit.

Who has this power? While the decision can be made by one or more psychiatrists, in no province in Canada is this necessary (see Roy 1917b). Rather, the laws require only a medical decision by a physician or physicians. Manitoba, Ontario, New Brunswick, and Prince Edward Island require only one physician's signature; Alberta requires the signature of one physician and a second signature of either a physician or a therapist; and the remaining provinces require the signature of two physicians (in British Columbia a medical commitment must in addition be supported by a relative or acquaintance of the patient). Some of these latter provinces also have emergency admission procedures which allow a briefer admission on one signature. Roy (1971b notes:

In Canada . . . patients are not given the benefit of a psychiatric assessment prior to hospitalization. This problem assumes serious proportions when one considers the generally low level of interest the average general practitioner manifests in psychiatry.

In a study of Ontario general practitioners published a decade ago (Clute 1963; pp. 306-7), it was found that half of them considered their education in psychiatry to have been unsatisfactory. Doctors who attended at all to mental health problems relied more on their personal life experiences than on their medical training. Using 1967-68 data, Hanly (1970; p. 115) concluded that the psychiatric expertise of general practitioners had not improved: " . . . the proportion of general practitioners who combine interest with requisite training is woefully inadequate." But Hanly's assessment of adequacy is in terms of training in a medical model of mental illness. We will consider later in this paper whether such adequacy is adequate enough.

Undoubtedly most formal committals to mental hospitals are made by psychiatrists. The civil libertarian critique of this legislation rests, however, on an assessment of what the law allows. That is, the civil libertarian is not willing to assume that the hospitalization system is governed and staffed by the psychiatric or medical equivalent of the philosopher-king. Rather, he asks that the maximal safeguards be placed on any process which results in deprivation of civil liberty. We have seen that many jurisdictions allow formal commitment on the basis of one signature. In addition the hospital may refuse to accept the patient. But presumably the one-signature regulation obviates the necessity for an extensive examination by the hospital so long as it admits the patient. When such application is made, it gives sufficient authority in Ontario

8-(5)   (a) to any person to convey the person who is the subject of the application to a psychiatric facility; and

   (b) to the authorities thereof to admit and detain him therein for a period of not more than one month.

In other provinces this period of authorized detention varies from fourteen days (Saskatchewan) to one year (British Columbia). Other provinces fall in between, with a typical period of one month (this applies to regular detention; emergency detention might be restricted to as little as twenty-four hours, as in Alberta, but enables regular detention to be arranged).

Let us underline this fact: with this legislation a person may be detained, forcibly and against his will, for as long as one month in a province such as Ontario, without benefit of trial. Using a medical model of mental illness, we allow these decisions to be made in a context where the customary safeguards of the right to be heard, the exclusion of hearsay evidence, the right to representation, and the presumption of innocence until proven guilty do not obtain.

Innocence and guilt? But we are talking about illness and disease, are we not? Evidence? But what would evidence be about? The commitment system works under a model of mental illness as a disease state. While danger or safety factors are generally prerequisite for formal commitment, these factors are not defined. A person may be considered dangerous, if a disease model is used, even if he has not actually done any action that is prejudicial to his own safety or that of others. He could be considered dangerous on the basis of verbal behaviour, or no behaviour, or anything that might lead a physician, employing a psychiatric model, to predict that he might be' dangerous in the future.

Under the criminal law we are not allowed to lock people up before they have committed offences. Even conspiracy must be ascertained as an act before a person can be convicted of it. And under the criminal system, the defendant is given the opportunity to have his day in court, with due process. (See Canadian Civil Liberties Education Trust, 1971.) He is innocent until proven guilty. What we have, in effect, are some magic words: "mental disorder"; "in the interests of his own safety or the safety of others." With these magic words, we suspend our libertarian safeguards and lock someone up.

There are methods of extending detention, renewal procedures which generally follow the same criteria for examination and assessment of mental disorder and danger; and as renewal follows renewal, the period of allowable detention becomes longer. For example, in Ontario, where first detention is for one month, first renewal is for two months, second renewal for three additional months, third renewal for six months, and fourth and subsequent renewals for one year. Of course most patients do not stay that long. They are "cured" and allowed by an authorized physician to leave; or their formal certification is not renewed and they become informal and can leave if they desire; or they can apply for a judicial hearing (on five day's notice in Nova Scotia) or a hearing before a review board (at any time, in Newfoundland or Saskatchewan, with a decision required in two weeks in Saskatchewan). But usually such hearings are not required to be conducted until the expiry of the first regular period of detention; thus, in Ontario, a patient is not entitled to a review-board meeting until he has been detained for one month.

One can only speculate about the effects of drug or electro-shock or other therapies, not to mention the identity-stripping functions of hospitalization on an individual's abilities to mount a solid argument to the effect that he has been cured. (See Goffman 1961; Rosenhan 1973; Erikson 1957; and Messinger, Sampson and Towne 1962 for data.) He has already been certified as mentally disordered and dangerous, and he must now prove that he is not. In short, by the time an individual gets to a review board, the presumption of innocence (sanity, safety) has been set aside, and he is presumed guilty (mentally disordered, dangerous). The burden of proof has been shifted to him.

We have looked at one stage of a four-stage process involving the route to identification and selection for psychiatric examination, the legal process of being involuntarily hospitalized, life within the hospital, and return to the outer world. Space limitations preclude a treatment here of the latter two stages, about which the reader is referred to Goffman's book, *Asylums* (1961), and David Rosenhan's article, "On Being Sane in Insane Places" (1973). In the remainder of this paper we would like to develop a critique of the developing use of the medical model of mental illness in justifying formal, or involuntary, commitment, in the light of some arguments and evidence put forth by some sociologists, "anti-psychiatrists," and civil libertarians.

Danger and Disease: The Medical Model

There are, of course, many differences among psychiatric practitioners as to just what mental illness is, its etiology, and its optimal treatment.

Nevertheless, certain common themes are discernible as underlying the current Canadian "reform" in legislation governing involuntary commitment of persons as mentally ill. These themes, we will argue, can be taken as defining a medical model of mental illness.

Thomas Scheff (1964) has outlined five assumptions of this medical model of mental illness. These assumptions are:

1. *The assumption that the condition of mentally ill persons deteriorates rapidly without psychiatric assistance.*

As Scheff has pointed out, it is still not clear that most psychiatric interventions are any more effective than no treatment at all. Eysenck (1952, 1960) has convincingly argued this for the neuroses; while Walker and Kelly (1960) have, in considering hospitalized schizophrenics, found no significant difference in improvement between an experimental group treated with short-term psychotherapy and an untreated control group.

2. *The assumption that effective psychiatric treatments exist for most mental illnesses.*

Although controlled studies are lacking here, the very plethora of competing conceptions of treatment (for Ontario data seen Hanly 1970) testifies to disagreement about the effectiveness of various treatments. (However, see Eysenck 1960, 1961 for a consideration of "behaviour therapy.")

3. *The assumption that, unlike surgery, there are no risks in involuntary psychiatric treatment: it either helps, or it is neutral; it can't hurt.*

On the contrary, there is very good evidence that involuntary hospitalization may adversely affect a patient's life, leading to loss of job, disruption of family life, and the burden of carrying a stigmatized label (Goffman 1961, 1963; Greenblatt et al. 1955; Rubenstein and Lasswell 1966). Hospitalization, we would argue, may carry the risks of turning a transitory crisis episode into a prolonged role career of mental illness and living with stigma (Cumming and Cumming 1965; Simmons and Freeman 1959; Simmons 1965; Freeman and Simmons 1958, 1961; Whatley 1959).

4. *The assumption that exposing a prospective mental patient to questioning, cross-examination, and other screening procedures exposes him to the unnecessary stigma of trial-like procedures, and may do further damage to his mental condition.*

It is probably true that exposing a patient to such procedures may damage his mental condition. But the failure to adequately screen potential candidates for the mental hospital carries the risk of unnecessary commitment. Thomas Szasz presents this argument very well:

> I believe it is possible that such a hearing is traumatic for a

person, as it is alleged to be. However, I feel even more strongly that to be placed in an institution without explanations of how one got there, why one got there, and for how long one will be confined, is even more traumatic. The question is not simply whether a given person is "mentally ill" and whether a hearing is "traumatic" – but rather what are our choices as to how we might deal with this person. If in the name of their allegedly traumatic experience we do what we now do – that is, confuse the patient and deprive him of the opportunity to effectively resist the commitment procedure – then I am 100 per cent against it . . . I think if a hearing is conducted with humanity and sensitivity, I don't see anything traumatic about it. (Mechanic 1969, p. 288)

5. *The assumption that there is an element of danger to self or others in mental illness; and that it is better to risk unnecessary hospitalization than the harm a patient might do himself or others.*

The element of danger is usually exaggerated both in amount and degree. Danger is not adequately defined. Cooper (1967, p. 25) discusses a patient detained because he had behaved aggressively and violently toward his parents – he was removed for the protection of others. On further investigation, the violent aggressive behaviour was found to consist of (a) breaking one tea-cup; (b) slamming the front door; and (c) stamping his foot once, but rather emphatically, on the garden path.

Lest this example seem trivial, we may note that Rubin (see also Greenland 1971), in a recent systematic review of the literature on the prediction of dangerousness makes the following points:

Even in the most careful, painstaking, laborious, and lengthy clinical approach to the prediction of dangerousness, false positives may be at a minimum of 60% to 70%.

Part of the problem may be that psychiatrists use mental disease as a concept which relates to treatment . . . and labeling of deviancy as mental illness or predicting dangerousness is just a convention to get someone to treatment. Once in treatment the concept of dangerousness is forgotten.

Psychiatry and psychoanalytic theory and studies have given very conflicting evidence having no predictive value.

Given the present reality it is unlikely that dangerousness can be predicted in a person who has not acted in a dangerous or violent way. (Rubin 1972)

Page and Yates, in two forthcoming articles, demonstrate that dangerousness was not adequately documented in Ontario before the legislative changes in 1967, and is still not documented. For a large sample of commitment certificates, they found notations alleging actual evidence of danger (for example "attacked wife") to have been made in just 8.9 per cent of commitments before the new legislation in 1967, and in a mere 4.4 per cent of forms for persons committed after the new legislation came into effect. Recall that in Ontario danger is a necessary condition for involuntarily, or formal mental hospitalization!

The five assumptions which we have initially reviewed may be taken as defining a medical model of mental illness; and we may interpret the current legislative trend in Canada as being based on, and more fully incorporating these assumptions. "Mental disorder" is customarily defined as "any disease or disability of the mind"; there is no question but that the involuntary commitment procedures are invoked in situations where the patient has no choice. The continuance of procedures rests on a conception of mental illness as a continuing disease state. There is no mention in the Acts of possible risk to the patient because of treatment although the commitment procedures rest on an estimation of presumed risk accompanying failure to treat (this presumed risk being danger to self or others). And finally, one can only assume that the failure to allow for careful questioning, cross-examination, and screening rests on the assumption that this would be stressful for the patient.

Mental Illness As Deviance

As we have indicated, we are not at all convinced of the accurateness of this medical model of mental illness. We would like to propose an alternative model – one which views mental illness not as a disease, but as deviance. We will borrow heavily from sociologists such as Howard Becker (1963), who view deviance not as a property of an act itself, but rather as behaviour which violates someone's conception of the rule and is identified as doing so.

Deviance, then, we see as rule-breaking activity; and we see mental illness as deviance. This perspective rejects, or at least plays down, earlier notions that deviants are people who are somewhat fundamentally different from "normal" people. The identification of a person's behaviour as rule breaking is taken to be problematical – all car thieves are not caught, most homosexuals keep their rule breaking a restricted secret, most pot-smokers avoid confrontations with legal authorities, etc. The significant question is not the understanding of rule breaking as such, for in a diverse society such as ours, we all break someone's rules some of the time. The important question is to try to understand how an individual comes to adopt a regular pattern of behaviour that is rule breaking.

The key link in this transition from occasional deviance to stable patterns of deviance is thought to be the labelling process (Lemert 1967, pp. 3-30). The imputation of a label has implications for the identity of the labelled. Through commonly known principles of person perception, people tend to see in others what they expect to see. A label defines the expectations, by suggesting that individual behaviours are to be taken as documents or indicators of some underlying essential quality of the self. Current and past behaviours of a person can be organized in terms of a label. Faced with the charge that he is some kind of different person (or not fully normal) the labelled person has two options – to attempt to fight the imputation of the label; or to accept it. Acceptance of the label implies living up to the expectations of the labellers and becoming mentally ill (Scheff 1964).

Fighting off a label requires the mustering of resources by the labelled. When a person has to organize aspects of his life in response to the labelling attempts of others, he acts in a power game. So, for instance, the upper class adolescent in juvenile court can muster the respectability of his family, not to mention the ability to employ a good lawyer in seeking dismissal of his case.

It is virtually axiomatic in the perspective of role theory which underlies this approach to deviance, that if a person is induced or coerced into playing a role, he alters his self-concept, or his indentity, in keeping with his behaviour. Thus, if an adolescent is defined by authorities, family, or neighbours, as a "bad boy," we would predict that he will tend to "live down" to the expectations which follow from the label.

We would argue, with Scheff (1964, 1966) and Goffman (1961) that this approach to understanding deviance applies well to mental illness. We wish now to review some evidence regarding mental illness that has been developed within this perspective, or which gives support to it. This is an alternative to the medical model of mental illness.

What is the human context of the person labelled mentally ill? How does the label come to be attached? By whom? And to what purpose? What does it signify for the labelled and labeller? The relationship between the family and the schizophrenic individual is not new; however, there has been a development in the study of schizophrenia (neatly summarized by Haley):

> A transition would seem to have taken place . . . from the early idea that the difficulty in these families was caused by the schizophrenic individual, to the idea that they contained a pathogenic mother, to the discovery that the father was inadequate, to the current emphasis upon all . . . family members involved in a pathological system of interaction (Haley 1959, p. 358).

It is this latter approach we have adopted. When you read through Laing and Esterson's book, *Sanity, Madness and the Family* (1964), it is surprising how often the delusional structures of the patients are recognizable in the patterns of relationships within their families. (See also Wynne et al. 1958.) Our view is that what comes to be labelled schizophrenia (and other psychotic disorders) is not a disease entity; that is, it does not submit to interpretation in terms of the medical model; rather, it is a certain, more or less specifiable, set of personal interaction patterns. It is not something happening *within* the individual; but it is an individual's interpretation of what is happening *between* individuals.

Cooper has offered the following tentative definition of schizophrenia as

> a micro-social crisis situation in which the acts and experiences of a certain person are invalidated by others for certain intelligible cultural and micro-cultural (usually familial) reasons, to a point where he is *elected* and *identified* as being "mentally ill" in a certain way and is then confirmed (by a specifiable but highly arbitrary labelling process) in the identity of schizophrenic patient by medical, or quasi-medical, agents (Cooper 1967, p. 2).

The point of focus is not the individual but the *group*. It is not argued that the "schizophrenic individual" does not exhibit bizarre, schizoid behaviour (breaking residual rules, in Scheff's terms), but that such behaviour is what Goffman would term a normal response to an abnormal situation; and that the focus of treatment should *not* be the individual, but the whole field of interpersonal relations within primary groupings such as (but not necessarily only) the family. Cooper has observed that quite often after interviewing the prospective patient with his family it is not he who is admitted, but another member of the family (in a significant number of cases, the mother). One gains the impression that the attribution of a schizophrenic label is necessary for the maintenance of the *status quo* within a given family system (Laing and Esterson 1964; Esterson 1970).

If we accept Kelly's (1955) view that man is continually trying to make sense of the world around him and continuously checking the sense he has made by testing its predictive capacity, then it will become apparent that the integrity of his self depends upon the integrity of the model he forms of the world. In a system of relationships, that integrity will also depend upon his experience of others' models of shared experience. In the family, to be *in* the family means sharing the same model of the family as the other members. This model of the family, as Laing has argued (1967, p. 119), may be the medium that each person uses to link his experiences with the others. Any attempt to restructure that model by one member results in a crisis and a necessary restructuring of the models internalized by the other members. In certain families such restructuring may be considered a threat to the family, to each individual's conception of his experience of what the family relations are. In Laing's terms:

> Acts of spontaneity may be defined *by the others* as acts of destruction, of sickness and illness, because they entail the breakup of the internal family structures of *the others*. Each must sacrifice himself, therefore, to preserve the [model] of the family (Laing 1967, p. 120).

In order to restructure his model the individual must seek to induce a restructuring of others' experience. Such restructuring may be resisted by what Laing (1965) terms "mystification," essentially, an action performed upon another to defend one's own person. A common form of mystification may be to deny that a person is responsible for his actions (or praxis) and to attribute them to some disease (or process). In this respect, "madness" is the substituting of an impersonal series of events for what one person does, and may constitute a systematic denial of another's experience. Bannister (1960), using Kelly's terminology, describes this process as "serial invalidation of constructs."

The symptoms of such a "disease" may be anything that makes the family anxious about the independent behaviour of one of its members. Laing and Esterson (1964, pp. 31-49) in their disucssion of the girl Maya describe how the customary needs of adolescence – sexuality, aggression, self-assertion, involvement outside the family – may be considered a threat to the family *status quo*, and labelled as symptoms of a disease. A label thus serves to invalidate the individual's future actions and experience.

This process, beginning in the family, has been interpreted in rulebreaking terms by Scheff (1966, pp. 31-54). With mental illness, Scheff argues, we are concerned in particular with residual rule breaking. This is the violation of expectations (or norms) which are not clearly defined. Such violations may be initially viewed as weird or bizarre behaviour, but they are usually attributed to the individual's being in a bad mood, having "gotten up on the wrong side of the bed," or to situational factors. The labelling process begins when for some reason residual rule breaking becomes the focus of attention. It is the change from saying, He's really not like that, to saying, You see? He's really acting strangely.

Formal, or involuntary, commitment is one further act of mystification, and invalidation, denying the individual's ability to act for himself and to determine his individual identity and integrity, by attributing his actions to the process of disease.

Conclusion: The Power Factor

We have seen that the move in Canadian legislation has been away from a legal framework governing commitment to a medical framework. In other jurisdictions where commitment is still done largely through a legal system, the power dimensions involved in the labelling process are clearer, because the legal system is a contest system. Several studies from such jurisdictions suggest the importance of power in determining involuntary commitment, and we would argue that the absence in the Canadian legislation of a legal format does not reduce this power domain but serves only to hide involuntary commitment from public scrutiny. Let us consider the findings of some of these studies.

Characteristics of the petitioners and their means of petition have been found to be related to the decision to commit. In one centre studied by Wilde (1968), of eighty-three cases adjudicated, 77 per cent of those for which an appointment had been made were approved, whereas only 23 per cent of petitions directly presented, with no prior appointment, were approved. The counter-argument is, of course, that appointments might be made in the case of more serious indications of mental illness as perceived by the petitioner. Wilde, however, attempted with an admittedly crude measure to allow for symptomatology, and found that it bore no relationship to commitment.

A study by Haney and associates (1969) of 127 cases from four Florida counties offers additional evidence as to the influence of petitioner characteristics on outcome of committal proceedings. They found the following characteristics to be important:

(a) Age: Older petitioners were more successful than younger ones in obtaining commitment. Younger petitioners were least successful in attempting to commit persons older.

(b) Sex: Female petitioners were more successful, on the whole, than male petitioners. Male petitioners, however, were equally successful in committing both males and females (50 per cent), whereas female petitioners were relatively unsuccessful in committing males (42.3 per cent) and more successful in committing other females (57.6 per cent).

(c) Marital status: Unmarried petitioners were more successful than married petitioners; but the highest per cent adjudged incompetent occurred with married petitioners seeking to commit unmarried.

(d) Education: Those with more than nine years education were more successful than those with less than nine years.

(e) Occupation: White collar petitioners were less successful than blue-collar petitioners; but non-working petitioners were least successful in obtaining commitment.

These investigators also called attention to the importance of status in effecting judgments of incompetency: variables associated with higher status led to greater success with the petition; and attempts to commit someone of higher status were less likely to be successful than attempts to commit someone of equal status.

Wenger and Fletcher (1969) have produced some evidence that the presence of a lawyer at a commitment hearing might make the psychiatrists more careful. In these hearings under study, a court referee presided, while two psychiatrists examined the patient and gave their judgments. It is interesting to note that the judges in all cases followed the advice of the psychiatrists. However, when a legal counsel for the patient was present, the hearing, and its outcome, were sometimes changed. Of eighty-one hearings, mean time of hearing increased from 6.15 to 16.84 minutes; and decision to commit changed as well. Of fifteen persons with legal counsel, only four were committed; of sixty-six persons with no legal counsel, only five were *not* committed. Conceivably the "sane" are more likely to obtain legal counsel; or might it work the other way around? Wenger and Fletcher attempted to control for condition of the patient on the basis of their own observations of the hearings. Gove (1970) has argued the inadequacy of this method. We might note, however, that this procedure placed the observers in the same situation as the so-called referee who had only the same information on which to base a judgment. They divided up the cases into three groups: those meeting legal criteria for commitment, those not meeting the criteria, and borderline cases. Of the seventy-two cases in which the patient was present for his hearing (nine not being present), forty-three were classified as borderline and 30 per cent were classified as not meeting the legal criteria. Presence of lawyers reduced chance of commitment in all categories, demonstrating that Wenger and Feltcher's finding of the protective function of legal counsel was not spurious.

If commitment to hospital rests solely on diagnosed mental illness then other factors ought not be involved. We have seen, however, that other factors may be involved. This leaves us with one of two choices; either

(a) these variables are associated with or are causative of mental illness, or

(b) factors other than mental illness affect the outcome of adjudication proceedings.

If we find the latter, then we would argue, from a consideration of civil liberties, that the strongest possible safeguards against such independent factors being operative must be built into the legislation governing commitment procedures. While judicial commitment procedures have their weaknesses, their strength is that they place commitment in a more public domain. They should thus be made more, not less, rigorous.

We would further argue for a shift in emphasis away from the individual and the whole notion of a disease entity, to a consideration of pathological family patterns, and the functions and consequences of the processes of mystification, invalidation, and labelling. This is not to argue for something new: the social process and deviance critiques of the disease model have been with us for a number of years. But these same years have seen, in Canada, a legislative trend toward a stronger foothold for those who ascribe to the disease model. Why this should be so is a question in the sociology of knowledge which cannot be explored here.

Notes

[1.] Letters were sent to all provincial ministers responsible for the administration of mental hospital legislation. All provided copies of the current Acts, and many provided additional data concerning hospital statistics, Annual Reports of the Departments of Health, and additional working papers. I am grateful for their co-operation. The Newfoundland Act cited herein, passed in 1971, has not yet been proclaimed (as of October, 1973), pending establishment of new regulations for its implementation.

[2.] These data represent patient movement for all reporting psychiatric in-patient facilities. They are provisional, and probably under-reported. Final figures will appear in the annual publication, *Mental Health Statistics, vol. 1, Institutional Admissions and Separations* (Ottawa, Statistics Canada).

[3.] See Shakespeare's *Hamlet,* act 2, sc. 2, line 93: "For to define true madness, what is it but to be nothing else but mad." See the title of this article.

Bibliography

Bannister, D. "Conceptual structure in thought disordered schizophrenics." *Journal of Mental Science* 106, no. 445 (1960): 1230-49.

Becker, Howard. *Outsiders.* Glencoe: Free Press, 1963.

Canadian Civil Liberties Education Trust. *Due Process Safeguards and Canadian Criminal Justice.* Toronto, 1971.

Clute, K. F. *The General Practitioner.* Toronto: University of Toronto Press, 1963.

Cooper, D. *Psychiatry and Anti-Psychiatry.* London: Tavistock, 1967.

Cumming, John, and Elaine Cumming. "On the Stigma of Mental Illness." *Community Mental Health Journal* 1 (1965): 135-43.

Erickson, Kai T. "Patient Role and Social Uncertainty." *Psychiatry: Journal for The Study of Interpersonal Processes* 20 (August 1957): 263-68.

Esterson, Aaron. *The Leaves of Spring.* London: Tavistock, 1970.

Eysenck, H. J. "The Effects of Psychotherapy." *Journal of Consultative and Clinical Psychology* 16 (1952): 319-24.

_____. *Behavior Therapy and Neuroses*. London: Pergamon Press, 1960.

Freeman, Howard E., and Ozzie G. Simmons. "Mental Patients in the Community: Family Settings and Performance Levels." *American Sociological Review* 23 (1958): 147-54.

_____. "Feelings of Stigma Among Relatives of Former Mental Patients." *Social Problems* 8 (1961): 312-21.

Goffman, Erving. *Asylums*. Garden City, New York: Doubleday, 1961.

Gove, W. R. "Who is Hospitalized: A Critical Review of Some Sociological Studies of Mental Illness." *Journal of Health and Social Behavior* 2, no. 4 (1970): 294-303.

Greenblatt, M., et al. *From Custodial to Therapeutic Patient Care in Mental Hospitals*. New York: Russell Sage Foundation, 1955.

Greenland, Cyril. "Evaluation of Violence and Dangerous Behavior Associated with Mental Illness." *Seminars in Psychiatry* 3 (1971): 345-56.

Haley, J. "The Family of the Schizophrenic: A Model System." *Journal of Nervous Mental Disorders* 129 (1959): 357-74.

Haney, C. A., et al, "The Interaction of Petitioner and Deviant Social Characteristics in the Adjudication of Incompetency." *Sociometry* 32 (1969): 182-93.

Hanly, C. *Mental Health in Ontario. A Study for the Committee on the Healing Arts*. Toronto: Queen's Printer, 1970.

Henderson, H. W. "(I) Mental Health Developments in Ontario." *Canada's Mental Health* 19, no. 2 (1971): 13-16.

Kelly, G. A. *The Psychology of Personal Constructs*. 2 vols. New York: Norton, 1955.

Laing, R. D. "Mystification, Confusion and Conflict." Chapt. 9 in *Intensive Family Therapy*, edited by Ivan Boszormenyi-Nagy and James L. Framo. New York: Harper and Row, 1965.

_____. "Individual and Family Structure." In *The Predicament of the Family*, edited by P. Lomas, pp. 107-25. London: Hogarth Press, 1967.

_____. *The Politics of the Family*. Toronto: CBC Publications, 1969.

_____ and A. Esterson. *Sanity, Madness and the Family*. Hammondsworth: Penguin, 1964.

Lemert, E. M. *Human Deviance, Social Problems, and Social Control*. Englewood Cliffs, N.J.: Prentice-Hall, 1967.

Page, Stewart, and Elizabeth Yates. "Involuntary Mental Hospitalizations: Semantics and Civil Commitment." *Canadian Psychiatric Association Journal*, in press.

_____. "A note on Semantics and Civil Commitment." *Canadian Psychiatric Association Journal*, in press.

McGregor, K. M. "Trends in Mental Hospitals." *Canadian Psychiatric Association Journal* 9, no. 4 (1964): 331-35.

Mechanic, David. *Mental Health and Social Policy.* Englewood Cliffs N.J.: Prentice-Hall, 1969.

Messinger, Sheldon E., H. Sampson, and R. D. Towne. "Life as Theater: Some Notes on the Dramaturgic Approach to Social Realty." *Sociometry.* 25 (September 1962): 98-110.

Ontario. *Forty-fourth Annual Report of the Ontario Department of Health, For the Year 1968.* Toronto: Queen's Printer, 1963.

_____. *One-Hundred and Fifth Annual Report of the Mental Health Division of the Department of Health of the province of Ontario. Calendar Year 1971.* Toronto: Queen's Printer, 1971.

Rosenhan, D. L. "On Being Sane in Insane Places." *Science* 179, no. 4070 (1973): 250-58.

Roy, R. G. "Canadian Laws on Voluntary Psychiatric Patients." *Canadian Journal of Public Health* 62 (November/December 1971a): 541-45.

_____. "Admission of Psychiatric Patients on Medical Certificates in Canada." *Canada's Mental Health* 19, no. 6 (1971b): 17-19.

Rubenstein, R., and H. D. Lasswell. *The Sharing of Power in a Psychiatric Hospital,* New Haven: Yale University Press, 1966.

Rubin, Bernard. "Prediction of Dangerousness in Mentally Ill Criminals." *Archives of General Psychiatry* 27 (September 1972): 397-407.

Scheff, Thomas J. "Social Conditions for Rationality: How Urban and Rural Courts Deal with the Mentally Ill." *American Behavioral Scientist* 7 (1964): 21-27.

_____. *Being Mentally Ill: A Sociological Theory.* Chicago: Aldine, 1966.

_____. "On Reason and Sanity: Some Political Implications of Psychiatric Thought." In *Transcultural Research in Mental Health,* vol. 2 of *Mental Health Research in Asia and the Pacific,* edited by Wm. Lebra. Hawaii: East-West Center Press, 1972.

Simmons, Ozzie G. *Work and Mental Illness: Eight Case Studies.* New York: John Wiley and Sons, 1965.

_____ and Howard Freeman. "Familial Expectations and Posthospital Performance of Mental Patients." *Human Relations* (August 1959): 233-41.

Smith, Colin M. "Mental Health Developments in Saskatchewan." *Canada's Mental Health* (1970): 15-20.

Statistics Canada *Mental Health Statistics. Patient Movement (Preliminary).* Ottawa: Statistics Canada, 1973.

Swadron, Barry B. *The Law and Mental Disorder.* Toronto: The Canadian Mental Health Association, 1973.

Szasz, Thomas S. *The Myth of Mental Illness: Foundations of a Theory of Personal Conduct.* New York: Hoeber-Harper, 1961.

_____. *Law, Liberty, and Psychiatry.* New York: Collier, 1963.

_____. *The Manufacture of Madness.* New York: Delta, 1970a.

_____. *Ideology and Insanity.* Garden City: Doubleday Anchor, 1970b.

Walker, R. C. and F. E. Kelly. "Short term psychotherapy with hospitalized schizophrenic patients." *Acta Psychiatrica et Neurologica Scandinavica* 35 (1960): 34-56.

Wenger, Denis, and C. R. Fletcher. "The effect of legal counsel on admissions to a state mental hospital: A confrontation of professions." *Journal of Health and Social Behavior* 10 (1969): 66-72.

Whatley, Charles D. "Social Attitudes Toward Discharged Mental Patients." *Social Problems* 6 (1959): 313-20.

Wilde, Wm. "Decision-making in a psychiatric screening agency." *Journal of Health and Social Behavior* 9 (1968): 215-21.

Wooton, Barbara. "The Place of Psychiatry and Medical Concepts in the Treatment of Offenders: a Layman's View." *Canadian Psychiatric Association Journal* 17 (October 1972): 365-75.

Wynne, L. C. et al. "Pseudo-mutuality in the family relations of schizophrenics." *Psychiatry 21* (1958): 205-20.

10
Tim Crawford Meets the Mind Police

Donald Cameron

"A teepee," said Tim, "is a very practical form of shelter. There's good ventilation, the fire is inside, and there's a lot of room in it."

In the seafood restaurant on the Restigouche River at Point à la Croix, Quebec, twenty-nine-year-old Tim Crawford was explaining why he had chosen to spend his summer in a teepee. You might think that nobody's business but his. You would be quite wrong.

"I'd been teaching at New Options, a free school in Halifax, and I'd planned my summer so that I would have a lot of time to myself, to bring together the experiences I had at that school, try to put them into a perspective and sort out the course of my life from that point. In the past two years I've felt myself drawn more and more towards crafts and away from more public, social work, and I wanted time to contemplate how that course would go for me if I chose to follow it.

"The teepee itself stems out of my concern for, I guess, finding the roots of human experience on this continent, which of course relates back to the Indians. I've felt that in transplanting a mainly European civilization to this continent something has been lost in relation to man's contact with his environment. I think this shows up with oil refineries and hydro plants and the exhaust from automobiles, things I worry about very much because they concern my own life and the lives of people who come after me. So I attemped to explore a way of life which seemed to me much more in contact with the fundamental environment, and to experience the elements that go into the way of life that one could live in a teepee. I was very happy in that teepee."

Until one July day his brother drove up in the deputy sheriff's official car . . .

The New Brunswick Mental Health Service considered him mad, literally *mad*. On August 20, as we sat with Tim's woman, Laura, eating fish and chips by the Restigouche, Tim was still an involuntary patient at the provincial mental hospital across the river in Campbellton. He had been certified, in the words of the New Brunswick Mental Health Act (1969) to be suffering "from mental disorder of a nature or degree so as to require hospitalization in the interests of his own safety or the safety of others."

I met Tim Crawford during 1969-70, when he was teaching high school in Sackville, New Brunswick. When the Sackville RCMP fearlessly smashed a major local drug ring (two teenagers sold some hashish) Tim was one of the few adults to insist that the police respect the rights of the high school students being interrogated. That spring he applied for a job at Fredericton's free school, The School in the Barn, of which I was a director. We interviewed and discussed a number of applicants – and offered the job to Tim. He was – he is – an exceptionally creative, gentle and sensitive man, a teacher of rare gifts. But he decided to do youth work in Montreal instead.

The following autumn he was back in the Maritimes, at New Options, living with Laura. By coincidence, Laura's father is Mount Allison University professor Herbert Burke, and the Burkes are among my closest friends. From time to time I met Tim at their house, the same thoughtful, honest man he had always been. It was good to see him.

The next I heard, he was in Campbellton.

"It goes back for years," recalled Tim, now officially sane, sitting at the Burkes' table, "the inability of family members to recognize each others' ways of life. I think that's the basis of it.

"The most recent events began when I was on the Miramichi at the cabin, on a vacation. My mother and sister lived nearby, and they came down one morning – my mother was very upset, and my sister wanted to know what I was prepared to do to help. I suggested we sit down and talk about it, which we did, and it was suggested that perhaps my mother and I go to Campbellton to seek psychiatric help for my mother. I thought that was unnecessary, just from my opinion of the state my mother was in.

"My sister then suggested that there was a mental health clinic in Chatham, and asked if I would go with my mother. I agreed – I've known that my present way of life upsets my mother, and so in a sense I'm a cause of her problems. I thought that seeing a psychiatrist with her would show her that although my way of life was different, there was room in the human experience for what I was doing, and that a psychiatrist would be able to distinguish that from sickness.

"So my mother and I went, we saw Dr. Fathy Tadros, and we talked with him for twenty or thirty minutes. He asked my mother what was upsetting her, and she said that it was mainly me, that she was worried about me and about my health, and about the way my life was going. I was terribly thin – in her opinion – and I wasn't eating well – in her opinion – and that's what was upsetting her. He asked me what I thought about politics, and I explained that I wasn't really too interested in politics, that my life was more geared to an immediate world around me. I explained that the political system of having mainly two parties I felt was not true to human nature, and to the way that people should govern themselves – to have a good and a bad, a right and a wrong, one side and the other side. He asked me how many sides there were to questions, and I said, probably an infinite number.

"Then at one point he turned in his chair, rather abruptly, to me, and asked me to come to the Hôtel Dieu Hospital in Campbellton for observation. I was stunned; I asked if it was absolutely necessary. He said, 'Yes, it is.' I asked why? and he said, 'Because it's my duty.' I was absolutely floored, both by the abruptness of this and by his absolute decisiveness. So I agreed; I agreed to do that. He immediately phoned for a room for me.

"Then we went outside, and the minute I got out of his presence I sort of sprang back to myself and realized that this was silly; we just hadn't talked enough. Nothing had been said about my work in Halifax, which was very trying work, and which had left me somewhat mentally exhausted, mentally fatigued, working in the North End of the city with kids who were dropouts from society, from their families, from school, from almost everything. I felt that going to Campbellton would only serve the purpose of my explaining this and it being understood, and then I would be back on my own path. I offered to come back the following week to the clinic to explain this, and he declined.

"So I went down to the cabin and spent the evening there searching very deeply into myself, looking at all sides of my life, looking at all the problems that I have had and did have at that time, and looking at the stars, and the water, and the trees, and looking at the cabin which I had built, and deciding that no, I won't do that, because I have plans for my summer and I'm going to carry out my plans. So the next day, or the day after, I phoned him and told him this, and saw my family and told them that I had made this decision for my own life, that I did not seek his help and that I felt it was a waste of time to go up there and explain what I was about, and what I'd been through, and what I was doing. They were very upset, and I felt that this was a very critical point – I sensed that – and so I made it perfectly clear that they either looked closely at me and saw what was standing in front of them, and agreed with my decision, or they did not, and if they did not we would not be together.

"My mother suggested perhaps seeing another doctor in Moncton, and I said there was no need for that. Then I went back to the cabin, stayed a few more days on the Miramichi, and moved down here to Sackville, to the teepee.

"I was invited back for my birthday, when my brother would be down from Toronto. My mother and my brother and I went out for dinner, and went back to the cabin. My brother and my mother became embroiled in an argument which I took very little part in; I don't really remember what they were discussing at all. I spent a lot of time out walking on the beach and wondering what kind of a birthday this was. The next day I went back to Sackville, and a day later I was walking along the road on the way to my teepee, and the sheriff's car pulled up with my brother and the deputy sheriff for this county in it, and they said that I had been committed, and to get in the back and go to Campbellton. I got in and asked to phone a lawyer, asked to phone friends, asked to visit the teepee – no, no, no. We went straight to Campbellton."

After one night in a locked ward, Tim entered the open ward he was to inhabit for twenty-nine long days. At once he phoned his friends: Brad Slauenwhite, another New Options teacher; Herb Burke; John Shuh, director of New Options; and, of course, Laura.

"I told them where I was," he remembered, "told them that I was fine, and that I had the strength of character and the strength of mind to see this through on my own if I had to, but that I sought their help, and that if there was anything they could do I completely authorized them to do it, because I wanted the hell out of there."

Tim's friends confirm that he did exactly that. But Dr. Claudette Durand, Medical Superintendent of the hospital, says flatly that he agreed to stay, presumably because Tim thought it "futile" to demand his release. Silence is consent.

But how does one resist such arbitrary power? Protest vigorously? *The patient shows symptoms of paranoia.* Insist that one is sane? *Patients often find it difficult to accept the reality of their own illness.* Use outside channels and maintain a low profile inside the hospital? *The patient is submitting willingly to treatment; we find it hard to understand why you people are so upset.* After one of John Shuh's visits, indeed, a hospital psychiatrist made the chilling comment that Shuh also showed signs of mental disturbance, and perhaps would benefit from treatment.

Though John Shuh was hardly mentally ill, he was certainly disturbed. A stocky twenty-eight-year-old ordained minister who sports a beard, long hair and granny glasses, Shuh had known Tim Crawford since the two were undergraduates at Mount Allison. In 1971 he had convinced Tim to come to New Options, and during the next year the two had become very close friends. When Tim phoned, Shuh at once set out on the four-hundred-mile drive to Campbellton, stopping for talks with the Burkes in Saskville.

"By the time I started up the North Shore of New Brunwick," Shuh reflects, "I really began to wonder just what in hell I *was* going to be able to do. I had a vision of how the thing was going to work out; I thought that if I were going to make a movie about the whole thing, I'd made it in these terms, you know, that I saw myself walking into the office of a face-less psychiatrist, and pulling four balls out of my pocket, facing off to him, and then starting to juggle them. He sort of nodded his head, and took out *five* balls, and started to juggle them. Then I took off a silk hat and pulled out a rabbit: he took off his silk hat and pulled out a chicken, and so on. The sense was that what was really going to be involved was working out of your bags of tricks, to see who could spring the definitive trick, the trick that would turn the whole thing. And that, in a very real sense, was the way things went."

Reaching Campbellton in the evening, Shuh went to see Tim. "He was on that occasion – as he was each time I saw him in the hospital – tremendously serene, very calm." Together they decided that Shuh would try to see both Dr. Tadros and a Dr. O'Callaghan, Tim's attending physician in the hospital. Next day Shuh found O'Callaghan at the Bathurst courthouse, seventy miles away.

"One of the things that struck me was that there seemed to be no way I could make any contact with O'Callaghan," Shuh says now. "He seemed to be tremendously threatened by the fact that I was snooping around and meddling. Furthermore – this was something that continued to amaze me – none of the psychiatrists could really understand why I was involved. I'd explain that I was there because Tim asked me to be there, and because I was his friend. They'd say, but the family has participated in the committal: don't you just trust that what the family is doing is in Tim's best interests? And I'd say, well, I know that the family is very concerned for Tim and that they've done what they've done out of that concern, but I just don't feel that Tim is sick; and I think that perhaps at this stage I know Tim better than his family does.

"Whenever I'd say that I didn't really feel that Tim was sick, they'd say, 'Well, are you a psychiatrist?' There was so much feeling expressed both by the psychiatrists and by Tim's family that the only person who could really judge Tim's sanity or insanity was a professional. That's one of the really disturbing aspects of the whole business. Tim's brother even told me at one point that he didn't feel that Tim was mentally ill, but because a psychiatrist hung a label on him he'd obviously taken that man's judgement over his own. It's really amazing that professionals have so usurped the expertise of friends and families that a psychiatrist, after a twenty-minute interview, can make a pronouncement which completely outweighs all the best knowledge and understanding of people who've known a person for years.

"So I didn't get very far with O'Callaghan. But the funny thing was that all he talked about was really that Tim was not sort of straightening up and taking a regular job, that he was out there living in the wilderness and not eating his green vegetables and all sorts of stuff like that – but he didn't really put any *psychiatric* tag on the thing. I kept saying to him, yeah, that's okay, people *should* eat their green vegetables, I agree with that, a balanced diet is very important. But if somebody is not eating a balanced diet it doesn't mean that you have the right to put him into a mental hospital. Finally, in frustration, I just said that I thought this whole thing was unconscionable, and that a number of people agreed with that, and that we were willing to make a public issue out of it. And at that point he got up and walked away."

Shuh went on to see Tadros at the clinic in Chatham.

"Tadros was the one who laid the diagnosis of schizophrenia on

Tim, and we went through his reasons in some detail. He talked of Tim's withdrawing from the world and from all people – this had obviously come from Tim's family, because when he went to Sackville to set up his teepee Tim didn't tell his family exactly where he was going. Now the reason he *didn't* should be quite obvious: he didn't want them hounding him and interfering with his life. He did let me know; the Burkes knew; I had been to see him and his teepee was next door to a number of other kids who were in a commune. A lot of his friends in Sackville knew where he was, and most of his friends in Halifax knew where he was.

"Tadros also had a thing about Tim moving from a practical area – his background and training had been in science, and he had had some work in meteorology – into abstract, poetic and philosophical considerations. This is quite true: this is what has happened to Tim. But it's far more indicative of a very broad cultural movement, the kinds of things that have been going on in the last ten years all across North America. One of the difficulties that I sensed was that of the three psychiatrists, one was French, one was Irish and one was Egyptian, and I really didn't have the sense that they had a tremendously acute perception of the cultural situation in North America at this point in our history.

"However, my conversation with Tadros, even though we disagreed on just about every point, was far more affable and open than it had been with O'Callaghan, and when I left Tadros suggested two things: first, that if Tim was currently out of a locked ward – which he was – I could get a psychiatrist in Halifax to write and say that he would take Tim under his care if he were released from the hospital. Tadros said that he suspected the hospital would release him on that basis. He also suggested that, failing that, it would be possible to get an independent psychiatric assessment – but suggested as well that an ordinary private practice psychiatrist wouldn't pull any weight. As he said, 'It's just his word against mine, so you've got to go into the big leagues and get a psychiatrist who is teaching at a university.' As it turned out, that was pretty astute political advice."

Talking by phone, Tim and Shuh agreed that the diagnosis "explained," as Shuh puts it, "his family's involvement, to a great extent. I was convinced at the time – and still am – that Tim's family was really operating out of a genuine concern for Tim. The whole process of diagnosis, I think, had been a vicious circle of misunderstanding, with the misunderstandings of Tim's family informing the misunderstandings of Tadros informing the family misunderstandings ... What had basically happened was that when Tadros said, 'This man's schizophrenic,' the family really got spooked. I don't think they would have wanted to go that route, of involuntary commitment, but they were scared, and when Tadros suggested that he be committed they went along. And in a very real sense, I can understand that. If I were really convinced that somebody needed to be hospitalized, particularly someone for whom I had love and concern – well, what do you do? One time Tim mentioned to me that his family talked to him about the parable of the Good Samaritan, and I think they really saw themselves as stopping to help when others had passed by on the other side."

Dr. Leslie Kovacs, a Halifax psychiatrist who has worked with New Options, sent a night letter to hospital Medical Superintendent Dr. Durand, agreeing to take Tim under his care. Next day Shuh sat in Dr. Durand's office as Kovacs followed up with a phone call. But Durand refused to release Tim without the family's consent. O'Callaghan refused to see Shuh at all. Shuh headed for Chatham to talk again with the family – and arrived just as Dr. Durand was speaking by phone to Tim's brother.

"From what I could judge," says Shuh, "she was basically telling him that any attempt to move Tim from the hospital at this time would be very bad for Tim, and should be resisted at all costs. When his brother got off the phone, he came out to the dining room where his mother was making me a cup of coffee, and I really felt that if it hadn't been for the presence of Tim's mother, his brother would have gotten into physical force to chuck me out of the house.

"He finally fumed out, and his mother and I talked. She very obviously perceived the whole thing as a kind of private family embarrassment which no one else had a right to become involved in, and she generally put across the sense that Tim's friends in Halifax were trying to manipulate Tim to achieve a political critique of mental health conditions in the north of New Brunswick. Now I think such a critique is necessary, and very important, but the north of New Brunswick is generally outside my range of both action and knowledge, and the reason I was there was because Tim had asked that I come. At every point – I tried to make this very clear to Tim's mother – I always phoned and talked with Tim about what I was doing, who I had talked to, what they had said, so that Tim was really on top of the whole thing. Nothing was done without his approval.

"In some ways I think Mrs. Crawford viewed herself as the central figure in a tragedy. She kept saying, 'Wouldn't you come to the person who was most involved?' and I'd say, 'Yes, I would; I just happen to disagree with your perception of who that person is, and my feeling is that Tim is it.' She'd say, 'Tim is not well,' and I'd say, 'Well, I disagree with your perception on that, too.' You'd go round and round in rings and never communicate."

For a persuasive independent assessment, Tadros had said, you have to go into the big leagues. You need someone like, say, Lionel Solursh.

Dr. Lionel P. Solursh, that is, M.D., D.Psych., M.R.C.P.(C), F.R.C.P.(C), of Toronto Western Hospital and the University of Toronto medical school. Apple-cheeked and precocious at thirty-six, Solursh has a string of qualifications that fills a typewritten page; his publications cover two more. He advises governments, chairs committees of the Canadian Medical Association, the Canadian Mental Health Association and the World Medical Assembly; he is the only Canadian consultant to the U.S. National Commission on Marihuana and Drug Abuse.

And so, on the sunny afternoon of August 20, we converged on Campbellton – John Shuh and two other friends from Halifax; Solursh and a social worker from Toronto; the Crawfords from Chatham; Laura from Campbellton itself, where she had stayed throughout Tim's confinement; and your humble narrator, from Fredericton.

By now the hospital, the Minister of Health, the Minister of Justice, the Ombudsman and the Premier had all been peppered by letters and phone calls. Tim's friends had considered – and rejected – the cumbersome process of a Review Board under the Mental Health Act. Shuh's probing had led the family to ask that Tim be denied both visitors and incoming phone calls, and the hospital had agreed. Since Tim and Laura were not married, his committal made his family legally responsible for him and thus cancelled his existence as an independent adult.

We sat on the low brick guard rail talking with one another, with Tim, with other patients. The afternoon ground on. Inside, Solursh was reviewing the case history, talking with Tim and his family and with Durand and O'Callaghan. A group of patients sang, accompanied by a rather good guitarist. The afternoon ground on. Tim showed us the wooden puzzles and the hooked rug he had made in occupational therapy. We asked one another what was going on inside. The afternoon ground on, interminably.

Mrs. Crawford emerged with her daughter Joan, and spoke to John Shuh. Then she asked to speak to me. What was my interest in this private family matter? Well, Tim was a citizen confined under law in a public institution, so the matter wasn't purely private. Who had asked me to write the story? It had been my initiative, undertaken in consultation with Tim and others. What protection did she have against what I might say? If what I wrote was not both true and in the public interest, she could sue for libel. *I am not interested in seeing my son used, I am interested in his welfare.* So am I, Mrs. Crawford. *Before you write anything, I think you should have a talk with me.* I'd very much like to do that. *Well, I certainly think you should.* But when I did visit her, she chose not to discuss it.

She turned to Shuh again, a tall, slim woman with silvery hair and fine features, a handsome woman in her trim tweed suit. *Now look here, John Shuh, if I hear any more of this business about Tim being imprisoned for his style of life, do you understand?* I could not hear what Shuh was saying. *I will not have my son used. I don't know whose idea it was to bring the press in. My only concern is for the welfare of my son.*

Mother, said Joan quietly, *Mother*. They got in their car and drove away.

The Halifax and Toronto contingents headed for home via the Moncton airport. Tim asked permission to have dinner with Laura and me, and we crossed the bridge to Quebec. Had I been Tim, I am not sure I would have had the courage to go back into New Brunswick. But he did, and I left him with Laura, two brave and weary young people.

"Thomas Crawford," wrote Solursh in his report, "is a bright warm young man who, at most, is a borderline schizophrenic, who is not now psychotic, and who has been playing the mental hospital game (meeting expectations, not taking medication, etc.) in a frustrating situation which he wishes to leave. He (and history from his family) provides no evidence of his currently being any danger to his life or property or that of others."

"What's interesting," John Shuh points out, "is that the hospital waited another week before releasing Tim. I think Durand wanted to emphasize that she wasn't about to be pushed around and that she wasn't going to release Tim before the thirty-day observation period was up. It's really rather a strange thing, because the agreement had been reached – in essence – that Sunday, that there was no reason for Tim to be hospitalized. And yet they kept him for another five days."

A borderline schizophrenic, Solursh explained two weeks later in his cramped office at Toronto Western Hospital, is someone who doesn't have "those classic symptoms of autism and affective disorder and ambivalence and the loosening of associations, that kind of stuff, but their history is such as to indicate that they've either been in and out of schizophrenic breaks or that they're close to one and could have it given sufficient stress – of almost any sort that's meaningful to the person. But what we were really seeing – and it's fairly typical – were symptoms of a family disorder."

And, Solursh pointed out, the question of lifestyle is really a pretext; if the family were not squabbling about that, it would be squabbling about something else.

No doubt. But in fact that *is* what they were squabbling about, and Solursh himself considered Tim's "unconventional social adjustment" to be a "symptom." The British psychiatrist R. D. Laing describes his fellow psychiatrists as "mind police," all the more dangerous for being well-intentioned. They only want to help people adjust, just as they do in the Soviet Union – and if that means subjecting them to imprisonment, electric shocks, lobotomies, aversive conditioning and psychotropic drugs, well, it's all done in their own best interests, eh?

And if the "patients" don't like these things, or, like Tim, object even to gentle jails?

Dr. Richard Short, Director of New Brunswick's Mental Health

Services, smiles indulgently. "A patient's thinking," he says, "is not all that logical."

I will spare you an account of my three days on the North Shore wading through the evasions and other defence mechanisms of three psychiatrists determined not to talk to me – though I will not soon forget the pinched expression on an angry O'Callaghan's red face; or the agitated Egyptian tones of Tadros offering yet another reason that we could not meet; or the clipped smile of Dr. Durand telling me she didn't understand my question (and she didn't; her English is at best uncertain) while trying to light a cigarette filter-first.

All roads led to Fredericton, to Dr. Short, a lean, stooped Scot with thinning hair who looks like a combination of doctor and bureaucrat – which of course, he is. He couldn't discuss Tim without Tim's permission. I showed him a letter from Tim. "Well," said Short, "if he really wanted us to discuss it he should have approached us directly." Did Short think the letter was not genuine, then? "No, no, but there was no way of knowing the circumstances in which it was written. In any case you should really talk to the doctors who were directly involved." "I'd be delighted," I replied, "but I haven't even been able to get the correct spellings of their names, let alone their views."

Short later provided the correct spellings, but literally nothing more. "All that the public is entitled to know," he argued, "is that the relevant authorities are satisfied of their competence. Who are you, Don, to judge their qualifications, or to judge whether a person is sane or not? Three psychiatrists saw the lad, and they agreed, even the consultant from Toronto." "But Dr. Short," I said, "if the New Brunswick psychiatrists were of Dr. Solursh's opinion, namely that Tim was no threat to anyone, why was he kept in hospital for a month?"

"Well," Short conceded, "perhaps the diagnoses differed in some details. And when Solursh saw him, he had been under treatment for two weeks." I had seen no startling change, though, and neither had Tim, his woman, his closest friends, his colleagues. "Well," Short smiled soothingly, "for people without professional qualifications, Don, these things are often difficult to see." "But look here," I protested, "your staff claims Tim had some pretty gross disorder which has now vanished, that he was dangerous in July . . . "

"Not necessarily dangerous, but in need of care and treatment."

But if he *wasn't* threatening "his own safety or the safety of others," the whole affair, surely, was entirely illegal?

Short thought we were getting off the track. "Would you," he demanded, "challenge your family doctor's opinion about a *physical* illness." "Certainly," I said: "when I don't trust a doctor, I *do* challenge him." Such impertinence in a mere patient momentarily reduced Short to speechlessness.

Short is very touchy about medical prestige. Transferring Tim to Halifax, he believes, would have been to concede that "our" psychiatrists were wrong. He told me he had been attacked for allowing Solursh to see Tim: that, too, threatened his staff. "I am perfectly satisfied," he said, "that we did what was correct." And he summed up with an astonishing claim. "Our only interest," he maintained, "is seeing that the patient receives the treatment he needs."

Mental Health Services, in short, has none of the instincts for self-preservation that characterize virtually every other bureaucracy under the sun. No interest, for instance, in upholding the status of psychiatrists, or in proving its staff was not "wrong." Evidently it is an even more remarkable organization than I had suspected.

Despite a further meeting with Short and Health Minister Lawrence Garvie, I discovered little more about the Campbellton Three. A Department of Health report admits that Fathy Tadros came from the University of Oran, Algeria, in December, 1970. Claudette Durand is rumoured to be Haitian, and O'Callaghan Irish. Other psychiatrists in the division come from Germany, India, and elsewhere. Some have enviable reputations – but there is a well-known anecdote about an Indian psychiatrist who believed an American was hallucinating because he reported "butterflies in his stomach." Language and culture are not irrelevant to psychiatry, and I would be happier if I had discovered at least *one* dull grey Canadian somewhere on the staff.

To work in Mental Health Services, a psychiatrist must satisfy both the Department of Health and the Medical Council of New Brunswick that he has trained in recognized institutions. For private practice among the middle classes, however, he must also pass the relevant Canadian examinations. The 1968 report of a Department of Health Study Committee on the provincial mental health services recorded that by December, 1967, only four of the division's twenty-three psychiatrists had passed them. And the division's psychiatrists were paid between $11,000 and $15,000, as opposed to Ontario's $18,000 to $22,000. Consequently, said the Study Committee, the division has "a poor reputation throughout the country." In particular, "the marked shortage of qualified personnel poses the biggest single problem in the treatment and care of mental illness in the Province of New Brunswick today." If that devastating judgment is not still true, why are Dr. Short and his colleagues so defensive?

But the competence of the psychiatrists is not, finally, so important as the question of insanity itself and its relation to liberty. On one man's authority, Tim Crawford was imprisoned for twenty-nine days. He had no opportunity to dispute the judgement before an impartial third party. He had not committed or threatened any illegal or violent action – and if he had, he could have been committed through the courts. If he was threatening his own well-being – and I doubt that he was – does that entitle us to force our good intentions on him? Under New Brunswick law – and it is not radically different elsewhere – *any* physician may commit anyone he thinks should be committed, at any time. Considering the social attitudes of doctors, how confident can we be that they will not use that power on any harmless eccentric, any hippie, and radical? Just who are they, those eight hundred and seventy-one New Brunswickers involuntarily committed last year?

Back in Sackville, I told Tim that Dr. Short had asked me how I would like it if someone challenged my credentials as a journalist. I was going to say that people do that all the time, and rightly so, when Tim cut me off.

"How would *he* like it," asked Tim Crawford, soft-spoken but passionate, "if someone challenged his credentials as a human being? Because that's what happened to me."

11
Memoirs of an Intermittent Madman:
A Declaration of Rebellion Against a Therapeutic Tyranny that Threatens All Who Find Their State of Consciousness in Conflict with the Norm

Carlton Brown

My name is Michael Kelly Jones, I shall pretend, as I did many years ago in a book called *Brainstorm*, and the writer whose by-line appears on this declaration is serving again, as he did then, as my ghost, my alter ego and guardian of my identity.

In *Brainstorm*, I described an astonishing experience I had gone through in the summer of 1940, when I was 27. Six and a half years earlier, I had married a slightly older woman because I had got her pregnant and was unwilling to let her have an abortion. It would have been her third or fourth. The entire marriage was beset by conflict of frequently violent intensity, but it lasted as long as it did because of my sense of responsibility for our daughter. I began drinking much more than I did customarily and treating my hangovers with bromides, spirits of ammonia, large quantities of black coffee and sniffs of Benzedrine inhalant. Meanwhile, I found myself undergoing a marvelous transformation. I became charged with mounting feelings of well-being, with greatly increased energy and with intimations that I was gifted with supernatural powers and insights into the secrets of the universe. My mind conceived ideas and received impressions with extraordinary ease and lucidity. My body became superbly light, agile, athletic, instantly responsive to my will. At first tentatively, then with mounting conviction, it came to me that I was soon to be revealed as a new embodiment of Jesus Christ, or else that I was a reincarnation of Joseph, who would father a new Christ child – or maybe a large brotherhood of them – under a new dispensation that would allow men and women to enjoy physical love with one another as freely as they chose, demonstrating that the doctrine of Immaculate Conception was simply a symbol for the miracle of all procreation. Out of the hell of my marriage, I was guided through stretches of purgatory, then into and out of enclaves of paradise, and finally to what I took to be an academy where my resurrected being would be given scientific study and final training for its divine mission.

It was, in fact, the psychiatric ward of a large county hospital. During the week I was held there for observation, I was given frequent doses of paraldehyde, a fierce-tasting, fiery liquid related to alcohol and ether that was then routinely given to alcoholics as a sedative and hypnotic and that had the effect on me of a triple shot of superbooze.. At the same time, the skillful, humoring nurses, attendants, psychologists and psychiatrists sustained my fantasies of rebirth and devine inspiration. When, at the end of the week, I was brought before a judge, I fervently agreed to my commitment to a state hospital, certain that I was being moved up to a higher level in God's hierarchy.

On the night of my admission to the state asylum, I was smoking a cigarette in the toilet when another inmate set off a thunderous slamming of doors in the corridor and then retreated to his room. Four uniformed screws rushed into the toilet and accused me of making the racket. When I denied it, one smashed me across the mouth with the back of his hand. I protested and all four joined in – throttling me, slugging me with their fists, knees and feet, dragging me along the hall and lashing me to a bed under a canvas restraining sheet.

After that beating, perhaps partly as a result of it, my messianic delusions began to diminish steadily and within a week or so had disappeared. I spent the next six weeks in two wards containing a total of 60 or 70 miscellaneous inmates. Among them were two boys of no more than eight or nine – looies, in hospital slang for luetic patients, whose central nervous systems had been permanently blasted by congenital syphilis. A few senile dotards. Others of intermediate age who showed pronounced signs of derangement and alienation. But these were a fraction of the total number. The majority were dried-out drunks, failures at suicide and losers in marital or familial strife. We were the sort of community of the displaced one might find in an Army barracks, a prison or a concentration camp. We played cards and bitched about the miserable food and the regimented routine. We exchanged guesses about how long we might be in for, and one of us spoke for many when he said, "The first thing I'll do when I get out is get myself a quart of rye and a yard of snatch."

Over the next few weeks, in separate interviews with two staff psychiatrists, I was told that I had undergone a psychotic episode, of the "manic-depressive" type. The first of these interviewers told me that I should have been discharged from the first hospital and not committed to this one. He added that my domestic situation had undoubtedly precipitated my breakdown and that I should not think of returning to it. His superior, however, who had final say in my disposition, pontificated: "You've made your bed, now you must lie in it," and continued, "We will not consider you completely cured until you are ready to make the best of your marriage."

My "mental illness" might have continued "uncured," and my imprisonment indefinitely prolonged, if my situation had not allowed me an alternative: release in the custody of my mother.

On my release, I sank into profound gloom and despair such as I had never before experienced, and that lingered for many months. The doctors at the asylum had not prepared me for this reaction and I got no usable advice on dealing with it from the thoroughly misnamed "mental-hygiene clinic" to which I was obliged to report for periodic checks during the following year. What I was able to learn about my "illness" in that time came entirely from books on abnormal psychology I found in the public libraries. Furtively I read every reference to manic-depressive psychosis, fearful that others would see what I was reading and identify me as one who bore the stigmata of that disease. The descriptions of symptoms seemed close enough to mine to corroborate the diagnosis, though as I read accounts of other disordered states, elements of them also applied to what I had experienced. And I recalled that a psychologist at the county hospital had said of me to a nurse, in a marveling tone, "He's everything—catatonic, manic-depressive, paranoiac, schizophrenic." (Later, when I revisited the county hospital and got permission to see my case record, I read the notation, "Final diagnosis: schizophrenic-catatonic. Improved." At the time of my visit, a new director of the county hospital revised the record to read "cyclothymic with episodes.") Altogether, though the texts convinced me that the extraordinary delusions that had arisen in my mind and the extraordinary behavior they had impelled were not the awesome and inexplicable phenomena I had at first taken them to be but typical manifestations of a distinct and quite ordinary "mental illness," less prevalent than schizophrenia, less severe in its effects and with a higher incidence of spontaneous recovery. I found no explanations of its causes, beyond a general agreement that they were to be found in early psychological conditioning and that a psychotic episode might be brought on by stressful, "precipitating" events. As to treatment, I learned that some authorities recommended psychoanalysis or "psychotherapy" of other kinds; others advocated shock treatments with insulin or Metrazol – later electricity – in both the elated and the depressed phases. The doctors at the county hospital had wanted to give me shock, but my wife and mother had withheld the necessary permission. From what I had seen of others' reactions to it, I judged that the beating I had been given might have produced a comparable effect.

By the time *Brainstorm* was published, at the end of 1944, I had been satisfactorily employed for three years, had remarried and had visited a young Adlerian psychiatrist every week or two for about a year, in search of clues to what had disordered me and advice on avoiding a recurrence.

During those three years, I found that my crack-up had heavily stigmatized me with some social and professional acquaintances but that others did not hold it as a blight on my character and ability. I continued my in-and-out career as editor and writer over the following six or seven years; my second wife bore us two children; I bought a house in the suburbs and I achieved the respectable preinflation salary of $12,000 a year.

During the second year of this marriage, I went through a second course of psychotherapy, with a renowned psychiatrist and author. It lasted approximately a year and seemed to have helped me "adjust" to sexual and emotional incompatibilities that had developed between my second wife and me. However, by the time our second child was born – a daughter, in 1950 – and increasingly thereafter, my wife had extraordinary difficulties in her relations with our three-year-old son and virtually refused to have intercourse with me, or, when she grudgingly allowed it, wouldn't respond to my most gentle and prolonged lovemaking.

At last, I entered into a love affair with another woman. At the same time, my immediate boss was planning to launch a publishing venture of his own – enlisting my clandestine aid, while contriving for a younger protégé of his, a step below me on the masthead, to succeed to the editorship when he resigned. Once again, I assumed that I was to blame for the troubled nature of my relationships and began a third course of head candling, this time thrice-weekly sessions of modified psychoanalysis with a young lay practitioner of a revisionist Freudian school. Although he prefaced the course by saying he would make no "value judgments" of my confessions, he ultimately pronounced some memorable ones, among them: "Your prick belongs in your wife." That statement, along with torments of conscience resulting from puritanical influences in my childhood, led me to break off the affair. I tried to return to my wife and to behave as a responsible executive and family man. I failed, again, and resumed the affair.

In the final pages of *Brainstorm*, I had confidently declared that if the premonitory signs of another "manic" seizure ever arose in me, I would be able to recognize and subdue them. This confidence seemed validated on two occasions, when I was under stress and drinking more than I could tolerate. On the first of these occasions, in the year before my second marriage, I experienced hallucinations and delusive thought, and on the second, some nine years later, less pronounced alterations of consciousness that I nevertheless recognized as ominous. The first time, I was able to arrest my course by giving up drinking and getting away from the incentives to it for a week. The second time I did it by getting off the sauce and onto phenobarbital for the first few nights of drying out.

Then, a year later, during a walk in the country on a lovely fall afternoon, my two-year-old daughter riding on my shoulders, I experienced a sense of rapturous unity with the universe that made me believe I might be off on another "manic" flight. I disclosed my fear to my wife and, by telephone, to my analyst. My wife reacted with such panic that our family physician was unable to calm her except with sedatives. My analyst assured me that my feelings of well-being were evidence of a genuine "rebirth." Between the anxiety my wife's panic raised in me, the continuing conflicts that I was involved in and my analyst's encouragement of my illusions, I was impelled to pursue my escape course until it ended with my capture and imprisonment.

This time I underwent ten days' observation in a suburban county hospital and then was transferred to a private sanitarium. To preserve its tax-exempt status, the institution waived its customary fee of $250 a week for one or two favored patients at a time, and through the influence of my boss (by then my ex-boss), I was granted a full scholarship. The subterranean admission ward, lined with barred cells in which we newcomers were lodged, was a worse hellhole than the state asylum had been. But I was soon moved to one and another of the upstairs wards, where I found myself among groups of 20 or 30 displaced gentlemen of whom only three or four appeared more than mildly distraught, living as captives in a celibate country club. There were two types of therapy: hydro- and occupational. The first consisted of high-pressure hosings, very hot and very cold, administered by an avid water gunner who deployed his healing tool with the zeal of a riot-control trooper. The second involved such traditionally sovereign psychiatric remedies as basket weaving and clay modeling. My doctor tapped his palms together as he talked, as though inviting one to a game of patty-cake. It would have been, I thought, as meaningful as our verbal exchanges.

My commitment by judicial order made it possible for my detention to be prolonged indefinitely. After two months – which I considered then and still do almost entirely unjustified by any psychiatric consideration – my custodians wanted to extend my scholarship for another month or more. At that point, I managed to speak with a state inspector who was making his annual tour. I was released at once. But I was a parolee for a year afterward and forced into a reconciliation with my wife. I felt – as I had 12 years before – that I suffered from an "illness" that originated in my own psychological flaws and must now "adjust" if I hoped to remain at large in the sane community.

So I tried. But this second breakdown had rendered me virtually unemployable. I went back to free-lancing, but even in my best years I could earn no more than half my previous income, which had, at its highest, never matched our expenses. There was more anxiety; disagreements with my wife over our steadily worsening financial situation, our children and our increasingly marked sexual and emotional differences. They combined to precipitate five more "psychotic episodes" over the ensuing years.

In 1956, episode three: ten days' observation in the same county hospital as before, followed by 90 days in a monstrous madhouse I shall call Hell Valley State Hospital.

In 1959, episode four: ten and 60 in the same places.

In 1963, episode five: 40 days in (I shall say) Mockrie State Hospital, in another state.

In 1967, episode six: ten days; and in 1968, episode seven: six months – same place.

Total time flushed down the institutional drains: some 18 months out of the past 32 years. I had experienced most of my detentions as profoundly debasing, occasionally brutal and needlessly prolonged punishment; and none had involved anything worthy of the name "treatment." Nevertheless, I assumed that society was justified in locking up its aberrant members until such time as they were again ready and able to conform to its standards and demands.

Then, during the past three or four years, I was introduced to five books in which I found strongly persuasive challenges to all of the assumptions that underlie the current practice of psychiatry and its social and legal applications. These books are *The Myth of Mental Illness, Law, Liberty and Psychiatry* and *Psychiatric Justice,* by Thomas S. Szasz, M.D., a psychiatrist and professor of psychiatry at the State University of New York at Syracuse; *Asylums: Essays on the Social Situation of Mental Patients and Other Inmates,* by Erving Goffman, professor of sociology at the University of Pennsylvania; and *The Politics of Experience,* by R. D. Laing, a British physician and psychiatrist.

These books hold the makings of an urgently needed Bill of Rights for the millions of us who have been, are now or may one day be subject to any of the many conditions of altered consciousness or behavior that our social establishment views as pathological and often insists on "treating" – usually without the consent of the treated – by methods that are of dubious efficacy at best and, at worst, cruelly dehumanizing and destructive. The radical criticisms these writers make are verified by many of my own experiences and observations.

In calling mental illness a myth, Szasz says that the term is "a metaphor which we have come to mistake for a fact" and is based on the false assumption that the conditions to which it refers are analogous to physical illness. Mental illness, Szasz writes in *Law, Liberty and Psychiatry*, exists only as a theoretical concept, which "derives its main support from such phenomena as syphillis of the brain or delirious conditions – intoxications, for instance – in which persons may manifest certain disorders of thinking and behavior. Correctly speaking, however, these are diseases of the brain, not of the mind." They are in the province of neurology, not psychiatry, which deals preponderantly with so-called functional disorders having no established basis in bodily malfunctions.

Szasz writes that "psychiatry – in contrast to the nonmedical branches of social science – has acquired much social prestige and power through an essentially misleading association with the practice of medicine." And its function as an agency of social control "is hidden under a facade of medical and psychiatric jargon."

Szasz doesn't offer "a new conception of 'psychiatric illness' or a new form of 'therapy.' My aim is more modest and yet also more ambitious. It is to suggest that the phenomena now called mental illnesses be looked at afresh and more simply, that they be removed from the category of illnesses, and that they be regarded as the expressions of man's struggle with the problem of *how* he should live."

In *Asylums,* Goffman cites the work of other researchers: "Clinical experience supports the impression that many people define mental illness as 'that condition for which a person is treated in a mental hospital.'" Dr. Karl Menninger has said, "At least three presidents of the American Psychiatric Association have publicly deplored the use of 'neurosis' and 'psychosis' as misleading. 'Neurotic' means he's not as sensible as I am and 'psychotic' means he's even worse than my brother-in-law."

Despite the imprecision of these and related terms, and the lack of scientific proof that the conditions to which they refer are, in fact, "illnesses," they are commonly taken to define distinct diseases for which psychiatric treatment is required. The question of whether or not and how such "treatment" is to be administered to the individual is largely determined by his social status and what sociologists call "career contingencies" – chance factors in his environment and associations. Szasz recalls that when the wife of Governor Earl Long of Louisiana had him committed to a public asylum of his own state, he freed himself by dismissing its superintendent.

In considering the various reasons held to justify such detentions – and to prolong them in the case of those lacking Governor Long's veto power – Szasz points out that "the so-called psychotic state of an individual is neither a necessary nor a sufficient cause for his commitment. Impecunious elderly persons, addicts and offenders are committed; yet, they are not usually considered to be psychotic." A reason commonly given for commitment is that the individual is a danger to himself or to others. But "there is no evidence that mental patients are a greater source of danger to society than [others]," Szasz writes. Goffman states that for every offense that leads to hospitalization, "there are many psychiatrically similar ones that never do." He concludes that "in the degree that the 'Mentally ill' outside hospitals numerically approach or surpass those inside hospitals, one could say that mental patients distinctly suffer not from mental illness but from contingencies."

Asylums is based on a year's field work in a public mental hospital of some 7000 beds and on wide reading of other studies of "total institutions." On this basis, Goffman rates mental hospitals as "storage dumps" and "places of coerced exile," whose inmates are reduced to "uniquely degraded living levels. . . . It is difficult to find environments which introduce more profound insecurities; and what responsibilities are lifted are removed at a very considerable and very permanent price."

All commitment procedures are based on the proposition that confinement in a "mental hospital" represents "treatment" of the socially troublesome behavior involved. But, Goffman writes, "current official psychiatric treatment for functional disorders does not, in itself, provide a probability of success great enough easily to justify the practice of institutional psychiatry . . . especially since the probability that hospitalization will damage the life chances of the individual is . . . positive and high."

Szasz speaks of "the violence – indeed, the brutality – and also the completely unproved efficacy, of such 'treatments' as lobotomy, convulsions induced by insulin, Metrazol and electricity and, more recently, the chemical strait jackets." These are, of course, the tranquilizers which – since their introduction in the mid-Fifties – virtually all mental-hospital inmates have been obliged to take. The most potent of these are generally, but by no means invariably, effective enough in relieving such conditions as excitement, confusion, agitation and anxiety. But none of them cures anything, and the forced taking of psychoactive drugs, since they make inmates more easily managed, is more of a service to the staff than to the inmate, as Goffman says in *Asylums*. Though the cruelly dehumanizing operation of lobotomy has mercifully been discontinued, the use of electroshock is still widespread – often, as Goffman writes and I have witnessed, "on the attendant's recommendation, as a means of threatening inmates into discipline and quieting those that won't be threatened."

On these grounds, Szasz ranks the "treatment" given asylum inmates, no less than their confinement, as punishment and coercion, not therapy. "Psychiatric hospitals are, of course, prisons," he states, and compulsory confinement in them constitutes "imprisonment without due process of law." Often, according to those who have undergone both, "mental hospitalization is worse punishment than imprisonment in the penitentiary" – a rating that a number of my bughouse buddies have ratified.

"The committed patient suffers a serious loss of civil rights," Szasz points out. "In many jurisdictions he is automatically considered legally incompetent: He cannot vote, make valid contracts, marry, divorce, and so forth. . . . [He] must suffer invasions of his person and body, cannot communicate freely with the outside world, usually loses his license to operate a motor vehicle, and suffers many other indignities as well." In most cases, an inmate held for longer than a limited period of observation suffers the further penalty of being put on parole (generally euphemized as "convalescent leave" or "trial visit") for a year after his release, with his civil and legal rights suspended and his status that of a ward of the state, subject to reimprisonment without necessarily being examined by a physician or psychiatrist.

In a similar summary in *The Politics of Experience,* Laing writes that "the 'committed' person labeled as patient . . . is degraded . . . to someone no longer in possession of his own definition of himself. . . .

More completely, more radically than anywhere else in our society, he is invalidated as a human being."

Goffman gives a description of this invalidating process that I find exactly applicable to my own experience. The asylum inmate, he writes, is often confronted by staff psychiatrists "arguing that his past has been a failure, that the cause of this has been within himself . . . and that if he wants to be a person he will have to change his way of dealing with people and his conceptions of himself." He writes further that mental-hospital staffs force the status of patient on a person by "extracting from his whole life course a list of those incidents that have or might have had 'symptomatic' significance . . . seemingly normal conduct is seen to be merely a mask or shield for the essential sickness behind it. An over-all title is given to the pathology . . . and this provides a new view of the patient's 'essential' character."

Goffman continues, "This dossier is apparently not regularly used, however, to record occasions when the patient showed capacity to cope honorably and effectively with difficult life situations." The record simply documents in summary terms the value system by which the inmate finds himself judged. Finally, his release will be contingent on his demonstration that he has achieved "insight" into the presumably pathological state that occasioned his confinement – in other words, that he accepts the institutions's view of himself – and, usually, that he is ready to attempt again to "adjust" to the same environmental circumstances that he may have every private reason to believe – but must not now declare – *drove* him out of his gourd.

If we who are labeled mentally ill are not "sick," then, how *are* our behavioral deviations, our alterations of consciousness, to be considered?

In *The Myth of Mental Illness,* Szasz proposes that "so-called mental illnesses may be like languages," like "various types of communications" employing both verbal and nonverbal methods; and that understanding their meaning may be like the problem of understanding a person speaking a foreign tongue. Freud, he points out, "regarded the dream as a language and proceeded to elucidate its structure and meanings."

In *The Politics of Experience*, Laing parallels Szasz in holding that "to be mad is not necessarily to be ill." He regards the term schizophrenia (and, by implication, psychosis and its other sub-categories) not as one that defines an illness, mental or physical, but as "a label that some people pin on other people under certain social circumstances." He describes the "double-bind" hypothesis, introduced by the anthropologist Gregory Bateson in 1956, which holds that a person might be diagnosed as schizophrenic as a result of being in "an insoluble 'can't win' situation."

Laing cites studies of the families of hundreds of "schizophrenics" by Bateson and other researchers in the United States and by himself and associates in England, all showing that the person so diagnosed "is part of a wider network of extremely disturbed and disturbing patterns of communication." He writes:

> It seems to us that *without exception* the experience and behavior that gets labeled schizophrenic is *a special strategy that a person invents in order to live in an unlivable situation*. In his life situation ... he cannot make a move, or make no move, without being beset by contradictory and paradoxical pressures and demands, pushes and pulls, both internally from himself and externally from those around him. ...
>
> Nor is it a matter of laying the blame at anyone's door. The untenable position, the "can't win" double-bind ... is by definition *not obvious* to the protagonists. Very seldom is it a question of contrived, deliberate, cynical lies or a ruthless intention to drive someone crazy. ... A checkmate position cannot be described in a few words. The whole situation has to be grasped before it can be seen that no move is possible, and making no move is equally unlivable.

This description of the double-bind, can't-win position applies accurately to the situations in which I found (or placed) myself before each of my flip-outs. I encouraged my ghostwriter to ask in his preface to *Brainstorm* why, in the clash between myself and a complex situation, it had been I and not the situation that had succumbed. This latter formulation, it now appears to me, is nearly equivalent to asking why a soldier, and not the situation he is in, succumbs to combat break-down. Of course, a soldier has much less freedom in getting into or out of his stressful situation than a civilian, and pressures from within himself can contribute little or nothing to its creation, but his reaction is no less individual a matter.

During World War Two – in which a substantial portion of all U.S. casualties were "mental" – individual soldiers reacted to the stress of combat by displaying one or several of the diverse behavioral phenomena that have been classified as "psychotic." Often, removal from the scene and relief from duty brought about recovery from combat breakdowns in as short a time as a day or two. It is evident that these breakdowns did not represent long-latent "mental illnesses" but temporary reactions that varied according to differences in temperament. It became an axiom that every man, no matter how "normal" or "healthy," had a breaking point; it was presumed that if he didn't crack up under one kind of stress, he would under another.

This presumption would seem to be equally tenable in regard to the reactions of individuals to social and emotional pressures in civilian life, and, indeed, is often stated as a tenet of common sense. But here the stresses involved are normally much less readily identified than those of combat. They are generally much more subtle, complex and, in Laing's phrase, "by definition *not obvious* to the protagonists." The situation that one person finds unendurably disturbing will usually not be experienced as such by others who have contributed to creating and maintaining it. They, in fact, may accept the view that any manifestations of disturbance are "symptoms" of "mental illness."

It seems highly likely to me, from my own experience and from observations of hundreds of fellow snake-pit inmates, that many seemingly irrational immediate reactions to stress might be as transitory as many instances of combat breakdown have proved to be, *if they were treated as such*. However, what happens all too often in civilian life is that such reactions, and even modes of behavior that family members disapprove of, are defined as manifestations of *mental disease* and are used to bring about the person's confinement.

If someone has once been branded psychotic, and has been subjected to the degrading punishment of psychiatric imprisonment, he is under the lasting threat that those close to him may interpret any anxieties he reveals of his fears as indicative of a "recurrence" of his "illness." They may, in fact, so interpret almost anything he does or says, and when they do, they are likely to reveal their attitude and intentions toward him, and so to arouse or increase his fears either of losing his mind or of being incarcerated again. When confinement is brought about against his will, and carried out by the police, as is often the case, the act itself is likely to provoke resistance, if only vocal, that will be added to his list of "symptoms."

This snowballing process seems to me to have been at work in each of my episodes of "manic" excitement. In two or three instances beyond the one I have mentioned, my wife began to show apprehensions that I believe were unwarranted – or, to say the least, premature – and to express them with such suspicion and hostility that I feared that she would have me put away again.

Fear often leads to panic, which produces alterations of behavior, which arouse further apprehensions in others, etc. Fear also releases adrenaline, giving the threatened animal or person a surge of self-protective energy.

In *Ten Feet Tall*, one of his absorbing narratives of medical detection, Berton Roueché writes of the power of the hormone compounds cortisone (adrenal) and ACTH (pituitary) to alleviate a great number of diseases, and also of the potentiality of these drugs to produce highly unpleasant side effects. He relates the harrowing experience of a New York schoolteacher whose life was probably saved by cortisone therapy for a destructive inflammation of the arteries, but who experienced extreme (and classically faithful) "manic" euphoria, overactivity and excitement as a result of it.

I read the story when it first appeared in *The New Yorker*, in the mid-Fifties, and not long afterward found myself incarcerated in the shit wards of the monstrous city of the damned I have previously referred to as Hell Valley State Hospital. I was certain that I had been helped by the cumulative interaction of suspicion and dread I have referred to, and quite possibly by supernormal energy from a fear-induced overproduction of adrenaline. The doctor in charge of the several hundred men quartered in my ward was a Jewish refugee from Germany and quite a humane man, as institutional hacks go. But when I suggested this possibility to him, he reacted with an intense scorn.

"Hah! What is this? You have discovered perhaps a new theory of manic-depressive psychosis?"

Well, why not? I hadn't found an old theory that made better sense. Psychiatrists who hold that "psychoses" are caused by as yet undiscovered biological malfunctions generally believe that these will prove to be glandular or metabolic, and some point to surpluses or shortages of certain chemical substances in the body fluids of "psychotics" as evidence. Researchers have found that the urine of "schizophrenics," but not of normal people, often contains a chemical similar to both adrenaline and mescaline. It is conceivable that the one thing those tested had in common was their state of stress and that the production of the chemical might be a reaction such as normal people would show in a similar situation. At any rate, in the absence of proof that such findings indicate causes rather than effects, their most useful explanation would seem to be Laing's:

> We know that the biochemistry of the person is highly sensitive to social circumstance. That a checkmate situation occasions a biochemical response which, in turn, facilitates or inhibits certain types of experience and behavior is plausible a priori.

Much of what Laing goes on to say suggests similarities between a psychotic "voyage of discovery" and the trips induced by psychedelic drugs. Following the synthesis of LSD, mescaline and psilocybin, researchers observed that these drugs produced alterations of consciousness like those experienced in the so-called psychoses, and it was supposed that further research with them might lead to the discovery of biochemical causes of mental disorders. Though this possibility has been increasingly discounted, it remains indisputable that many varieties of "psychotic" experience have been temporarily duplicated in the varieties of psychedelic experience on record.

Laing describes a "schizophrenic" episode as an entry into "the inner space and time of consciousness," as contrasted to the usual sense of living in "the outer world." It is a "journey [that]is experienced as going further 'in,' as going back through one's personal life, in and back and through and beyond into the experience of all mankind, of the primal man, of Adam and perhaps even further into the beings of animals, vegetables and minerals." It may be "part of a potentially orderly, natural sequence" that, if allowed to, would result spontaneously in the voyager's return from inner to outer and an "existential rebirth." But, Laing writes, "This sequence is very seldom allowed to occur because we are so busy 'treating' the patient." Instead of the mental hospital, he proposes, we need "an *initiation* ceremonial, through which the person will be guided with full social encouragement and sanction into inner space and time, by people who have been there and back again. Psychiatrically, this would appear as ex-patients helping future patients to go mad."

Though this proposal will seem shocking to those who regard madness as a necessarily pathological process, it need not be to those who admit the validity of Laing's and Szasz's view of madness.

Bateson writes that one comes back from a "psychotic" voyage "with insights different from those . . . who never embarked on such a voyage." This observation parallels the testimony of psychedelic trippers that their outlooks and insights have been lastingly changed by the experience. The terms Laing uses to describe the schizophrenic voyage, in the lines I have quoted and in further impressionistic and poetic passages of *The Politics of Experience*, are also similar to those that have been used to describe psychedelic states of consciousness. His recommendation of an "initiation ceremonial" virtually duplicates Timothy Leary's proposal to psychedelic voyagers. "You have to go out of your mind to use your head," as well as the insistence of Leary and others on the importance of the setting and auspices of the trip – and of having a knowing guide – in determining whether it will be heavenly or hellish.

In my "manic" highs, I experienced many of the alterations of consciousness that are produced by the psychedelic drugs. Though these self-generated trips may have represented voyages into inner space and past time, in the sense that they returned me to a childlike, atavistic state of unrepressed thought, emotion and action, they have been directed toward increased awareness of and participation in the outward world, toward a dissolution of the ego and a transcendental unity with the universe. My impulses have been outgoing, generous, expansive, responsive, seraphic and loving. Only when my ebullient acts and expressions have met with suspicion and opposition, with active threats of their suppression by capture and imprisonment, have I reacted with opposition, and then never to a menacing degree.

"So-called mental illnesses," Szasz states, "can be understood only if they are viewed as occurrences that do not merely happen to a person but are brought on by him (perhaps unconsciously), and hence may be of some value to him." He further proposes that "the behavior of persons said to be mentally ill is meaningful and goal-directed – provided one is able to understand the patient's behavior from *his* particular point of view." Similarly, Laing asserts that madness need not be all breakdown. "It may also be breakthrough. It is potentially liberation and renewal as well as enslavement and existential death."

Any individual, whatever his reaction to stress, follows particular patterns and trends of thought, behavior and emotion that are distinctly his own. In *Law, Liberty and Psychiatry*, Szasz makes a comment on some moral implications of this point that perfectly expresses my attitude toward my experiences of madness:

> If psychology and sociology were taken seriously ... we should have to conclude two things: first, that insofar as it is always possible to regard antecedent events as explanations of human behavior, men should never be blamed (or praised) for what they do; second, that insofar as men are human beings, not machines, they always have some choice in how they act – hence, they are *always* responsible for their conduct. There is method in madness, no less than in sanity.

This statement might seem to support the inclination of institutional psychiatrists, as Goffman has described it and I have experienced it, to argue that the "mental patient" has brought about his own "illness." It does so only if, in the second clause of the statement, the phrase "responsible for their conduct" is misread as "*to blame* for their conduct." To hold one responsible for his conduct is not necessarily to deny that his behavior may have been appropriate to his situation, that it may have been motivated by creditable impulses or that it may be directed toward healthy rather than pathological goals. To blame him for his conduct is, of course, to find nothing but fault in his personality. As this blaming process is applied in institutional psychiatry, it is an instrument of domination and subjection. Szasz's insistence that human beings are *always* responsible for their conduct, mad or sane, corresponds to the emphasis of existentialist philosophy on man's responsibility for creating his own nature and destiny by means of the choices he makes.

It's probable that some of the phenomena of altered consciousness that occur in "psychotic" episodes, like some of those occurring in psychedelic and mystical states, may be untranslatable into verbal terms, and so may be inaccessible to "rational" investigation and elucidation. They may thus be comparable to dreams, which often cannot be remembered on awakening, and at best are only partially conveyable in words. Apart from what meaning may or may not be found in them by Freudian methods of analysis, dreams are thought to discharge psychic energy and gratify unconscious needs in a psychologically beneficial way. It may be that many of the experiences of madness are and will always remain beyond the reach of objective investigation and explanation but may nevertheless serve purposes of maintaining balance or awarding satisfactions in the only partially penetrable domain of the id. Existentialist philosophy also holds that anguish and despair are unavoidable elements of the human condition and that reason alone is inadequate to the explanation of man's problems.

The goal toward which I now believe each of my excursions into madness has been directed has been the overthrow of repression, imposed from the outside by social demands and erotic and emotional denials, and from within by the standards and inhibitions that make up the conscience or superego. Oppressed by circumstances of my own and others' making, by failures and insufficiencies and frustrations, I have repeatedly hurled my being into a desperate total thrust outward and upward into joy and freedom – and overshot the mark.

Though at the time of each of my later imprisonments I have felt intense resentment toward everyone concerned with bringing it about, it has not persisted for long. I have come to acknowledge that – lacking the sort of guidance through such excursions that Laing has advocated, and having been unable to cut them short myself as I did in the two instances referred to earlier – some *temporary* restraint of my actions was probably advisable. Although there were considerable variations in the length of time between the onset of each of these excursions and my imprisonment, each of them came to an end within one or two weeks after the jailing took place. What I believe accounted for this outcome was my removal from the disturbing situations from which the flights took off. To allow an acutely troubled person such a reprieve from besetting pressures may, of course, be a considerable service to him. But what benefits it offers are greatly outweighed by the heavy risk of further detention to which he is subjected.

What happened in the last two instances of my confinement is vividly illustrative of this process and its attendant risks. In August of 1967, not long after I had told my second wife of my determination to separate from her and start divorce proceedings, I was carried away, very much against my will, to Mockrie State Hospital, where I had been committed twice before – once involuntarily, in 1963, for 40 days, and the second time of my own volition, in 1964, for one week. (On that occasion, I felt in urgent need of a respite from a tough laboring job and a succession of long, late evenings with friends down for vacations of sunning and drinking.) I'd found the admission building of M. S. H. – in a state to which we had moved in 1960 – a fine place of its kind, and learned that the institution had been rated fifth or sixth in excellence among all the nation's public asylums, by whatever body makes such determinations. I had no dread of the place itself that August, but the means of my reinduction into it were atrociously assaultive and needlessly forcible. I felt largely vindicated and vastly relieved when the young psychiatrist in charge of my case authorized my discharge after ten days' observation, against my wife's strenuous protests. Legally, a lawyer friend told me, this meant that I had been found not in need of psychiatric care.

The following April, I'd been separated from my wife for seven or eight months and had asked my lawyer to begin divorce proceedings. The hearing hadn't been scheduled, however, when it appeared that I was losing my mind again. My wife blew the whistle on me once more. This time the doctor told me that I was "less disturbed" than I had been the previous August. The estimate was debatable, but I was not about to debate it. From all he could learn from a telephone conversation with my wife, and from my edited account of the events she described, the worst he could charge was that I had shown "poor judgment." It was enough, along with my status of repeater and some other entirely nonpsychiatric factors, to serve as justification for my being given a "prolonged judicial commitment" – an indeterminate sentence such as has doomed many thousands of people to living out their lives in the miserable shitholes which the back wards of even such a highly rated asylum as this one continued to be.

After two months in the admission building, I was transferred to the oldest – 100-odd years – most dismal, dirty and neglected of the institution's eight or nine buildings, above the main entrance of which is still visible in faded lettering its original name, Mockrie Insane Asylum. There I spent four of the most agonizing and heavily degrading months of my life, in the company of 400 or 500 of the state's most wasted and unwanted men and women. I might be among them still if I hadn't been lucky enough to meet what at first seemed an impossible condition of my release: that I find a job in the city two miles from the madhouse and work at it for two or three months while continuing to live in the institution. No one on the staff had any leads to offer, there was nothing I could qualify for in the want ads and I had no money for taxi fares to and from the city.

But I *was* lucky enough to find a job, with a painting contractor willing to take a chance on a certified loony, to hold it for over two months, and then to surmount a further obstacle the doctor put in the way of my release. I made it out and continued working at the least congenial labor I have ever done and living in the most charm-forsaken city I have ever been stuck in in a long lifetime. By the terms of my parole, which ended October 10, 1969, I was free to move elsewhere in the state but not out of it, nor to drive a car, vote, proceed with my divorce or to appear *likely* to violate any "laws, ordinances, conventions or morals of the community" (to quote a statute that Szasz cites as justifying commitment in this and other states).

I accept the tough existential truth that my choices in the past have brought me, step by stagger and lunge by lurch, along the route I have traveled. One's field of choices tends to become narrowed over the years in the best of circumstances, and after a lifetime of making choices that have been judged wrong by supposedly expert examiners and custodians, one's confidence in his ability to make the right ones diminishes.

Nevertheless, in reflecting on the critical decisions of my life, and on the seeming impasse to which the whole sequence of them has brought me, there isn't one I can think of – given the sum of what I was at the time of making them and the alternatives that confronted me – that I could have made differently. I find it pointless to judge any of them right or wrong, good or bad, in terms of what it led to; each was, in the full context of its making, *necessary*. I honor the responsibility that, as I see it, went into each of them and accept the responsibility for the results of each.

Indeed, it was responsibility that dictated my choice of continued exile and isolation and that will guide whatever steps I take out of it. If some unfathomable and irrepressible force should lead me to choose to lose my mind again – or to launch another expedition into madness in quest of it – I want no one I love or have loved to be burdened with the obligation of putting me back into bedlam, where, with less luck next time, I might live out my days with the legions of once-human beings turned into zombis by shock, chemicals and indifference. If the choice must be made, I want it to be unequivocally clear that it has been mine, so that it may be said of me, and I may say of myself, there, now, is a *responsible, self-made* madman.

DIFFERENTIAL REACTION TO LABELLING

One result of being labelled an outsider is being viewed as a certain kind of person, one who is basically different and less moral. Kitsuse has suggested that the imputation of deviance is documented by *"retrospective interpretations*, . . . a process by which the subject reinterprets the individual's past behavior in light of the new information concerning his . . . deviance" (1962:96). The deviant may soon discover that others' reactions to him centre about his deviant identification, that he is treated as being generally, rather than specifically, deviant (Becker, 1963; Simmons, 1969). As has often been shown, being labelled as deviant has important consequences for one's further social participation and self-conception, the most significant being a change in the individual's public identity (Becker, 1963; Goffman, 1963).

Made aware that he is tagged as a deviant, the individual responds to others' novel conception of who and what he is and is not. Stigmatized as morally inferior and different, the person typically engages in actions to manage his differentness. At one extreme he can choose to accept the labellers' definition of him, come to see himself as the kind of person they believe him to be, and thus assume a deviant identity. For example, the diagnosed patient, with others' encouragement and support, may choose as the wisest course of action under the circumstances to accept the mentally ill designation. At the other extreme, the deviant label is rejected and the individual's identity remains unaltered. In his well-known study on delinquent youth, Reiss (1961) discovered how teenage youths could engage in homosexual activity without finding it necessary to identify themselves as homosexuals. Along similar lines, Sykes and Matza (1957) argue that by employing techniques of neutralization – "justifications for deviance that are seen as valid by the delinquent but not by the legal system or society at large" – delinquent youth can effectively offset the larger society's definition of them as incorrigible and immoral. It is important to emphasize that either extreme, occurring over a period of time, involves a highly complex series of interchanges between the individual and those viewing him as different. While either outcome is logically possible, it is more realistic to conceive of this process as one in which both sides are involved in a negotiated relationship.

The nature of the individual's response to his labelled and stigmatized condition will be largely affected by whether he must face his problem alone or if he has access to a group of others who face the same or similar problems. When similarly labelled individuals are not afforded the opportunity to share their common situation, their efforts at attending to their discredited condition may be termed individual adaptation. In contrast, members of organized deviant groups, with the opportunity to coordinate a series of strategies by which to create and sustain certain self-conceptions, experience a sense of common fate, and form a subculture – "a set of perspectives and understandings about what the world is like and how to deal with it, and a set of routine activities based on those perspectives" (Becker, 1963:38). For example, in his study of a maximum security prison, Sykes (1958) describes how the inmate subculture represents the prisoners' collective attempt to mitigate the consequences of prison deprivations. In a similar vein, Leznoff and Westley contend that "the primary function of the homosexual group is . . . that it provides a social context within which the homosexual can find acceptance as a homosexual and collective support for his deviant tendencies" (1956:257). Thus, through its various activities, the homosexual subculture has been able to provide "a working philosophy for the active homosexual, explaining to him why he is the way he is, that other people have also been that way, and why it is all right for him to be that way" (Becker, *ibid.*).

While the deviant subculture provides its members with various supports for continuing a particular line of activity, it may, over time, become politically active. Members of the subculture realize that in order to remove the negative conditions surrounding their everyday life and to improve their low status in society they must assert themselves as a political force. This may take several forms, including attempts to influence the public to reconsider its punitive stereotyping of the group and to develop a better understanding of its members, and/or organized activity for legal reform (Schur, 1965:95-96). The Gay Liberation Movement and various militant poor people's groups, which have organized campaigns both to request and demand greater opportunities for themselves, exemplify a politicized reaction to the manifold consequences of being labelled.

A common theme running through the articles we have selected is that for those labelled deviant their relations with others undergo marked changes over time. It is this temporal accent which suggests the utility of viewing the adaptations to these reactions as a career. The articles in this section focus around the strategies utilized by deviants in managing their emergent career. The first two papers investigate individual adaptation. Petrunik, writing about stuttering and intermittent fluency, describes the tactics and management strategies stutterers have developed in dealing with their speech disability. The author argues that the stutterer's very desire and effort to be normal constitute a major stumbling block to the possibility of his actually becoming a normal speaker. Himmelfarb and Evan's paper discusses the management of stigma, concentrating specifically on obesity. The authors focus their attention on the management techniques of people who have accepted, to some degree at least, that they are fat. Turning out attention to individuals' affiliation with a deviant subculture, Sawchuk examines the sequence of actions which ultimately result in the individual's entry into and acculturation to the homosexual community. He notes that socialization into the homosexual community involves the sequential processes of self discovery, sensitivity to the personal consequences of being a homosexual, learning to manage this new identity, and labelling oneself a homosexual in the presence of other such people. In the final paper, Felt deals with the emergence of militant poor people's groups and describes the process by which a low income individual becomes a militant poor person. His analysis suggests that for a majority of participants the process can be analytically described as four stages, each of which is a necessary but not a sufficient condition for the succeeding one.

References

Becker, H.S. *Outsiders: Studies in the Sociology of Deviance.* New York: The Free Press, 1963.

Goffman, E. *Stigma.* Englewood Cliffs, N.J.: Prentice-Hall, 1963.

Kitsuse, J. I. "Societal reactions to deviant behavior: problems of theory and method." *Social Problems*, 9 (Winter), 1962, pp. 247-56.

Leznoff, M. and W. A. Westley. "The Homosexual Community." *Social Problems*, 3 (Spring), 1956, pp. 257-63.

Reiss Jr., A. J. "The social integration of queers and peers." *Social Problems* 9 (Fall), 1961, pp. 102-20.

Schur, E. *Crimes Without Victims.* Englewood Cliffs, N.J.: Prentice-Hall, 1965.

Simmons, J. L. *Deviants.* Berkeley, Calif.: The Glendessary Press, 1969.

Sykes, G. M. *The Society of Captives: A Study of Maximum Security Prison.* Princeton: Princeton University Press, 1958.

Sykes, G. M. and D. Matza. "Techniques of neutralization: a theory of delinquency." *American Sociological Review*, 22, 1957, pp. 664-70.

12
The Quest for Fluency:
Fluency Variations and the Identity
Problems, Management Strategies
of Stutterers*

Michael Petrunik

In an effort to deal with the problems posed by stuttering and intermittent fluency, stutterers have developed a variety of tactics or management strategies. These can be classified as *avoidance* and *concealment* strategies, *repair* and *overlooking* strategies and attempts to make stuttering an *asset*. Some schools of speech therapy argue that most of these tactics serve only to amplify the stutterer's troubles and that the only way out of the vicious circle of the disorder is to embrace the role of "stutterer". But because of the attachment of individuals to the fluency standards of "normal" demeanor in their society and because stuttering is an intermittent, not a fixed, phenomenon, such a solution is seen to have great costs. The stutterer's very desire to be normal and his efforts to be normal then seem to constitute a major stumbling block to the possibility of his actually becoming a normal speaker.

Stuttering is a puzzling disorder of human communication that has confounded man's attempts at explanation and cure for thousands of years. It is estimated that stutterers constitute slightly under 1 per cent of the population of modern industrial societies. There are indications from a few cross-cultural studies (Bullen 1944; Lemert 1967; Stewart 1959) of a much lower incidence in many so-called primitive societies. Not only do the incidence and form of stuttering vary with different societies but also the frequency of stuttering varies with the social context, contingencies in interaction, and changes in identity or role. Despite these points and despite the fact that research on stuttering (Bluemel 1913, 1932; Johnson 1944; Van Riper 1931, 1937, 1971) has been important in the formulation of the well-known sociological

* Data for this paper were gathered through analysis of the literature on stuttering, interviews, case histories, diaries, participant observation, and the author's own experience as a stutterer. I would like to thank both the therapists and clients who participated in the different speech-therapy programs under study for their assistance and co-operation. I would also like to note that many of the themes developed in this paper owe a great deal to my earlier work and to long discussions with Cliff Shearing of the University of Toronto, Criminology Centre (Petrunik and Shearing 1971-1972).

model of primary and secondary deviance (Lemert 1951, pp. 75-76; 1967, pp. 40-41), stuttering has received little attention from sociologists.[1]

In this paper, stuttering is analyzed as an unintentional, recurring, form of deviation from the "situational proprieties" (Goffman 1963 b, 1967) or social standards which define the "normal" way of speaking and co-ordinating the movements of the face and body in social interaction. Individuals who are seen to unintentionally and chronically deviate from the fluency standards may be defined as stutterers or as abnormal in some way. Depending on their social context, culture, and status, these individuals are subject to penalizing social reactions of varying degrees.[2] (See Van Riper 1963, p. 311; Lemert 1967, pp. 135-53, Johnson 1959, p. 239.)

An important factor influencing both social reactions to stuttering and the ways in which individuals who define themselves as stutterers attempt to deal with stuttering and the possible reactions of others is the intermittency or fluctuation of stuttering. Most stutterers are part-time normal speakers, and some rarely stutter or are rarely seen to stutter, by others. The degree of variability and anticipation of stuttering, which depends upon the situation and the speaker's definition of self and others (Sheehan 1970, p. 13; Heltman 1939; Bloodstein 1949, 1950; Siegel and Hauger 1964) is often so great that many stutterers feel that they project themselves not only as "normal speakers" and "stutterers" but also as different personality types in different situations. Because stutterers, like most individuals in society, wish to be seen by others as at least "normal, competent persons," they try to convey favourable impressions of themselves and to regulate these impressions (Goffman 1959). However, the actual occurrence of stuttering may discredit such efforts; the stutterers therefore face the problem of experiencing great anxiety about the possible breakdown of their speech in situations where they are either actively or passively projecting themselves as "normal speakers."

Some "Natural" Methods of Adaptation to Stuttering

Most stutterers try in various ways to conceal the fact that they stutter. Though they feel they cannot control the *reality* of their stuttering they try in various ways to present the *appearance* that they are fluent speakers and "normal" persons.

The basic types of tactics that stutterers use, either singly or with the co-operation of others, are *avoidance* and *concealment* strategies, and *overlooking* and *repair* strategies. They often follow a sequence in that if avoidance and concealment strategies fail, the stutterer will try the overlooking and repair tactics.

Avoidance and concealment strategies are designed to avoid the possibility of stuttering and to prevent others from noticing that one is a stutterer. In doing so one is able to tacitly indicate to others that one is a fluent speaker and in general "a normal competent person." For example, a stutterer by not speaking in a situation may hope to be seen as a "quiet person," "a good listener," or a "shy person." However, he faces the possibility that he may be labelled as a member of some category he sees as less desirable than the category "stutterer" (for example, "nervous," "odd," "rude," "affected," "silly," "strange," "stupid," "crazy," or "retarded"). Such possibilities pose dilemmas for a stutterer. Should he reveal himself as he really is or should he let it pass? What costs are involved?

Overlooking and repair strategies are used when the individual has breached the fluency expectations and wishes to influence the way in which others will interpret this, or when he wishes to forewarn others about the impending breach. The stutterer's fellow participants may co-operate with him in such strategies in order to prevent the various types of alienation (Goffman 1967) that may arise when stuttering occurs, or to prevent any participant from becoming flustered, going out of play, or bringing the encounter to an end with a resounding crash (Goffman 1961, 1967, p. 101). The chief concerns of the stutterer in using repair strategies can be summarized as follows: How can one maintain a positive self-image and how one can project a favourable image to others despite the "deviant" appearances one is presenting, or is surely going to present?

Avoidance and Concealment Strategies

The first group of tactics we will consider involve ways in which the stutterer tries to avoid using the medium of speech, and if he feels it is necessary to justify his avoidance. The principle which founds this set of tactics is that if you do not talk, your fluency will not be questioned, and if your fluency is not questioned then neither will be your identity as a normal competent person. Some of these tactics are as follows:

1.   The avoidance of modes of interaction where speech must be used as the means of expression; for example, the avoidance of structurally problematic communication media such as telephones and intercoms. The telephone is the nemesis of many stutterers who will often walk great distances or write letters to avoid the use of the telephone.[3]

2.   Avoiding roles or jobs which demand a great deal of speaking, poise, contact with the public, and use of the telephone.

3.   The establishment of routines; for example, eating in the same restaurant and ordering the same items so that one may avoid the possibility of being revealed in new situations.

4.   The avoidance of situations in which the pressure of fluency and performance norms are very strong; for example, speaking to a large audience or to people of high status.

5.   Avoiding speaking by concurring with others. Some individuals who go to a restaurant with others achieve this by saying, "I'll have the same," when someone else orders.

6.   The use of commercial facilities which are socially and physically structured so as to reduce the amount of interaction (particularly speech) with personnel in order to achieve quick service and efficiency. Some examples are cafeterias, liquor outlets in Canada, automated laundries, supermarkets, and all other types of self-service stores or shops.

7.   Avoiding the necessity to speak by using other channels of communication. Sometimes the stutterer will avoid speaking by the use of written notes (for example, doctor's prescriptions and shopping lists) or by pointing to what he wants.

8.   Using the typical meaning of the setting one is in to communicate one's desire without speaking. This strategy relies on the expectation that others will treat one's desires as obvious merely because one is in a particular setting geared to provide specific services. For example, to be present in a homosexual bar may indicate that one is available to be "picked up." Most members of society will use the typical meaning of a setting for communication, but, unlike the stutterer, with no apparent awareness that it is a technique.

9.   The stutterer's purposeful avoidance may be accompanied by a variety of accounts or excuses should his actions be questioned. Stutterer may provide reasons for his generally low degree of participation in voluntary associations and social activities (Lemert 1951) by denying that it has anything to do with his stuttering, but rather that it is a matter of choice or simply a matter of the kind of person he is.

When the stutterer does not want to or is unable to avoid situations where he must speak, he is still able to exercise some control over what he will say and how he will say it. This involves attention to matters of syntax, vocabulary, tone, rhythm, pace, and pronunciation. What we are witnessing here is a type of camouflage strategy. The speaker is attempting to convey "normal appearances" (Goffman 1971) to others by putting forth semblances of either "normal disfluencies," gestures, or slight idiosyncracies. In the extreme form such tactics may involve assuming a different character or identity, or consciously practising an artificial, highly structured way of speaking (as some stuttering treatments, such as the Kerr method,[4] advocate). The following is a summary of some of the practices that are used:

1.   Practising saying difficult words before entering into a speaking sit-

uation – perhaps using a mirror or a tape recorder as an aid.

2. Practising positive thinking – telling oneself that one will be calm and relaxed or that one will not stutter.

3. Avoiding certain words or a certain order of words that one believes will be difficult to say by substituting words or by circumlocution (for example, the well-known British actor who asked for information about which bus went to Marble Arch in London by saying, "Can you tell me which bus I take to go to that Arch which is of marble made?")

4. The use of "starters," "fillers" (postponement devices) and "releasers" – that is, words (*actually, like, well, so, yes*), sounds (*ah, er, uh, um*), gestures (pointing one's finger), and stances and sudden movements (stamping one's feet, slapping one's thigh) which individuals use before difficult words, in between words to give them an easier approach or an opportunity to substitute, or during a block to help bring it to an end. Some of these may be very noticeable and bizarre, others very subtle as the following report from a young Chinese-Canadian woman indicates:

> I often began sentences with *um* or *uh* to help get started. The sound *s* has never been a problem so I'd try to start sentences with a word beginning with *s*. One of my most frequent tactics which usually works is to begin a phrase with the word *so*; . . . I can never say for instance, "What did you do this week-end"? But I can say, "So, what did you do. . . . ?"

5. Looking away while speaking or speaking while others are looking away.

6. Pretending to think during pauses.

7. Writing words on a black board or piece of paper while saying them.

8. Feigning a cough or yawn while blocking.

9. Talking while moving or talking to the rhythm of a sound or movement.

10. Speaking while there is background noise, such as a radio playing or a tap running.

11. Altering one's breathing or speaking with one's residual breath.

12. Controlling the tone or pitch of the voice; for example, speaking in a deep or high voice, speaking in a sing-song fashion, speaking in a monotone, or speaking nasally.

13. Speaking with a fixed rhythm or pace.

14. Altering the pace of speech.

15. Assuming a drawl or an accent.

16. Talking while pretending to concentrate on some other kind of activity.

17. Speaking with an object in one's mouth; for example, a pipe, cigar, or pencil.

18. Using a mechanical device to facilitate speaking (McKenzie 1955).

19. Assuming a different role or identity. This phenomenon can be dramatically noted in actors and entertainers who stutter in everyday life but speak fluently on stage or in front of a microphone. The basis for this strategy seems to be the tendency of some stutterers to feel that their "stuttering self" is their "real," or "true," self. Any mechanism which enables a stutterer to distance himself from this self-image and provides him with a new one may aid him to speak fluently. (See Sheehan 1970, pp. 12-13.)

Passing: The Case of the Interiorized Stutterer

Though the use of these strategies that we have considered may enable an individual to avoid stuttering and to avoid being recognized as a stutterer, his problems are not solved in any final sense. The very reason such strategies are used is the individual's belief in the possibility that he will stutter. He need not actually be seen by others as a stutterer to see himself as a sutterer. This point is dramatically made by the case of "interiorized stutterers" (Quarrington and Douglass 1956) – that is, individuals who, by developing large vocabularies, verbal dexterity, and a variety of other devices which enable them to change words and vary their syntax in an unnoticed fashion, are generally seen by others as "normal speakers."

The interiorized stutterer is an excellent illustration of what Becker (1963, p. 11) refers to as the "secret deviant." Although such persons see themselves as stutterers, they are usually not recognized as stutterers by the general public and sometimes even by their families and close friends. They become known only to speech therapists when they seek help for their stuttering problem. In the world of stuttering therapy they have achieved a certain notoriety. Many stories circulate about their exploits; for example, individuals buying houses on streets whose names they can say easily; individuals changing their names to ones they can say without fear of stumbling, and so on.

The case of James A. illustrates quite well some of the proto-typical features of the interiorized stutterer.

James A. is a self-employed businessman in his early forties. Although he has discussed his stuttering problem with his wife, he has in the past taken pains to conceal stuttering from his children and from friends and acquaintances. He says that when entertaining he tries not to drink too much or to become too fatigued so that he will not lose control over his speech. At work, many situations in which he anticipates difficulty are handled by his secretary – for example, he will have her make certain phone calls for him. At one time he fired a secretary who had been working with him for a number of years because he thought, by her facial expression, that she had noticed him stammering. He had tried a number of kinds of speech therapy including a brief stint at the type of non-avoidance therapy advocated by Van Riper and used in Toronto by Ernest "Van" Douglass. He did not stay in therapy primarily because he felt he could not reduce fears by openly stuttering and discussing stuttering. In 1970 he attended a course teaching stutterers a new method of speaking. (This course was similar to the Kerr method discussed in footnote.[4]) Though he had not used the method as a whole outside of the course, he claims that he occasionally uses certain techniques from the course. Basically, he had incorporated them into his old manner of speaking.

By using starters and fillers and by controlling facial or bodily strain, the interiorized stutterer can strategically produce the appearance that he is a "normal speaker" producing "normal speech." This sense of normality, however, is tied to situational constraints. Such strategies are used effectively when the individual is talking about matters in which he is not expected to give a routine and automatic reply and in which there is considerable leeway in the way he can answer as, for example, in the following interchange:

A.:   Where is the Borden building?
B.:   It's on—uh—let me see now [quizzical expression] on—ah—Spadina near—uh—College.[5]

To use these strategies, however, when he is asked for his name or address is to create the impression that "something is fishy" or that he is a non-serious (a joker or "wise guy") or non-competent (stupid, crazy, or retarded) person. These charges are based on the assumption that one's name and address are not the sort of information that any serious, competent, or trustworthy person need ponder. By using word shifts and fillers instead of struggling to get his words out the individual may put in question his competence or sanity, not his ability to speak. For example:

> On the first day of a course for stutterers, individuals were going through the ritual of introductions. One nervous-looking man came up to the group, and we began to introduce ourselves. As he put his hand out he said, "My name is—uhh—actually—my name is Jim." Afterwards, one of the other men, with a highly noticeable stutter, shook his head and said, "What a fool! I'd rather stammer my head off than avoid like that. It looks ridiculous. People must think he's crazy."

One context that gives interiorized stutterers, and stutterers in general, trouble is the border crossing. To pause, use fillers, or show nervousness when asked a routine question, such as Where were you born? is to invite the inference that one is hiding something. Since border guards or customs officials are concerned with detecting individuals who are smuggling or seeking to make an illegal entry, they are on the look-out for any signs individuals might give off (Goffman 1959). The following incident illustrates the possible outcome of such a situation:

> The border guard asked me where I was born. Because I was afraid I would stutter on Nova Scotia I hesitated and started to hem and haw; "Let me see now—its the—uh—Maritimes—uh—." The outcome of all this evasion was that they made a thorough search of my car and even threatened to slit open my seat covers.

For the typical interiorized stutterer the concern with presenting himself as a "normal speaker" seems to be far greater than it is for more visible stutterers.[6] Since success is based on constant vigilance and wariness, the interiorized stutterer experiences much tension and anxiety. Since he passes so well, he has more to live up to, and the costs of disclosure are much greater. He is perpetually on guard waiting for a fatal slip.

Remedial Strategies

Remedial strategies (Goffman 1967 and 1971), refer to the techniques of disguising or controlling stuttering once the stutterer, and possibly others, have perceived that stuttering has occurred, and to the providing of "reasonable" accounts for actions that could be interpreted as stuttering or as some other form of impropriety. They involve ways in which stutterers attempt to save face by influencing the interpretations of others as to (a) what type of behaviour they are witnessing and (b) what should be done about what is happening.

Remedial activities are not always distinguishable from avoidance strategies in kind, but rather in use. Some of the techniques used to prevent or avoid stuttering may also be used to remedy or control stuttering and its possible consequences. The issues now are not, Am I seen as a stutterer or as some type of abnormal person? but, How bad a stutterer am I seen to be? What type of abnormal person, and how abnormal, am I seen to be? and What consequences will stuttering have in my relationships with others?

Tactful Overlooking

One common remedial tactic is the overlooking or ignoring of acts which might breach situational proprieties. This involves the tacit message to others that they should ignore them too. When an individual stutters in interaction, it is common that most adults will co-operate with him in this *tactful overlooking* (Goffman 1967, p. 16). Sometimes the breach can be so blatant that to achieve such a state would seem to be extraordinary. Yet it happens a great deal. By the use of such a method the tacit claims and virtual identities of the interactants are supported: in the stutterer's case, that he is a normal competent person; in the case of the other, that he is a decent tactful person. (See Goffman 1963a, pp. 2-3.) To do otherwise would mean that the taken-for-granted grounds of interaction would be disrupted (Garfinkel 1967). A new definition of the interaction would have to be sought with the possible consequences of embarrassment and uneasiness for all involved.

Tactful overlooking is usually achieved through the loss of eye contact. Sometimes the stutterer alone averts his eyes, and sometimes it is only the other. At other times, there is a mutual loss of eye contact while the stutterer is struggling to say a word. Normally, mutual glances during a conversation, accompanied by an expression of attentiveness or slight nods of the head, reaffirm attentiveness and involvement. The period in which eye contact is broken by the participants can be viewed as a sort of "time out" from the interaction, a way of excluding stuttering and its disruptive influence from the conversation and maintaining the conversation's "integrity."[7] During this period, the other may assume an air of nonchalance, shuffle some papers, fiddle with an article of clothing or some other object, or survey the immediate surroundings – all actions which tacitly indicate that he is not *in* the conversation. As soon as the word is out, eye contact is restored, and the participants continue their conversation as if nothing unusual happened (Emerson 1970).

The meaning of the loss of eye contact can be described in another way. Both stutterers and members of their audience may avert their eyes in order to hide feelings of embarrassment or shame. The phrase "the eyes are the mirror of the soul" indicates that the eyes are often regarded as expressing one's deepest feelings. To avoid looking into another's eyes at a time of crisis, then, may be to spare him the indignity of being seen in a moment of nakedness. Further, the loss of eye contact provides both the stutterer and others with the opportunity to regain composure before returning to the conversation. To insist on maintaining eye contact may be to insist that the other witness the shame and fear of the stutterer or to catch the other's expression of embarrassment and discomfort which he would rather not be seen. Eye contact at such a time may also create a greater sense of intimacy than the participants regard as appropriate for the occasion.

The consequence of mutual, tactful overlooking during a severe period of stuttering is that public recognition of what each person privately knows, and knows that the other knows, is avoided.[8] When eye contact is maintained the stuttering becomes a public object or mutual focus for the interactants, and seems to demand an account or comment by either or both persons.

Repair Strategies

For various reasons the interactants may not want to use the tactful overlooking method. Various repair strategies and accounts may then be used. Perhaps the chief way stutterers attempt to repair the possible damage stuttering might cause is through the use of *accounts* (Scott and Lyman 1970). Sometimes these are given at the beginning of an encounter to tell others what is going to happen and how they might respond to it. For example, one university professor who stutters, starts off each term by telling his students about his stuttering and encouraging them to give their reactions to stuttering and to ask questions about it. Another professor who stutters begins his classes with a period of voluntary stuttering so that he will not set up expectations of fluency which he may later fail to meet. Sometimes accounts are used after a situation by the stutterer or his intimates to explain the behaviour that has occurred. The stutterer may also attempt to offer explanations for his disfluencies, when and where they occur, and while they occur, through the use of interjections, asides, or facial expressions. The following repair strategies indicate the stutterer's desire to influence the opinions of others by specifying mitigating circumstances for his difficulties and by indicating that these difficulties are not to be taken as representative of his speech in general or of the kind of person he is:

> We went to the shh – shhh—s's always give me trouble – show last night.
> I was talking to K – K – K – en – Wow! I had a hard time on that one – and he was saying. . . .
> Boy, I'm having a hard time today. I must be really tired.

A variant of this technique is the use of humour. (See Goffman 1961, p. 50; 1967, p. 21.) As a repair strategy, humour can be regarded as an effective form of "role distance" (Goffman, 1961), a way, perhaps, of saying: Do not take this display seriously; I don't get too concerned about it. This is well illustrated by the comments of Pat, a young stutterer from Prince Edward Island:

> I use humour a lot now. If I'm having a problem, I'll make a comment like, "Boy, it's a problem having a big mouth like mine and not being able to use it." When I have a hard time getting a word in a store, I'll say something like "three tries for a quarter." Once a waitress started guessing when I blocked giving my order, and kept on guessing and guessing wrong. Every so often, I

would smile and say "You just keep guessing." Everyone was laughing; but they were laughing at her, not me.

Making Stuttering an Asset

Another strategy, which is less commonly used, is based on the fact that although stuttering is usually viewed as a liability, it may in some situations prove to be an asset. For example, in Great Britain a slight stammer is regarded, in some circles, as very distinctive and indicative of good breeding. British lords, diplomats, and intellectuals have been known to purposefully cultivate a delicate stammer (Shenker 1970). Stuttering may also become an asset for those individuals who talk about their stuttering in order to achieve greater intimacy with others. By revealing personal foibles, individuals make themselves appear more human. Another instance is the use of stuttering as an excuse to avoid situations that might be unpleasant. Conversely, a few individuals have used their stuttering to achieve success in occupational roles – for example, many well-known figures in stuttering therapy and research,[9] and some entertainers and public figures whose stuttering has become a trademark. Two examples of the latter are the legendary comic Joe Frisco and the British humorist Patrick Campbell. In his autobiography Campbell makes this point with characteristic wit:

> While making the ginger ale commercials I looked upon my stammer as a nuisance that would have to be played down as much as possible if we weren't to have endless takes. . . . Although I didn't care to think about this aspect of it too much I did realize that my stammer fitted rather neatly into their campaign, the essence of which was never to mention the whole word "Schweppes," but merely to present the first syllable, "Sch – –," and that was quite enough for me in every way. It wasn't until a year later that I realized my mistake. [At this time Campbell was asked to advertise butter. Again he tried to control his stuttering. The producer called him aside and said] " . . . I don't quite know how to put this – but could we have a little more of your trademark on the word 'butter' " . . . I'd been trying to suppress the very thing it seemed that everyone wanted (Campbell 1967, pp. 212-13).

Campbell, however, acknowledges that such an asset is in the end not really worth it. The infrequent and fleeting gains cannot offset the losses that recur day after day each time the stutterer opens his mouth or even thinks about opening his mouth to speak:

> . . . If I was offered by some miraculous overnight cure, the opportunity never to stammer again, I'd accept it without hesitation, even

though it meant the end for me of television (Campbell 1967, p. 213).

Non-Avoidance Therapy

The *non-avoidance approach* is based on the secondary-deviance theory that efforts to control or hide stuttering feed-back into the stuttering process to maintain or exaggerate it. Therapists who follow the non-avoidance approach advocate the management strategies of public avowal of one's stuttering, careful monitoring of one's behaviour and attitudes, and "faking" stuttering or stuttering voluntarily.[10] The logic of the approach is that if one can give up one's efforts to control or hide stuttering, many of the most serious problems associated with stuttering will disappear or be minimized. First of all, if the stutterer can lose his concern about whether others see him stutter, he will experience less anxiety and tension and will therefore feel free to participate more actively in work and recreational activities and in the general social life of his community. Secondly, if stutterers do not attempt to control or avoid stuttering, their struggle responses will decrease and their disfluencies will be less bizarre and disturbing to others.

The non-avoidance approach is widely used in speech clinics in North America; also, some of the important writings in speech therapy (such as the works of Van Riper and Sheehan) advocate such an approach. Recently, voluntary organizations of stutterers have been developed in North America, Europe, and New Zealand (Borkmann 1971a, 1971b) which are similar to the many other self-help groups of deviants (largely modelled along the lines of Alcoholics Anonymous) that have come into being in the last few decades (Sagarin 1970). Some of these groups (for example, the National Council of Adult Stutterers of Washington, D.C.) have their own journals which serve as a form through which stutterers can share their experiences, educate other stutterers about speech therapy (largely non-avoidance therapy, at least in the United States), and present humorous anecdotes and inspirational reports to help stutterers react more positively to their circumstances. These groups give presentations on the mass media and speak to public service clubs both to educate the public and to increase their own self-confidence and competence in communication skills. As of yet, only an infinitesimal proportion of stutterers are members of stutterers' organizations, and it seems (although I have no data on this) that many stutterers are not even acquainted with non-avoidance therapy. Even when stutterers are aware of the non-avoidance solution, this study indicates that they dislike it or have great difficulties accepting it. First of all, because of their attachment to situational proprieties, stutterers experience a great pressure to strive to be fluent. The general public, unaware of the possible benefits of voluntary stuttering, praises and rewards fluency. Some stutterers, even when it is pointed out to them that their voluntary stuttering is less severe and disruptive than their involuntary stuttering, would rather stutter only involuntarily. As the following comments from interviews and one of Van Riper's patients indicate, to intentionally stutter and to go against the fluency expectations of a society is a hard thing to do:[11]

> I don't mind stuttering when I have to, but when I don't have to, it half kills me.
>
> (Van Riper 1954, p. 288)

> I didn't like voluntary stuttering. I wasn't even able to tolerate the sound of doing it when I was speaking to myself.
>
> (Author's interviews)

> I like to be fluent and I always hope and try to get by. I don't want to stutter if I can help it. I was never any good at doing repetitions. Of course I didn't practice them. I hated doing buh-buh-buh. . . . It looks phoney. People don't know very much about stuttering, but they don't think that's stuttering. Even in the others, I didn't like repetitions. It just didn't seem natural.
>
> (Author's interviews)

Though this dislike of voluntary stuttering is common with many individuals whose stuttering is very visible, it is especially so with those who successfully pass themselves off as fluent speakers much of the time. Because voluntary stuttering, in effect, means announcing to the world that one is a stutterer, the stutterer who passes fears that the potential gains derived from voluntary stuttering might be offset by the sure and immediate loss of his status as a "normal competent speaker."

Secondly, even if voluntary stuttering is attempted, certain problems may result. One problem is related to the distinction some speech therapists make between voluntary stuttering and faking stuttering. They contend that faking stuttering may serve as a crutch – playing the role of a stutterer by assuming an artificial stuttering pattern, rather than presenting oneself as one really is by exposing one's "real" pattern of stuttering. Some stutterers feel, however, that they cannot stutter voluntarily. Since stuttering is something that "happens to them," they can only fake stuttering. This feeling may lead to great frustration as in the case of the stutterer who angrily reported that his therapist had accused him of playing the role of stutterer and of not just surrendering to his real stuttering.

Therapists do not always discourage faking stuttering. There are various reasons for advocating this practice; for example, to advertise publicly that one is a stutterer (Aldrich 1968); to learn to become detached from stuttering; and to learn easier ways of stuttering. However, this manner of stuttering may not seem natural and may convey a playful or non-serious air since the signs of struggle others associate with stuttering may be conspicuously absent. A number of stutterers report that friends and family complain about this purposeful stuttering after a while with remarks such as "Stop that, you're just fooling around." Situational propriety requires that unintentional breaches from normal behaviour be forgiven. With seemingly intentional breaches, this is not so.

Even though the non-avoidance approach promises greater social and personal adjustment, it involves certain difficulties. First of all, we are socialized to try to present ourselves to others as attractive and competent. Stuttering, however, is generally viewed as undesirable, unattractive, and indicative of physical or emotional pathologies. Secondly, stuttering is often highly variable, which means that active work may be involved in visibly displaying it to others. Such work is likely to seem tiresome and distasteful. Finally, stutterers often view their speech difficulty as something that is not fixed, that may one day just miraculously disappear. In short, for many stutterers the long-range goal of better adjustment gives way to the more immediate losses involved in voluntary stuttering and to the temptations to avoid and conceal stuttering.

Conclusion

Stutterers, and those who interact with them, engage in various management tactics which point to expectations that bind all "competent members" of a society. Certain of these tactics are merely common practices of etiquette which serve to protect the "integrity" of social situations and of participants involved. However, other methods such as avoidance, concealment, overlooking, and repair may pose special problems for the stutterer. In his very efforts to be or to appear to be a "normal competent person" – *in the context of a society where fluency is rewarded, and disfluency penalized, concealed, or treated with a conspiratory silence* – the stutterer may cause many of his own problems. The stutterer's efforts to avoid or cover up his speech disfluencies often tend to perpetuate the very behaviour he is trying to escape. Voluntary stuttering is another option for the stutterer; but because stuttering is intermittent, and voluntary stuttering may seem unnatural, this method is usually difficult to carry out. As the stutter moves into adolescence and adulthood, the likelihood of permanent remission decreases, and the route out of stuttering becomes more problematic.

Notes

[1] It is noteworthy that accounts of the development of the "labelling" or "societal reaction" perspective in sociology overlook the considerable body of work carried out by speech pathologists prior to 1950, particularly at the University of Iowa. Lemert's notion of primary and secondary deviance seems to be an obvious extension of the notion of primary and secondary stuttering developed many years earlier by Bluemel and Van Riper. Wendell Johnson's semantogenic approach to stuttering (Johnson 1938, 1944, 1946, 1955, 1956a, 1956b, 1958, 1959; Berlin 1960; Williams 1957) is a classic example of the application of the labelling approach which has been overlooked by sociologists, with the exception of Lemert and Borkman 1971a, 1971b.

[2] Here we refer to reactions *as they are evaluated by the stutterer*. Some of these are "pity," "condescension," "embarrassment," "amusement," "ridicule," "condescension," and negative labelling. Lemert (1967 p. 139), referring to the work of Sapir (1915), gives a good example from the practices of the Nootka Indians: " . . . when a person who had a speech defect was addressed or talked about, his defect was imitated or mocked, with changes in word forms – such as suffix changes – which carried implication of smallness, childishness, animal quality, or of some physical defect."

[3] Toronto Globe and Mail, 1970. For a detailed discussion of the difficulties stutterers face because of the structure of telephone interaction see Petrunik and Shearing, 1972.

[4] See Huxham 1953. The "Kerr method" refers to a method of speaking taught by W. C. Kerr in a two-week course, as a "cure" for stuttering. The method essentially involves a standardized temporal ordering (time-on/time-off sequence) of speech. Each word is syllabilized and there are split second pauses between each syllable; for example, I-am-a-u-ni-ver-si-ty stu-dent. The individual is told to stand in a ram-rod straight fashion with his head up high. Unfortunately, such a manner of speech, though technically fluent, does not meet the expectations for normal speech in North America. Its effects have been described as mechanical, stilted, and artificial.

[5] The device used here is the "mental lapse," the conveying by facial expressions and by talk that one cannot think of the right word.

[6] In some instances individuals may be constrained to pass because of their social position or work. A resident surgeon who was an interiorized stutterer was told by his chief surgeon that he could not attend speech therapy because, if word got out that he stuttered, a "halo effect" might take place and others might lose faith in his competence as a surgeon.

[7] "Time out" is discussed in Goffman 1961 pp. 36, 40; in Scott and Lyman 1970, p. 33; and in a different sense in Cavan 1967 and MacAndrew and Edgerton 1969.

[8] See Sheehan 1970, p. 267; Sacks n.d., p. 38; Schlegloff 1968, p. 34; Goffman 1961, pp. 19-26.

[9] Some of the well-known figures in stuttering therapy and research who stutter or stuttered at one time include Charles Van Riper, Wendell Johnson, Joseph Sheehan, Dean Williams, Lon Emerick, Henry Freund,

Dominick Barbara, William Dennison, Ernest Douglass, and Ronald Muirden.

10 Sheehan (1970, p. 7), a major advocate of non-avoidance therapy, even contends that the experience of fluency by adult stutterers may insidiously serve to perpetuate stuttering: "The experience of speaking normally may set up a role expectation for fluency and actually lead to more stuttering. On the other hand, when the individual stutters and thereby enacts more fully the role of stutterer, the fear-producing role expectations for normal speech are diminished. In this manner enactment of the stutterer role leads to fluency, and vice-versa."

11 It should be noted that voluntary stuttering, despite the difficulties mentioned, has proved to be a successful route out of the quicksand of stuttering for some individuals who have managed to persist in their efforts. A dramatic case is cited by `Lon Emerick in *Journal of the Council of Adult Stutterers* (Winter 1972-73), p. 19:

> "We once worked with a young exchange student who almost completely extinguished her stuttering by doing negative practice. [Stuttering on purpose.] We were enmeshed in doctoral examinations so we gave her a hand counter and told her: "There are 100,000 people living in Lansing; see how many you can talk to and show your stuttering." When I saw her seven days later she was haggard and worn but grinning broadly and not stuttering. Having taken us literally she had worked around the clock. Incredibly she had confronted 947 listeners! And she was totally unable to stutter involuntarily."

Bibliography

Aldrich, Rosemary. "Advertising Stuttering." *Journal of the National Council of Adult Stutterers* (May-June 1968): 2-3.

Antonio, R. "On Ignoring the Subtle Dimensions of Labelling: The Case of Mental Disorder." Paper prepared for 23rd Annual Meeting of the Society for the Study of Social Problems, 24-27 August, 1973.

Aron, M. "Nature and Incidence of Stuttering among a Bantu Group of School Children." *Journal of Speech and Hearing Disorders* 28 (1962): 116-28.

Becker, H. S. *The Outsiders*. New York: The Free Press, 1963.

Berlin, C. I. "Parents' Diagnoses of Stuttering." *Journal of Speech and Hearing Research* 3 (1960): 372-79.

Bloodstein, O. *A Handbook on Stuttering for Professional Workers*. Chicago: National Society for Crippled Children and Adults, 1959.

_____. "Hypothetical Conditions Under which Stuttering is Reduced or Absent." *Journal of Speech and Hearing Disorders* 15 (1950): 142-53.

_____. "Conditions under which Stuttering is Reduced or Absent: A Review of Literature." *Journal of Speech and Hearing Disorders* 14 (1949): 295-302.

_____ et al. "Diagnosis of Stuttering by Parents of Stutterers and Nonstutterers." *Journal of Speech and Hearing Disorders* 17 (1952): 308-15.

_____. "The Development of Stuttering: I – Changes in Nine Basic Features; II – Developmental Phases; III – Theoretical and Clinical Implications." *Journal of Speech and Hearing Disorders* 25 (1960): 219-37, 366-76; 26 (1961): 67-82.

Bluemel, C. "Primary and Secondary Stammering." *Quarterly Journal of Speech* 18 (1932): 187-200.

_____. *Stammering and Cognate Defects of Speech*, New York: Stechert, 1913.

Borkman, T. "Participation Patterns and Benefits of Membership in a Self-Help Organization of Stutterers." Research paper, Catholic University of America, 1971a.

_____. "Stuttering as Social Deviance: A Study of Self-Help Organization of Adult Stutterers." Paper read at School of Public Health Seminar, 8 January 1971b, at U.C.L.A.

Bullen, A. "A Cross Cultural Approach to the Problem of Stuttering." *Child Development* 16 (1945): 1-87.

Campbell, Patrick. *My Life and Easy Times*, London: Anthony Blond, 1967.

_____. *The P-P-Penguin Patrick Campbell.* Harmondsworth, Middlesex: Penguin Books, 1965.

Cavan, S. *Liquor License: An Enthnography of Bar Behavior*. Chicago: Aldine, 1967.

Clifford, S. "Stuttering in South Dakota Indians." *Central States Speech Association Journal* 16 (1965): 59-60.

Douglas, J. ed., *Introduction to Sociology: Situations and Structures*. Toronto: Collier-MacMillan, 1973.

Davis, Fred. "Deviance Disavowal: The Management of Strained Interaction by the Visibly Handicapped." *Symbolic Interaction*, edited by J. Manis and B. Meltzer, pp. 189-204. Boston: Allyn and Bacon, 1967; and *Social Problems* 9 (Fall 1961): 120-32.

Dennis, Nigel. "A Bicycle Built for Two." *Encounter* 15 (1960): 12-22.

Douglass, E., and Quarrington, B. "Differentiation of Interiorized and

Exteriorized Secondary Stuttering." *Journal of Speech and Hearing Disorders* 17 (1952): 377-85.

Emerson, Joan. "Nothing Unusual is Happening." In *Human Nature and Collective Behavior*, edited by T. Shibutani. Englewood Cliffs, N.J.: Prentice-Hall, 1970.

French, P. "The Stammerer as Hero." *Encounter* 28 (1966): 67-75.

Garfinkel, H. *Studies in Ethnomethodology*. Englewood Cliffs, N.J.: Prentice-Hall, 1967.

Glaser B., and Strauss A. "Awareness Contexts and Social Interaction." In *Symbolic Interactionism*, by J. Manis and B. Meltzer. Boston: Allyn and Bacon, 1967.

Glasner, P. J., and Rosenthal, D. "Parental Diagnosis of Stuttering in Young Children." *Journal of Speech Disorders* 23 (1957): 288-95.

Goffman E. *Encounters*. Indianapolis: Bobbs-Merrill, 1961.

_____. *The Presentation of Self in Everyday Life*. Garden City, N.Y.: Doubleday-Anchor, 1959.

_____. *Stigma*. Englewood Cliffs, N.J.: Prentice-Hall, 1963a.

_____. *Interaction Ritual*. Garden City, N.Y.: Doubleday-Anchor, 1967.

_____. *Behaviour in Public Places*. New York: The Free Press, 1963b.

_____. *Relations in Public*. New York: Basic Books, 1971.

Heltman, H. "Psycho-Social Phenomena of Stuttering and their Etiological and Therapeutic Implications." *The Journal of Social Psychology* 9 (1938): 79-96.

Huxham, H. H. "Stammerers." *The Spotlight* (Durban, South Africa) (January 1953): 24-25.

Johnson, W. "The Role of Evaluation in Stuttering." *Journal of Speech Disorders* 3 (1938): 85-89.

_____. "The Indian Has No Word for It: Part I, Stuttering in Children; Part II, Stuttering in Adults." *Quarterly Journal of Speech* 30 (October-December 1944): 330-37, 456-65.

_____. *People in Quandries*, New York: Harper, 1946.

_____. ed. *Stuttering in Children and Adults*. Minneapolis; University of Minnesota Press, 1955.

_____. "Perceptual and Evaluational Factors in Stuttering." In *Handbook of Speech Pathology*, edited by L. Travis. New York: Appleton-Century-Crofts, 1956a.

_____.et al. *Speech Handicapped Children*. Rev. ed. New York: Harper, 1956b.

_____. "The Six Men and the Stuttering." In *Stuttering: A Symposium*, edited by J. Eisenson. New York: Harper and Row, 1958.

_____. *The Onset of Stuttering*. Minneapolis: University of Minnesota Press, 1959.

Katz, J. "Deviance, Charisma, and Rule-Defined Behavior." *Social Problems* 20 (Fall 1972): 186-202.

Lemert, E. "Sociological Perspective." In *Stuttering: Research and Therapy*, edited by J. Sheehan. New York: Harper and Row, 1972, 172-87.

Petrunik M. and Shearing, C. "Telephone Troubles: Interactional Breakdown and Its Management by the Stutterer and His Listener." Research paper, University of Toronto, 1972.

Sacks, Harvey. "Social Aspects of Language: The Organization of Sequencing in Conversation." Unpublished manuscript, n.d.

_____. Unpublished lectures, University of California, 1966-1970.

Sagarin, E. *Odd Man In: Societies of Deviants in America*, Chicago: Markham, 1970.

Sander, Eric. "Application of Descriptive-Behavioral Language Principles to Stuttering Therapy."mimeographed. Louisville: University of Kentucky, n.d.

Sapir, E. *Abnormal Types of Speech in the Nootka*. Anthropological Series. Ottawa, Canada, Dept. Mines Geol. Survey Memoir C2, 1915.

Schegloff, E. "The First Five Seconds: Sequencing in Conversational Openings." Ph.D. dissertation, University of California, 1968.

Schur, E. *Labeling Deviant Behavior*. New York: Harper and Row, 1971.

Scott, M., and Lyman, S. *A Sociology of the Absurd*. New York: Appleton-Century-Crofts, 1970.

Sheehan, J., ed. *Stuttering: Research and Therapy*. New York: Harper, 1970.

Shenker, Israel, "Stammer Becomes Fashionable." *The Globe and Mail*, Toronto. (November 12, 1970).

Siegel, G., and Hauger, D. "Audience Size and Variations in Stuttering Behavior," *Journal of Speech and Hearing Research* 7 (1964): 383-88.

Snidecor, J. "Why the Indian Does Not Stutter." *Quarterly Journal of Speech* 33 (1947): 493-95.

Stewart, J. "The Problem of Stuttering in Certain North American Indians." *Journal of Speech and Hearing Disorders.* Supplement 6 (1959): 1-87.

"Stutterers Challenged by Telephone Calls." *The Globe and Mail,* Toronto (September 9, 1970), p. 10.

Travis, Lee, ed. *Handbook of Speech Pathology and Audiology.* New York: Appleton-Century-Crofts, 1971.

Trice, H., and Roman, P. "The Self Reaction: A Neglected Dimension of Labelling Theory." Paper presented at the American Sociological Association Meeting, 1969.

Turner, Ralph. "Deviance Avowal as Neutralization of Commitments." *Social Problems* 19 (Winter, 1972): 308-22.

Van Riper, C. "Speech Defects among the Kalabash." *Marquette County Historical Society* 8 (December 1946): 333-37.

_____. *The Nature of Stuttering.* Englewood Cliffs, N.J.: Prentice-Hall, 1971.

_____. *Speech Correction: Principles and Methods.* Englewood Cliffs, N.J.: Prentice-Hall, 3rd ed., 1954; 4th ed., 1963.

_____. "The Effect of Devices for Minimizing Stuttering on the Creation of Symptoms." *Journal of Abnormal and Social Psychology* 32 (1937): 63-65.

_____. "Symptomatic Therapy for Stuttering." In *Handbook of Speech Pathology and Audiology,* edited by Lee Travis. New York: Appleton-Century-Crofts, 1971.

_____. *Do You Stutter?* New York: Harper and Row, 1939.

_____. "The Growth of the Stuttering Spasm." *Quarterly Journal of Speech* 23 (1931): 70-73.

Williams, D. "A Point of View About Stuttering." *Journal of Speech and Hearing Disorders* 22 (1957): 390-97.

Wingate, M. E. "Evaluation and Stuttering" *Journal of Speech and Hearing Disorders* 27 (1962): 106-15; 244-57; 368-77.

13
Deviance Disavowal and Stigma Management: A Study of Obesity

Alexander Himelfarb and John Evans

This study investigates the management of stigma – in this case, obesity. We concentrate on the management techniques of individuals who have accepted, at least to some degree, that they are fat. After briefly discussing some of the critical issues regarding "stigma" and "impression management," we present a description of the particular management techniques employed by the obese.

Data for this study are derived from a larger study, undertaken by one of the authors (Himelfarb), which involved participant observation research among groups of obese in a weight reduction programme. Fortunately for the purposes of this research, both authors have continued a more intimate, though less formal, research programme – being fat and managing it – and are thus able to draw from this first-hand data as well.

Most of us are usually concerned with presenting ourselves as "normal" members of society, and for this, we typically receive support. Although we are not necessarily aware of making a presentation, the process involved is by no means simple. In fact, the normal presentation of self relies on a common stock of taken-for-granted rules and on a set of sophisticated skills. When, for whatever reason, these rules and skills are not shared, interaction becomes problematic. When normality is denied we typically attempt its reaffirmation or terminate the interaction. The stranger may not possess the knowledge or techniques necessary for successful presentation. This is a dilemma we all experience from time to time. In fact, both the stranger and the sociologist are confronted with a major difficulty in attempting to acquire this knowledge: for the most part, it is taken for granted and hence not easily articulated.

We therefore have to devise special techniques to gain access to this taken-for-granted knowledge. One of the best methods for uncovering it consists simply of focusing on breakdowns – those instances in which a presentation is challenged or denied, or in which an actor feels dissatisfied with his own performance. Davis expresses this point well:

> . . . it can be said that our understanding of a mechanism is often crude and incomplete until it breaks down and we try to repair it (Davis, 1964: 135).

When break-downs are recurrent, the repair and management of identity becomes a matter of explicit concern. This is so in the case of individuals who feel they have a discreditable personal attribute.

The techniques of repair and management, however, will differ between those who judge their stigma to be visible and those who do not (Goffman, 1963:48). More specifically, those who feel that their stigma is invisible to others will generally employ techniques to keep it so; while those who feel that their stigma is visible to others will attempt to reduce its visibility, assert normality in spite of it, or actually discount it.

Since we are concerned with the role of the actor, it is important to point out that visibility is seldom a clear cut issue. That is, depending on the situation, the actor may be quite uncertain as to how others see him. For example, one obese person commented, "Almost every morning I have to ask my wife whether I look fat today. I can never tell. She usually says no, but I don't always believe her." In addition, many fat people commented, "Some days I wake up and feel fat while other days I feel fine." It is important to stress, then, that the specific management techniques employed will depend on the actor's definition of the situation. As we have indicated, this definition may change from day to day. In fact, much of the initial interaction between a stigmatized and a normal individual involves a search for the appropriate management techniques.

A related and equally important question is, impression management for whom? Management techniques are usually described as procedures utilized in presenting a positive image to others. Is this all that is involved? It would seem that in many cases an actor is as concerned with the impression he conveys to himself as with the impression others receive. Some obese people, for example, inform us that they do not like to be nude even when alone. Also, obese people are adept in their avoidance of scales. In each case it seems that these actors do not wish to be confronted with their own obesity.

We suggest, after Cooley (1903:151), that man's self-conception is a reflection of how he imagines others see and evaluate him. Even when man is alone, he can and does imagine how others would see and evaluate him. In any case, it seems evident that he will usually attempt to present himself in the best possible light for the benefit of both others and himself. Thus, it is important to stress that when we make the distinction between management techniques in public and private places, we do not mean to imply that public management techniques are for others' benefit alone or that private management techniques are for the benefit of self alone. The meaning of the concepts "self" and "other" can only be understood in terms of their relationship. Forcing a neat separation is nearly always misleading.

In some situations an obese person may experience some doubt about how fat he appears to be. If, in these situations, he judges his management techniques to be successful, that is, if he feels that he is not being perceived or treated as a fat person, he may come to doubt the extent of his stigma:

Sometimes when a girl treats you nice – just like anybody else, you start wondering, maybe they don't really think you are grotesque – maybe it's all in your head.

Hiding the Fat

Perhaps the most widespread technique for the management of obesity consists of attempts to hide or minimize the appearance of fatness. The most obvious and the most frequently used technique is to cover it. For the obese person his coat is his shield:

Being fat is so embarrassing that I wear my coat almost everywhere I go – even in the movies where it's dark.

Or, as a Weight Watchers' member describes her first appearance at a meeting:

I registered with all my fat tucked into a coat and oh! did I feel sloppy when I took that coat off to be weighed.

For many fat people their entire wardrobe seems to reflect this shielding function. Baggy pants, baggy sweaters, long skirts, and waistless dresses are always "in." More sophisticated camouflage involves making use of patterns and tailoring to "increase" height and "decrease" width; hence the preference for vertical stripes over checks in the selection of clothing. It seems unnecessary to emphasize the role of foundation garments in compacting fat.

However, one of the difficulties with props such as clothing is that there are occasions when one is expected to remove them. What begins as a relatively simple management technique becomes more complex and affects more and more areas of the individual's life:

I joined the 'Y,' but didn't enjoy it because I couldn't undress for the shower.

I used to swim, but now I can never go to the beach.

What's a bikini!

It is perhaps ironic that many of the activities we engage in to keep trim are out of bounds for the obese. Thus, joining a gym group, swimming, and exercising in public are avoided by many of the obese.

Perhaps more serious is the fact that for many of the obese, sex is purely theoretical; at the very least, sex presents embarrassing moments. As we would expect, sexual problems are frequently of central concern. For example, the conversation at a "men only" reduction group frequently revolved around the relationship between obesity and sexuality:

When I'm with a woman I lie on my back, my hands behind my head, stretching with every muscle – and hope that I don't have to move.

and from the same man:

You run the danger of being seen as a male chauvinist since you're always saying, "Will you get me a cigarette?" "Will you get me a drink?"

Would you believe that I've been married to my wife for twenty years and I'm still embarrassed about getting undressed in front of her.

It is clear from the example of our male respondent that fat people take certain physical postures which they hope will serve to hide their fat. For example, fat people will often sit on the edge of the chair so that the fat is not spread out; also, getting up may thus be made less difficult. Similarly, fat people will often wrap their arms around their middles when standing.

In summary then, it appears that the most frequent management techniques are camouflaging the fat; avoiding situations in which camouflage must be discarded; and, if these situations cannot be avoided, taking up postures which themselves attempt to hide the appearance of fatness.

Regardless of the camouflage, there is a generally held belief that numbers don't lie. For example, many obese people do not like to be measured for clothes. This may mean, as many of our informants report, that the obese person will frequently send someone else to purchase his clothing. For much the same reason, many obese people find mail order houses useful. The obese are also reluctant to reveal clothing size. One respondent protected herself from inadvertent disclosure by tearing off all her clothing labels. When discussion of clothing size cannot be avoided, many of our informants report that they lie about it. In fact, there seem to be size barriers beyond which many are reluctant to go: "When I got to size 40 I stopped buying pants."[1] What seems to be an extreme example of this same concern for numbers occurs when individuals "fit" into clothes which they themselves consider too small: "I was so happy to get into a size 14, I didn't mind not breathing."

Of course, it comes as no surprise to learn that the overweight are reluctant to reveal their weight:

Only my husband knows how much I weigh. If people ask, I like to have them guess – they often guess less!

I've only told one person my weight – and I lied to him.

Again, situations may be encountered which make it difficult to withhold this information. As one would expect, these situations are avoided as much as possible. For example, many of our informants reported that they avoided doctors even when they felt they "really should go."[2] Similarly, many of the clients of the reduction programme who are weighed each week reported this to be an uncomfortable experience:

> This is the first time I have weighed myself in public. It's painful.

This is not to suggest that when these numbers become public they cannot be denied:

> I don't weigh that much on the doctor's scale.

> Of course, I was fully dressed and I even had my purse!

> I shouldn't have had dinner just before I got weighed.

All these examples illustrate the importance of withholding information which would vitiate the camouflage (Goffman, 1963:91); when the information does "get out," an attempt is made to alter its meaning.

One of the more interesting findings is that camouflage and other management techniques are not designed solely for others. Part of the reason for this may be that confidence in camouflage is impaired if one constantly reminds oneself of the fact of his obesity. As we have already mentioned, some obese people dislike being in the nude even when alone. In addition, they may avoid their own private scales. They may even avoid their own reflection:

> When I walk down the street I can't look in shop windows – I might see myself.

> The two greatest villains are my tailor and his mirror.

This backstage behaviour is a most important part of our preparation for interaction. That is, we often prepare ourselves to believe in the performance we are about to give.

When we have no confidence in our performance, when our management techniques seem to have failed, we may avoid interaction. This may involve social or even physical withdrawal. As we have seen, some social withdrawal is common even for those who think their management techniques are relatively effective. For those who have lost confidence in their performance, social withdrawal may be more extreme:

> I tended to withdraw into myself. To be in a corner or on the sidelines at parties.

When the individual feels he is grotesque, to others and to himself, physical withdrawal may seem to be the only answer:

> I would go home and lock the door and wouldn't even go out for groceries.

Being Normal

Camouflaged fat can be exposed not only by uncovering it; it can be exposed as well by "acting fat." There are a number of behaviour patterns associated with obesity, which a person who runs some risk of being seen as obese does well to avoid. We identify and discuss three patterns of "obese" behaviour: behaviour which most people see as the cause of obesity; behaviour generally seen to be the consequence of obesity; and behaviour generally taken as proof of the consciousness of obesity.

Eating "too much," eating "too often," and eating the "wrong" foods are all seen as causes of fat.[3] It is not surprising, therefore, that many obese people take these common perceptions into account in preparing their presentations:

> When I am out in public I tend to eat less than I ordinarily would. No, it is when I am alone that I overeat.

> You know what I like best about the movies? It's dark so I can sit there and feed my face.

> French fries! I'd never eat those in public.

Obviously, what is going on is an attempt on the part of the fat person to eat like a normal person.

Control of public eating may be relatively easily accomplished. However, managing behaviours which are perceived as consequences of being overweight may present greater difficulties. It is difficult to be normal if you simply cannot walk easily up a hill. In order to protect the veracity of your normal presentation, you avoid walking up the hill. If you must, perhaps you *run* up the hill, so that you have every reason to puff.

> When I'm at the office I work harder and longer than anybody else. I never stop going. There's no way I'm a fat person at the office.

Behaviours such as these are frequently described as overcompensations. We have no quarrel with this if the overcompensation is seen as a stricter interpretation of performance rules because of a greater sense of vulnerability and a greater awareness that this is, in fact, a performance.

Precisely because the obese person is presenting himself as normal, it is important that he not spoil the presentation by admitting to consciousness of fat. For example, many obese persons will not buy diet foods:

> I never used to buy diet pop. That would have been admitting I was fat.

> I never told anyone about attending Weight Watchers.

> I used to get my wife to buy Metrecal for me. She hated it – people would think it was for her.

> I stopped ordering salads when people asked if I was on a diet.[4]

These, then, are techniques for being normal – "passing" (Goffman, 1963:73).[5] We have previously mentioned that visibility is not a clear cut issue. In many situations, then, passing will appear to be a possibility. But all fat people encounter situations in which passing does not work or is simply out of the question. It is to these situations that we now turn.

Being Almost Normal[6]

> It is a fact that persons who are ready to admit possession of a stigma (in many cases because it is known about or immediately apparent) may nonetheless make a great effort to keep the stigma from looming large. The individual's object is to reduce tension, that is, to make it easier for himself and the others to withdraw covert attention from the stigma, and to sustain spontaneous involvement in the official content of the interaction (Goffman, 1963: 102).

As Goffman points out, those techniques used for minimizing the impact of stigma in interaction are often similar or identical to the techniques used for passing. Thus, all of the management techniques previously discussed apply here as well. The obese man who works harder than everybody else does so, not to hide the fact of fat, but to say, I'm normal despite it – I'm almost normal. The obese person may, in fact, be making two statements: I am not that fat, and However fat I am, we should not let it become central in our interaction. In this section we will be concerned with techniques which are primarily directed at saying, It's not that important.

The best way of demonstrating that it is not that important is to minimize the concern one shows for one's fat – hence, the jolly fat person:

> But we all know what it feels like to be singled out as a 'fatty.'

> When we were fat, and somebody made fun of us, we were always ready with a quick comeback, or we laughed it off. But inside we hurt, we felt like crying, like building a wall around us.

> At a convention my husband introduced me to a business acquaintance. This person said, "Oh, this is your bigger – oops! – better half." Straight away I said, "Bigger and better."

A related, but bolder, technique is to take the initiative, to make the first comment or joke about your girth:

> When I meet somebody new, I usually like to tell a joke about my fat. That way it's over with.

What this technique does, as our informants are aware, is to get out of the way comments about weight which would otherwise "hang in the background of the entire conversation." At the same time, it serves to demonstrate the individual's willingness to discuss his weight, and, hence, by inference, his lack of concern over it. *– but less concerned*

Another way to be almost normal is to have normal friends. Having fat friends may serve to underline your own fat. On the other hand, as should by now be obvious, interaction with "thins" may not always be easy. Demonstrating your lack of concern over an issue which concerns you is taxing. Fat people generally welcome the opportunity to be off stage and "be themselves." This may be possible with other "fats." Though many of the activities at "fat farms" may be unpleasant, many of the customers enjoy the opportunity to relax their performance. Perhaps the best compromise between "fat farms" and thin friends are understanding normals:[7]

> I have this one friend, I can talk about my fat or not; she talks about it or not. It doesn't seem to matter.

Again, we note with interest backstage behaviour which may serve to maintain or increase the individual's confidence in his ability to perform well in the future. For example, several of our informants reported consciously looking for people fatter than they:

> Whenever I sit on the bus, I'm always hoping that someone *really fat* will get on.

A more subtle point is raised by another informant who commented:

> I really like watching fat people talking to their friends. It's fascinating to see how both handle it.

In the first example, it seems the fat person is attempting to assess how fat he really is – hoping he really isn't. In the second example, the individual seems to be assessing, more generally, the importance of fat in interaction. It is clear that such information would be helpful in developing smooth performances. In addition, we may speculate that these informants are searching for information which would allow them to deny, with confidence, the centrality of their obesity.

Accounts

At this point, we must deal with those situations in which obesity becomes central. In these situations, the fat person often feels called upon to do some repair work; that is, he may feel compelled to account for his fat. Account giving (Scott and Lyman, 1968) is a form of management used to help save face (Goffman, 1955) and to allow interaction to proceed more smoothly. Of course, such accounts are not manufactured on the spot each time interaction difficulties occur, but are constructed on the basis of past experience and the specifics of the present situation.

We distinguish among three classes of accounts: denying the fact; denying its importance; and denying responsibility for it:

> I have a large frame, big bones. Just look at my wrist!

> It's really weird. I look so much fatter with my clothes on.

> It's just baby fat.

All of these accounts serve to deny the fact of fat. These people agree that they may give the appearance of fat; however, it is not really fat. That this type of account is common is reflected in their choice of words to describe themselves to others. Such labels as heavyweight, big, large, stocky, bulky, portly, and pleasantly plump, contain implicit denial. That these terms, or others like them, are the ones we are most likely to use in interaction with our fat friends suggests that we are often willing to support this type of account.

Other accounts serve to deny the importance of the fat. In fact, some of our informants do this directly. They may agree that it is undesirable, but insist that one should not be obsessed with weight. Many claim that their fatness is a temporary condition and therefore not very serious:

> I always put it on in the winter and take it right off in the summer.

Others insist that fat is ubiquitous. They make reference to the fatness of most people, suggesting that their fat is only relative:

> Just look at the statistics; almost everyone in North America is overweight.

They may make reference to particular groups of fat people:

> I just got back from Hawaii. Those people are really fat – not just fifty pounds overweight.

They may cite particular people:

> I'm lucky; I'm fat but I don't really look it. It's worse for my friend; she's fat and she looks even fatter.

> Those roller-derby girls have to be fat to get their job done, and they get it done for sure.

In this last account, citing successful or famous fat people may serve as a strong demonstration that fat is not too important.[8]

When fat cannot be denied or minimized the individual can still offer an account – in this case, the denial of responsibility. When a fat person insists that he "eats like a bird," has "only one meal a day," "never eats lunch," etc., he is denying responsibility for his weight. He may, however, find it necessary to offer some further explanation. This may involve attributing his obesity to biological or physiological factors:

> My parents were fat, their parents were fat. I just feel sorry for my kids.

> I got this metabolism thing.

Many obese women are in the fortunate position of being able to provide an account which is not only seen by many as legitimate, but even to their credit – pregnancy. Unfortunately, its legitimacy may be questioned if it is used as a permanent account.

Another way of denying responsibility is to cite environmental factors as the cause of obesity:

> I learned my bad eating habits from my parents. It's awful what parents can do to their kids.

An account which involves a greater degree of complexity is the "sad tale":

> It was the first time I was away from home. The classes were all so large, and I didn't know anyone. I had to eat in restaurants all the time. Everyone seemed so unfriendly. In the end, whenever I got lonely, I just ate.

The sad tales do not completely deny responsibility for obesity, but rather assert that the circumstances were greater than any individual. The assertion is, then, that anyone in similar circumstances would be similarly affected – "After all, I'm only human."

A more subtle way of handling the issue of responsibility is to dissociate yourself from your past. If you make public the fact that you are dieting, you assert that you should be judged on the basis of your present display of will power, rather than on past sins. In other words, you are not necessarily denying responsibility, you are disowning the fat person you used to be. More generally, statements of self-abuse may also serve to separate the "real you" from the "fat you."

Another account takes the radical posture (Matza, 1964:41) that fat is where it's at. Such accounts do not apologize for being fat, they flaunt it. For example, fat fashion shows and fat is beautiful groups are relatively recent additions to the liberation theme. In addition, they have received support from fat celebrities[9] who insist that fat is a sign or result of character, spirit, love of life, or some other rare and desirable quality.

Summary and Conclusions

It should be evident that the primary stigma management technique is the disavowal of deviance. Disavowal of deviance may involve techniques ranging from the denial that the actor belongs in the deviant category to denial that the category is, in fact, deviant. Of course, most actors do not make exclusive use of techniques at the extremes. Rather, depending upon the specific nature of the interaction, the same actor may try to hide, cover, minimize, or even disown his stigma.

Studying the management of obesity requires no special justification; it is interesting. Such a study, however, attempts primarily to make explicit certain implicit features of everyday interaction: everyone performs; controls vital information; hides negative attributes; and tries to account for performance failures. By studying the obese, we are studying everyday interaction.

We began with the assertion that presenting a normal face to the world is important for most of us. In presenting this face, nearly everyone feels the possibility of being discredited. In studying the obese, we are studying ourselves.

Notes

[1] Many respondents reported that it was when they reached these barriers that they decided to take some action to reduce their obesity.

[2] Many informants stressed as well that they wished to avoid doctors because they often felt abused by them.

[3] This is not to suggest that other factors are not seen as causes; these are

the causes which the fat person can attempt to deal with in public.

⁴ This irony may be more meaningful to our thin reader if he imagines, for example, the adult who refuses to take swimming lessons because he does not want to be seen as a non-swimmer.

⁵ By "passing," we do not intend to imply that the passing is successful, only that it is attempted.

⁶ Goffman (1963:102) discusses many of these techniques as techniques of "covering."

⁷ See Davis (1964), for an excellent discussion of the processes whereby normals become understanding. See also, Gowman (1956).

⁸ Compare Lucas' (1969:199) discussion of "precedent citation" as a technique of neutralization.

⁹ For good examples of the radical defense, see the "works" of Victor Buono and Totie Fields.

References

Cooley, C. H. *Human Nature and the Social Order*. New York: Charles Scribner's Sons, 1903.

Davis, Fred. "Deviance Disavowal: The Management of Strained Interaction by the Visibly Handicapped." *The Other Side: Perspectives on Deviance*, edited by Howard S. Becker. Glencoe: The Free Press, 1964.

Goffman, Erving. "On Face-Work." *Psychiatry* 18(1955):213-31.

_____. *Stigma: Notes on the Management of Spoiled Identity*. Englewood Cliffs, N.J.: Prentice-Hall, 1963.

Gowman, A. G. "Blindness and the Role of the Companion." *Social Problems* 4 (July 1956): 68-75.

Himelfarb, A. In progress "Stigma, Selves, and Others."

Lucas, Rex. *Men in Crisis: A Study of a Mine Disaster*. New York: Basic Books, 1969.

Matza, David. *Delinquency and Drift*. New York: John Wiley & Sons, 1964.

Scott, M. B., and Lyman, S. M. "Accounts." *American Sociological Review* 33 (February 1968): 46-62.

14
Becoming a Homesexual

Peter Sawchuk

In virtually every major North American urban centre a significant proportion of the male homosexual population participates in and forms a loosely organized collectivity that may be termed a community.[1] This is not a community in the traditional sense; rather, I use the term in the sense of a community of understanding involving shared perspectives and expectations, and arising out of the continuing shared activity and interaction of the members and their common commitment. Hooker states with respect to this use of the term:

> If . . . one is permitted to use the term [community] to refer to an aggregate of persons engaging in common activities, sharing common interests, and having a feeling of socio-psychological unity, with variations in the degree to which persons have these characteristics depending on whether they constitute the core of the periphery then it is completely germane to homosexuals (Hooker 1967, p. 171).

The process by which an individual becomes a member of the homosexual community typically follows a pre-entrance period of self-identification, during which the individual identifies himself as a homosexual. The decision to manage this identity by participation in the organized group life of fellow homosexuals, marks the beginning of a process of socialization, whereby the individual's homosexual identification is reinforced by the various activities, people, places, events, and beliefs that compose the homosexual community. The result of this process is a socialized member who, in varying degrees, identifies with the community and is subject to its norms, values, and contingencies. The entrance phase is referred to as "coming out" and begins when the individual makes public his homosexual identification in the presence of other homosexuals.

Self-identification as a homosexual has upon occasion been equated with entrance into the homosexual community. For example, Burgess states:

> His full development as a homosexual comes only when he identifies himself as a homosexual. This typically coincides with his entrance into the homosexual world. His recognition of himself as a homosexual has a special term in the jargon of this society, it is called coming out (Burgess 1949, p. 234).

This equation fails to distinguish between the process by which an individual comes to identify himself as a homosexual and the manner in which he chooses to manage this identity. It appears however, as Achilles (1964) has noted, that the processes of self-identification and group affiliation are generally distinct. An individual may identify himself as a homosexual long before he chooses to enter the homosexual community. Similarly, many individuals define themselves as homosexuals and yet choose to remain isolated.

In considering the lines of development by which an individual becomes a member of the homosexual community, I am, as Becker states,

> . . . not so much interested in the person who commits a deviant act once, as in the person who sustains a pattern of deviance over a long period of time, who makes deviance a way of life, who organizes his identity around a pattern of deviant behavior (Becker 1963, p. 30).

A highly useful concept in this regard is that of "career." This concept refers, in the current context, to the sequence of movements or changes in position that occur over time and that are common to members of a social category. This concept allows one to focus on the relation between changes in self-concept and the complex of personal relationships and experiences an individual moves through. In large part I am concerned with the moral aspects of an individual's career, that is, the subjective changes in the way the individual views himself and others (Goffman 1961a, pp. 127-38). This paper then considers two phases of an individual's career as a homosexual: the process by which an individual comes to identify himself as a homosexual, and the process by which an individual becomes socialized and integrated into the homosexual community.

The study upon which this paper is based was conducted in the city of Montreal. Participant observation and unstructured interviews were the method used to collect the data. As a participant observer I "hung out" with a group of participants, primarily in gay bars, and subsequently recorded my observations. My original access to the homosexual community was through an informal source. Space does not permit a complete discussion of my research role; nevertheless, I should point out that without the assistance of those individuals who provided social introductions and who acted as my guides in the homosexual community it is doubtful this project would have been completed.

Interviews were informal and open ended. I interviewed twelve individuals. This is a rather small interview sample; nevertheless, it does reflect, in part, some of the difficulty one encounters in finding individuals willing to discuss the broad range of personal matters required for a career analysis. Interviewees ranged in age from seventeen to forty, while the majority were in their twenties. All respondents were males. Occupationally the sample ranged from those in executive positions, to students, to those employed in a variety of service and clerical occupations. This sample is, of course, in no way random; it is, however, fairly representative in the sense that in addition to including individuals of varying personal experience as homosexuals, it includes individuals whose involvement in the homosexual community is central to their lives and those for whom it is more peripheral.

Awareness of Being Different

Becoming a homosexual initially involves a process of self-discovery. The homosexual, unlike those who are stigmatized very early in life, usually becomes aware of his stigma during adolescence. This discovery involves the recognition of a subjective attraction to members of one's own sex, often occasioned or verified through a sexual encounter. Psychoanalytic theories trace the origins of homosexuality to early childhood psycho-sexual development in the context of the family; however, from a sociological point of view the recognition of intrinsically rewarding, subjective, homosexual attractions and accompanying experiences may be regarded as the beginning of the individual's homosexual career. A respondent comments on this discovery:

> (What first made you think you might be gay?)

> Well, little things like one thing I remember, like on the bus, if I was sitting next to a good-looking guy I'd get excited, you know what I mean? Actually that happened a lot, I remember thinking that there must be something about the movement of the bus that was sexually stimulating. Or, well, like when I'd masturbate I found it made it better, you know, more exciting, to think about guys.

The individual, by this stage in life, is likely to have internalized the conventional or "normal" (in the sense of typical) perspective regarding an appropriate sexual orientation; hence, the recognition of homosexual attractions can lead to a sense of personal conflict and make self-acceptance problematic. The individual may define his homosexual feelings negatively and attempt to follow a conventional sexual pattern. Those who are successful in this endeavor may attribute their homosexuality to an adolescent phase and terminate their careers as homosexuals. In many cases, however, this does not present a desirable or practicable alternative.

Failure to develop a conventional sexual orientation can have a powerful impact on the individual's self-concept. Cory describes how he struggled against his homosexual orientation and made resolutions to refrain from homosexual activity. Failure to do so, however, reinforced the notion of the centrality, permanence, and immutability of homosexuality:

> . . . I had learned a cruel lesson, and one worth learning. No teacher but life itself could have convinced me that homosexual passions do not come and go at will but cling relentlessly to the last breath of life (Cory 1951, p. 9).

To the extent that the individual finds conventional sexual alternatives and responses impracticable or unappealing, the notion of the centrality of deviance and homosexuality is fostered. This experience leads to the realization that he is indeed different and contributes to the process of self-redefinition as a homosexual.

The individual's sense of being different may be further compounded by the social situation in which he finds himself. First, unlike the racially or ethnically stigmatized, such an individual is not supported by conventional primary groups and group traditions which provide established methods of identity management. Rather, the individual is likely to feel isolated and estranged from his family and conventional associates:

> Most gay people feel caught in an insoluable dilemma, if we disclose our homosexuality to our parents we will risk anger and pain. Yet, if we hide it we must drift apart avoiding any contact that might uncover our essential selves (Altman 1971, p. 40).

Furthermore, the lack of social support, that is, his having to handle things on his own, may further compound the individual's sense of isolation and alienation. A respondent comments:

> No, why should I tell them [parents]? They never told me anything about sex. No, really, I really resent that. I had to find everything out for myself. I don't see why I should tell them now.

Secondly, unlike other types of stigmatized individuals, such as the physically handicapped, homosexually oriented persons are frequently held responsible for their sexual orientation. An element of volition is imputed to their sexual preferences. As Altman says, " . . . there remains always the suspicion that we could rid ourselves of it, if we wanted to enough" (Altman 1971, p. 40). To the extent that a homosexual shares this view he faces the additional problem of managing guilt.

Identification and Accommodation

An important aspect of an individual's career as a homosexual involves the learning process through which he becomes aware of the personal consequences of being a homosexual. Through various experiences he learns or infers what it means to others for him to be a homosexual and how their reactions can affect him personally. The individual may have a vague and general prior awareness that homosexuality is socially disapproved of or, to use Matza's term, "banned";[2] however, the significance of these experiences is that he comes to realize the consequences and implications that "the ban" entails for his own life.

One type of experience involves what may be termed public reactions. Generally these occur in the context of passing encounters between unacquainted homosexuals and heterosexuals. In such an encounter the homosexual who is identified as such may sense varying degrees of moral disapproval; and he may find he is not accorded the approval and acceptance forthcoming an ordinary individual in good standing. The individual may realize that the actual consequences of this type of reaction are generally limited; the heterosexual actors do not represent official agencies nor do they exercise significant control over his personal biography; hence, these encounters often merely amount to "embarrassing incidents." Nevertheless, the individual who is involved, or who perhaps witnesses such an encounter, realizes that to identify oneself as a homosexual is to risk transforming a routine encounter into an embarrassing situation:

> I had to go to this doctor for a physical; my mother took out an insurance policy on me so I needed a medical examination. Anyways, he was filling out this form, you know – T.B., heart disease, and then he asked, "Have you ever seen a psychiatrist?" So, I figured what the hell, he's a doctor, he's no fool, not some Joe on the street, why shouldn't I tell him, I don't have to lie. So I said yes. And he says, "For what reason?" So I said, "I went because I'm a homosexual." And this stupid nurse standing there, her mouth dropped open and she stared at me like I'm some kind of a freak or something. It was horrible. The doctor was pretty much okay, he just dropped his eyes to the form and got all stiff and quickly went on to something else. But it was ridiculous, it made me feel like some kind of freak.

A second type of experience involves the reactions of significant others. These include heterosexuals involved in significant relationships with the individual, such as parents and employers. In certain situations the individual may learn how these persons regard the type of person he can be proven to be; and based upon their response he infers how they may react toward him should they become aware of his sexual orientation. A respondent provides the following example:

> I was in the car with my father and some guy cut him off, so he started screaming at the guy "You goddamn cocksucker," and I thought to myself, "You fool, that's what I am, a cocksucker."

These reactions are seen by the individual as potentially consequential; he realizes that a negative response from these parties could have disruptive implications for the relationships upon which he is both emotionally and practically dependent.

Finally, the individual may learn how various agents of social control regard and treat those whom they consider to be homosexual. The reactions of these agents may be seen as most consequential by the individual because of the societal authority they represent and can invoke:

> I was walking in the park, up the road near _____ Avenue. I was just taking a walk, but these two police on horses came over and stopped me. One of them said, "There are a lot of queers around here and they might try to pick up a young guy like you." I was so surprised I just said, "Oh." Then the other one said, "We try to keep the queers over here. If you want to walk, try the other side; there are a lot of girls over there."

Realizing the significance others attach to being a homosexual contributes to making the individual's sexual orientation of special significance to him as well. He comes to regard himself as a special kind of person, a person for whom life holds special contingencies and discrediting possibilities:

> Attentive to the methods of deviation even before their concrete appearance, the wrong-minded subject acts in terms of them. He takes into account the meaning of ban and, for that reason, proceeds to become somewhat more deviant. (Matza 1969, p. 148)

The process of developing a deviant identity and commitment is further advanced by an important career contingency – the experience of being publicly labelled a deviant.

This can set into play a self-fulfilling prophecy whereby the individual comes to regard himself as others do and organizes his life around this new identity and the deviant behaviour. A similar outcome may occur when the negative response is merely anticipated. Homosexuality, unlike certain forms of physical stigma, is not readily apparent. The homosexual may choose to pass for a heterosexual. The homosexual who is not labelled, but who sees himself as potentially discreditable, faces problems of information and impression management. In many cases, as Kitsuse (1962) points out, the expected hostile response is not forthcoming; however, to the extent that a negative social response is anticipated, and consequently disclosure is feared, the individual's behaviour is likely to be designed to maintain secrecy and avoid labelling. In this way, the individual may come to organize his life in a particular way around the deviant behaviour:

> Well, for example, like on the street, I'd worry about the way I'd walk and, you know, once you become self-conscious about

something like that it's next to impossible to act natural. Or like once at school I was carrying my black brief case, the one from Europe, and this character in one of my classes came up and says, "Oh, is that your new purse?" I didn't know what to say, I thought, "Christ, he must know."

The individual who fears disclosure must pay special attention to how others will interpret the cues he emits and the appearance he presents. To preclude "giving himself away," he watches himself in the same way he believes others do. He engages in a conscious deception – pretending to be the kind of person he would have others believe he is, but that he has reason to believe he is not. As Matza states, "He is engaged in a remarkable project of imitation – being himself as he thinks he is ordinarily" (Matza: 1969 p. 153). In the process of keeping his secret he comes to alter his conception of those from whom the secret must be kept. Again, Matza comments:

> . . . he has created some distance between himself and right-minded associates. Acting with guile, he has misled them; he has worked the bluff. Even if only slightly he has alienated himself from their company. Spurred by ban, the subject has behaved deceptively. In that process he is led to discover certain features of the right-minded – their gullibility, their misunderstanding and perhaps even an over-assiduous interest which may later be conceived as a sign of hypocrisy. (Matza 1969, p. 154)

A basic problem for the individual who attempts to "pass" is that he can never be entirely certain how well the deception is working. A consequence of this uncertainty is that when he experiences social rejection, the basis of which is vague, ambiguous, and ill-defined, he may infer that he is being rejected because homosexuality is known or suspected. The following comment illustrates how an individual may infer the basis of rejection:

> I really don't like to go to his house.

> (Why not?)

> His parents, they make me feel uncomfortable. I don't really know if they suspect something or not. Once they almost caught us in bed together, we heard them coming and got dressed, but it's like maybe they sense something. Like I get this feeling the way his mother and sister look at me that they know all about me. Maybe they think I'm corrupting their son or something. It just makes me nervous to go there.

It appears that the concern with information control, and the consequent organization of everyday behaviour in a particular way to prevent disclosure, make the concept of homosexuality and deviance increasingly significant and contribute to its centrality in the individual's self-concept.

During the process of self-redefinition as a homosexual, self-acceptance may be made difficult by a sense of personal conflict, isolation from family, anxiety regarding discovery, and a sense of guilt. Individuals who experience these problems may seek professional help in an attempt to learn more about their sexual orientation, and to seek an adjustment to it. Most often this is likely to involve a psychiatrist, although doctors and religious leaders may also be consulted. However, to the extent that an individual finds this experience unrewarding, discouraging, or frustrating, it is likely to convince him further of the immutability and centrality of his sexual orientation. The individual who finds himself cast in the role of patient or psycho-neurotic in such therapeutic encounters may find it easier and personally less costly to continue his deviant behaviour:

> I finally decided to see a psychiatrist, so I went to the mental health service at school. I told my friends I was going because of depression, because I didn't want anyone to know; but actually I really was depressed. But, anyway, he really made me mad, you know. He'd never tell me anything. I'd do all the talking and he'd just nod and then after four weeks he told me my problem was fairly serious and that I'd have to see him on a private basis. He meant pay him! So I said the hell with that. I wasn't about to become a mental patient for his benefit.

One further feature of the individual's identity transformation remains to be considered – its retroactive character. The individual who redefines himself as a homosexual reinterprets his past experience in the light of his new self-concept. In this way the validity of his new self-definition is conformed: he comes to realize he has always been a homosexual:[3]

> Now I realize I always liked sleeping with other men. Like even when I was a kid I remember I used to like to sleep with my cousin, and like to sleep really close. I never had sex with him or anything like that, it's just that I didn't know it then but now I see what was really going on.

Entrance into the Homosexual Community

The individual who identifies himself as a homosexual is faced with the problem of managing this identity. There are several alternatives. He may repress his homosexual feelings. He may attempt to conform to a heterosexual pattern while confining homosexual activity to anonymous sexual encounters (Humphreys 1970). He may, while defining himself as homosexual, isolate himself from the homosexual community. Or, he may enter the homosexual community. The factors involved in choosing a particular strategy would appear to involve the extent to which the individual is constrained by conventional commitments and social controls and his ability to compartmentalize and neutralize these commitments and controls.

An individual enters the homosexual community by publicly labelling himself a homosexual in the presence of other homosexuals. This is referred to as "coming out" or "making one's debut." Most frequently this public declaration takes place in the "gay" bar, although other gatherings, such as parties, may provide the setting.

An individual may enter the bar alone or in the company of initiated friends. If he enters alone the initial visit is often accompanied by considerable apprehension and uncertainty. "Coming out" is a crucial turning point in the individual's career, a decision the total consequences of which are often unknown. Accordingly, initial visits are often tentative, exploratory ventures. One respondent describes his initial visit as follows:

> I was petrified. You go in there and you pray that no one says anything to you. If someone talks to you you're terrified, and if some queen decides to play it up, you want to die. Like now I can handle any queen. I can out-bitch any of them. They're harmless, they'd never do anything there. But if you're new and don't know, you could die of fright.

Unfamiliarity with the standing behaviour pattern can lead to further tension. Situations that constitute "normal trouble" in the bar can provide the basis for apprehension:

> I remember the first night I went. I ordered a coke and you know unless you order liquor they don't hear you, so the waiter says again in a loud voice, "What do you want?" I was very embarrassed. Now it's all different. I feel very at home in the bars, but at first it was very frightening.

> I was going up the stairs to the L____ and this queen comes over and says, "Shall I rape you now or later honey?" I was so shocked, I didn't know what to say. Of course, they were only kidding but when someone says that to you it shocks you.

The individual who enters the "gay" bar with others who are already acquainted with the community, and to whom he has already identified himself as a homosexual, usually finds the experience less frightening. In effect, he is sponsored and this eases his introduction into the community and speeds his integration with it. Furthermore, he is likely to receive advice on how to conduct himself and, in general, what to expect. This information gives him a greater amount of control over the new situation.

Entrance often takes the form of a "coming-out" ceremony, in that the newcomer's entrance may be the focus of interest and entertainment. During field observation I observed the following:

> A young man entered the "gay" bar accompanied by another young man with whom he was living at the time. The entrant's partner was a habitué at the club. They sat at a table and about five minutes later were joined by four other habitués who were all friends of the entrant's partner. The young man was introduced and it was mentioned that it was his first time in a gay club. One friend said, "Oh, so you're making your debut?" All attention was focussed on the new-comer. There was a great deal of joking, story telling, and laughing, in the course of which the habitués translated the terms they were using and explained the events that were transpiring in the bar around them. When other friends approached they were introduced to the new-comer and informed that it was his "debut." Some offered congratulations in a joking manner. At one point the entrant and his partner went over to the bar at the suggestion of the partner. At the bar the partner instructed the newcomer regarding his social demeanor: "You're talking to these guys like they're the people at school, and they're not! You can't come on too friendly or they'll think you want to make it with them. You've got to be more cool."

The individual who "comes out" finds his feelings of apprehension and uncertainty regarding this decision diminished by several important discoveries. He learns that homosexuals in the community are generally young and attractive and not, in the main, effeminate; that the homosexual population, judging by the varied representation in the bars, is extensive; and that the opportunities for sexual contact are many. Furthermore, especially if he is young and good-looking, he discovers that not only is he accepted, but by virtue of being new, he is popular and is actively sought out. These discoveries increase the likelihood that the individual will accept the "gay world" and define participation in it positively.

A further factor influencing acceptance is often the marked contrast between this stage of the individual's career and the pre-"coming out" period. A respondent who had recently "come out" states:

> After years of having sex, maybe once a month in some bathroom around ..., and all the frustrations and anxiety, it's wonderful to come out of your closet. Suddenly you know all these people, you're having lots of sex, it's terrific for the first few months. A lot of people go overboard, I know I did. The gay life is so fantastic and interesting, all these people, more friends than you've ever had before, friends from all over the world. It's incredible.

Socialization into the Homosexual Community

As the newcomer participates in the homosexual community, the process of discovery and learning continues. The more experienced members that the individual meets act as tutors; under their guidance he becomes acquainted with the complex of places, activities, people, and events that compose the "gay" life. As this new world opens up before him, he comes to realize the opportunity it provides for varied sexual and social experiences. He learns to regard the "gay" life as exciting and intriguing. In short, he learns the rewards of participation. Similarly, he acquires the skills necessary for participation. He learns various contact or "cruising"[4] techniques, types of sexual activity, ways of avoiding problems with the police, the homosexual argot, and the location and particular features of the public setting that serves the homosexual collectivity. Finally, the individual incorporates the community's ideology. This system of ideas supports homosexual activity and thus neutralizes feelings of guilt and inferiority, and contributes to greater self-acceptance.

The "coming-out" period is marked by a high degree of involvement and participation in the homosexual community. This is largely due to the realization of the aforementioned rewards of the "gay" life. The pattern of participation involves bar going, parties, and affairs. Concurrent with this greater involvement with homosexuals is a withdrawal from heterosexual groups. This can lead to problems with respect to the neglect of conventional associations and responsibilities, such as family, friends, job and school.

Furthermore the homosexual group rewards this withdrawal and provides a rationale for it. The entrant is told that "straights" and "gays" are essentially different. Homosexuals are reported to be more sensitive, talented, adventurous, cosmopolitan, and open-minded; while heterosexuals are generally considered boring, narrow-minded, conventional, and perhaps hypocritical. As the entrant incorporates the perspective of the homosexual group vis-à-vis the out-group, he learns to redefine himself in terms of his new group affiliation. He is "gay" first and foremost:

> (How do you view "straights"?)

> Well, I suppose it sort of varies for different periods but I went through this thing for a long time where you know – "Oh, straights are all boring" – because I'd just gotten into getting to know homosexuals and I didn't like anyone else. Now, most of my friends are straight but when I started thinking about it I had to admit my homosexuality is the most important thing about me.

The "coming out" period ends once the individual has been socialized, trained, and integrated into the perspectives, practices, and structure of the homosexual community. This process usually lasts a few months and is terminated when the individual is no longer considered a "new face," but must compete with other members on a more or less equal basis in the sexual market:

> At first the gay life is simply incredible; but after maybe three months you get over it. I've sat in D's on a crowded night and I'd slept with every person in the place. All these faggots would be sitting by the door tearing their hair waiting for a new face. It can get boring after a while.

Conclusion

Homosexuals are persons whose identities are stigmatized; like other stigmatized individuals, they face problems of self-acceptance and identity management. For the individual who comes to identify himself as a homosexual, participation in the organized group life of fellow homosexuals provides a method for dealing with these problems. The individual's self-identity and his commitment to it are reinforced and stabilized by his interaction with the homosexual community. He learns through more experienced members how to manage his homosexual activity and identity with a minimum of difficulty: the former through the acquisition of various skills; the latter through the incorporation of a new ideology which encourages self-acceptance and supports continued participation.

Notes

[1] Female homosexuals form communities as well (see Simon and Gagnon 1967); however, the focus in this paper is upon the male homosexual community and the careers of male homosexuals.

[2] Matza (1969) provides a more complete discussion of the effect of "ban" on the individual, the process of signification and the entire process of becoming deviant.

[3] Similarly, Goffman (1961) in discussing the mental patient's moral career mentions how once the individual comes to regard himself as a mental patient he comes to adopt a view of his past that is consistent with this self-definition.

[4] The term "cruising" refers to the search for sexual partners.

Bibliography

Achilles, Nancy. "The Homosexual Bar." Master' thesis, University of Chicago, 1964.

Altman, Dennis. *Homosexual: Oppression and Liberation*. New York: Outerbridge and Dienstfrey, 1971.

Becker, Howard. *Outsiders: Studies in the Sociology of Deviance*. New York: The Free Press of Glencoe, 1963.

Burgess, Edward W. "The Sociologic Theory of Psychosexual Behaviour." *Psychosexual Development in Health and Disease*, edited by P. Hoch and J. Zubin. New York: Grune and Stratton, 1949.

Cory, Donald. *The Homosexual in America*. New York: Castle Books, 1951.

Goffman, Erving. *Asylums*. New York: Doubleday 1961.

Hooker, Evelyn. "The Homosexual Community." In *Sexual Deviance,* edited by J. Gagnon and W. Simon, pp. 167-84. New York: Harper and Row, 1967.

Humphreys, L. *Tearoom Trade*. Chicago: Aldine, 1970.

Kitsuse, John. "Societal Reactions to Deviant Behaviour: Problems of Theory and Method." *Social Problems* 9 (Winter 1962): 247-56.

Matza, David. *Becoming Deviant*. Englewood Cliffs, N.J.: Prentice-Hall, 1969.

Simon, W. and J. Gagnon. "The Lesbians: A Preliminary Overview." In *Sexual Deviance,* edited by J. Gagnon and W. Simon, pp. 247-82. New York: Harper and Row, 1967.

15
Becoming a Militant Poor Person in Canada

Lawrence Felt

The rediscovery of extensive poverty in Canada became a familiar topic to many Canadians in the late 1960s. Countless articles in the mass media on the plight of some Canadians, and numerous provincial and federal government sponsored studies, including a prestigious Senate investigation, can be offered as indications of the extent of concern. I stress the rediscovered nature of this concern with poverty because the most cursory investigation of Canada's past suggests that the recognition of poverty as a social problem is a cyclical phenomenon occurring periodically only to become ignored and later rediscovered.[1] (The social processes underlying this cycle of concern, while exceedingly interesting, are beyond the scope of this essay.) Despite the current popularity of poverty, there is little, if any, evidence that significant inroads have been achieved in combatting it.

Such concern with poverty in Canada has not occurred without some impact being felt by those Canadians designated through government studies and programs and media exposés as "poor." One important consequence with which this essay deals is the emergence of "militant poor people's groups" throughout Canada. These groups are composed of lower income people who, through the organizations they have formed, mount wide-ranging campaigns to request and, if necessary, to demand greater opportunities for themselves and other "poor" Canadians, and better treatment from the institutions of the larger society with which they must continuously deal, for example, the agencies concerned with public welfare, manpower, and unemployment insurance. The adjective "militant" is offered by members of such groups themselves to denote both their anger and frustration and their willingness, if necessary, to confront representatives of the larger society through picketing and sit-ins to make headway in their cause.

THE CAREER OF THE MILITANT POOR PERSON

This essay describes how a low income individual becomes a militant poor person. My theoretical perspective will focus upon the low income individual as he or she progresses through a sequence of stages from a period prior to any contact with militant groups to a full participation and identification with such groups. In focusing on these stages, I will stress the interrelationships between three factors: (1) the impact of the larger society on low income individuals and militants, in particular with respect to the labelling of some people in society as "poor" and the provision of anti-poverty programs; (2) the changing organizational affiliations of individuals who eventually become militant; and (3) the change in self-conception (identity) that occurs in these individuals and how it relates to participation in militant poor people's groups. I shall attempt to account for the variance in the degree of militancy and/or the perception of what action is needed to combat poverty by specifying what I believe to be crucial differences in the stages of different individuals and groups.

The general theoretical framework utilized above is usually known as symbolic interactionism.[2] The sequence of progression culminating in full participation and identification with a group and its activity is termed a "career."[3] Henceforth we will simply refer to the career(s) of the militant poor person. This symbolic interactionist perspective stresses the acquisition of categories of thought and action and their social supports which guide individuals in their relations with the world in which they live. In short, we are examining the process of a particular variety of consciousness formation in one sector of the population. It should be stressed that such a perspective makes no attribution of "deviance" or "abnormality" to the type of behaviour under investigation. The perspective would be employed in an identical way if one wanted to understand how a young person becomes a "good student" (assuming agreement could be reached on the meaning of "good") or some other social identity. The logic of this perspective, then, is that whether some activity is "deviant" lies not with the activity itself, but rather with the interaction between that activity and institutions or individuals in the larger society who desire to designate such behaviour as deviant.

Research Strategy

The data for this analysis comes from a number of sources. Between 1966 and the present, I have been involved in varying degrees with a number of militant poor people's groups, first in the United States and then (since 1969) in Canada. I stress the world "involved" because my relationship with these groups has been, and is, one of co-operation and assistance rather than a perhaps more typical one of researcher/ subject. I have never made a formal study of militants. It is highly questionable whether anyone offering his or her formal credentials could ever gain the access and trust needed for any worthwhile research. Furthermore, my own values are such that I would not have considered it proper simply to study these people – many of whom became friends – even if it had been possible. I saw and still see my role as someone with certain skills that might be of use to a group of individuals whose cause is in general agreement with my own values. For this reason, some might consider my data "impressionistic." The sources used in this analysis include:

1. A file of materials produced by various individual members of such groups, for example, letters, position papers, etc.
2. Group position papers, newspapers, newsletters.
3. Hundreds of conversations I have had with different members of different groups at various stages in their individual careers.
4. My own observations of dozens of meetings that I have attended.
5. Discussions with individuals who have either never joined such groups and refuse to do so, or have joined and then dropped out.

Despite the lack of systematic evidence, I feel that the data collected provide a basis upon which to build some provisional explanation of participation in such groups.

The purposes of this discussion are three fold. First, as a sociologist, I am interested in systematically comprehending as much of the social world as possible. Groups such as the militant poor peoples' have become rather numerous social phenomena in the last few years and thus have become an object of professional investigation. Secondly, the public seems to have a great many misconceptions about militant low income groups and the people who are most active in them. For example, lack of proper motherly concerns has been imputed to female participants and laziness and drunkenness to male participants. This analysis serves the purpose of debunking such conceptions and of providing a provisional characterization of the values and concerns of participants. Thirdly, some argue that the movement of militant poor people has reached a crisis point: it has not attempted to make the fundamental changes in society that these critics say are necessary to overcome poverty. Additionally, many people are withdrawing from such groups. An understanding of how people become members of these groups may allow us to make some useful comments about this alleged crisis.

The reader will note a certain tension between the three purposes to which this analysis is addressed. The second and third are decidedly partisan, while the first appeals to the supposedly neutral goal of understanding for its own sake. I do not wish to digress into a discussion of "neutrality" as an axiom of social research at this point. I do wish the reader to note that the researcher is trying to understand as a sociologist a set of social processes while offering general support to the cause being examined. I would argue that it is only through one's commitment as a sociologist that the attempt does not regress into a polemical muddle in which questions of fact and interpretation become buried under harangue and conjecture.[4]

Stages in the Career of a Militant Poor Person:

The process of becoming a militant poor person can be broken down into four stages for a majority of the participants:

1.   The non-affiliated low income citizen stage.
2.   The stage of initial contact with an on-going citizen's group (or a group of individuals in the process of forming one).
3.   The stage of participation in group activities without identification with the group.
4.   The participation and identification stage.

Each of these steps is a necessary but not a sufficient condition for the succeeding one. The term "career contingency" is used to specify the conditions upon which passage from one stage to another depends.

Some members of militant groups do not fit as readily into the four stage career. After we examine the "typical" career, we will develop some alternate career patterns which also lead to participation and identification with militant groups.

1. The non-affiliated, low income citizen

Large sectors of the Canadian population have incomes insufficient to acquire a "minimally acceptable standard of living"[4] as determined by nutritionists, economists, and other formulators of government policy. Depending upon how one defines this standard, the number of Canadians below it range from a low of four to a high of nine and one-half million people.[5] People below such a standard are officially designated as "poor" and singled out for various anti-poverty programs.

Eventual participants in militant citizen's groups are not drawn equally from all parts of this "poor" population. A majority of eventual participants are either welfare recipients, usually women with young children, or individuals with physical limitations that restrict the type of work they can perform, most often middle-aged and elderly males. Individuals working full time at the minimum wage, which still places them below the poverty standard, participate infrequently in such groups, even though estimates usually suggest that these people compose around 60 per cent of those designated as "poor."[6]

There are a number of reasons for this over-representation in some categories of "poor." The fear – real or imagined – of losing one's job as a result of participation serves as an important determinant. Another reason for the under-representation of the so-called working poor is the unwillingness of many such individuals to identify themselves as poor. Numerous opinion poll studies[7] suggest that a very high percentage of low income, full-time employees earning wages which place them below poverty standards simply reject the label "poor" in describing themselves. Rather, they perceive themselves as working class or ordinary workers. My own experiences support these findings. Low income workers with whom I have discussed possible participation in militant groups, while not nearly as hostile as some commentators have suggested,[8] have frequently expressed the opinion that such groups are not organized for people like themselves, but rather for "poor people," such as welfare recipients, the physically disabled, and the elderly. There is, of course, a self-fulfilling process at work here. As few employed people join initially, there is little inclination within the group to advance causes that assist the low income employee, except in a very general way. This result tends to reinforce the original perception that such groups are set up for "somebody else."

A further limit to participation by low income workers is the practical constraint of little available free time. During the day, employed workers are at work; consequently, evenings are the only time left for social activities. While groups normally have general meetings in the evening, many activities occur during the day. This is particularly true of protest activities. The reason for this is quite obvious – those institutions of the larger society which are the object of protests – for example, welfare offices, schools, and manpower centers – are open only during the day. On numerous occasions I have seen employed people gradually cease to participate because of what they said was an inability to keep up with what the group was doing and to influence its strategy and general outlook because the informal decision making was occurring during the afternoons. Since these afternoons were also the crucial socializing times where friendships were established and informal prestige and influence emerged, employed people saw themselves as giving up their only free time to organizations in which they felt increasingly isolated.

There are other reasons why welfare recipients and the unemployed should constitute a majority. During the late 1960s a large number of attempts were made by social workers to organize welfare recipients. The war on poverty in the United States and its spillover into Canada[9] and the partly independent development of *animation sociale*[10] as a philosophy of community participation and development in Quebec provided the major intellectual rationale for this effort. Welfare recipients were selected as the object of organization because of their numerous attempts to organize themselves in order to redress grievances and because of a sense of moral outrage on the part of social workers at the conditions of welfare assistance.

If one were to summarize in a phrase the various life styles of individuals in their pre-militant life, it would be "individualized coping." By the term "life style," I mean the hopes and fears – limited and grand, present and future – as well as the strategies – individual and collective – available for realizing or preventing them. "Individualized coping" refers to a mode of existence in which only very limited resources can be allocated to future goals because of a routine succession of everyday crises which must continuously be conquered, usually without any outside assistance. Mrs. P. provides her own description:

> You were always moving from one disaster to the next. Your assistance check didn't come, the radio or television would break down, the plumbing would go, the grocery store wouldn't give you credit, somebody was getting sick, the family allowance check was a couple of days late and you didn't have any money or food in the house.... You didn't have anyone to turn to either. Maybe a friend or two but she usually had the same things happening you did.... I remember wanting to take a training program but I never had the time or energy.

With meagre financial resources, day to day existence becomes a delicate juggling act between assistance checks – a balancing act constantly being disturbed by a new and unexpected complication.

Although a great deal of one's time must be spent handling these routine emergencies, large amounts of idle time remain for reflecting about the future. Despite accusations in the media about welfare recipients being relatively content with their status and income (the "lazy bum" syndrome) and some social scientists deploring the lack of future orientation[11] of many low income people, the overwhelming majority of welfare recipients who participate in citizen's groups desired to vacate public assistance even from their first admission to it. According to the present leader of one citizen's group:

> There is hardly anyone who ever wants to stay on welfare. The people from the agency [welfare] pretty often treat you with contempt as if you weren't human same as them.... They [welfare] don't really try to help you off either.

Some of the ways in which they hoped to leave welfare were through acquiring a full-time job or at least training, getting married, or going back home. The routinization of crises, however, severely limited the opportunities for acquiring training, a job, or even for meeting new people from whom a husband could be found. Welfare agencies and to a certain extent manpower training programs, do not attempt to provide any institutional support for moving into the labour force. The lack of child care facilities, elaborate red tape surrounding entrance into re-training schemes, and the failure to integrate such training into the labour force demand—all operate to make movement into the labour force difficult.*

Those who are elderly or physically disabled also cope in the individualized fashion as described above. In these cases as well, financial payments are markedly insufficient to allow individuals or families to live at a level anywhere near the poverty standard. Many – including the retired – desire to gain jobs or training to allow some degree of employment to augment their meagre pensions. The lack of institutional support thwarts their aspirations.

Further problems arise because boredom and isolation often accompany economic hardship. In the words of Mr. C., a partially disabled labourer:

> Not only didn't I have anywhere enough money, I didn't see anybody any more. After I got hurt, I saw some of the guys for a while, but they stopped coming. I just used to sit around all day being moody and then mad . . . I had the Mrs. and that's all.

With no one to talk to and unfilled time, feelings of self-pity, sadness, and guilt all emerge. As Mrs. N. said:

> You start feeling sorry for yourself and feeling somehow or other it's your fault things are the way they are. I guess you don't really believe it but there it is.

Essentially, these individuals see themselves as blameless, as victims of circumstances beyond their control. However this conception is often difficult to maintain because of the lack of organized support from others.

The image that emerges from this brief portrait of the future activist is that of an isolated, frustrated individual, unhappy with his (her) status of welfare recipient, unemployed or retired person. This unhappiness results from the insufficient income attached to the status and from the "demeaning" treatment from the institutions that confirm the status. The unhappiness of the welfare recipient is also the result of his acceptance of a set of general societal values which stereotype welfare as an unacceptable status. According to these values, welfare should be limited to absolute emergencies and be brief in duration. Furthermore, even the "legitimate" need to receive such aid implies a certain amount of personal failure. Acceptance of such values merely aggravates an already frustrating situation.

* See S. Arnopolois, *THE MONTREAL STAR*, February 1-15, 1971 for an exposé of Canadian Manpower Training in Montreal and its lack of support for people with lower incomes, desiring to move into the labour force or to upgrade themselves. Such exposés exist from other parts of the country as well.

2. Contact with militant group

The portrait of the future activist that has been developed does not appear to differ significantly from the countless descriptions of welfare recipients, unemployed workers, and low income pensioners completed in recent years.[12] It is the second stage – developing contact with an ongoing group or participating in the formation of a new group – which begins to differentiate militants from other low income individuals. Since the processes involved in contacting on-going groups and establishing new ones are rather different, it is useful to discuss each in turn.

Individuals make contact with on-going militant groups in a variety of ways. A frequent occurrence is the accidental meeting of a group member and a non-affiliated person. Residential proximity or use of the same laundromat or corner store are frequent reasons for such meetings. A friendship may develop and through this initial contact, the non-affiliated individual meets other friends of the new acquaintance, who are likely to be group members as well. Before groups become widely known, initial contact is predominantly of this informal kind.

If the group has been well publicized (usually through word of mouth and newspaper stories), initial contact may occur as a result of the individual seeking assistance for some particular problem, or, in rarer cases, through referral by some social service agency to which the individual has gone for assistance. People typically seek out such groups with some reluctance. Often the group is solicited only after all other remedies to the problem have failed. The major reason for such reluctance is that individuals at this stage in their career see militant group members as "rabble rousers" and "hollerers" flaunting the fact that they are poor while receiving public assistance. In one person's words:

> [I was always told] . . . if you're poor and you have to go on assistance, you don't announce it, you try to hide it.

Such groups seemingly represent a challenge to the identity the individual has developed to neutralize any stigma attached to receiving assistance, being unemployed, or being poor. The magnitude of this challenge is all the greater since the identity of a "blameless" individual is often mixed with guilt and is without significant social support because of isolation.

A professional service agency refers people to militant groups only under fairly specific conditions. One condition is that the group must have a reputation for being able to provide certain kinds of "responsible" assistance. For example, some groups undertake "food drives" in which free food is solicited from supermarkets and individuals and is then distributed to emergency cases. The media usually publicize such activities widely. The second condition is the existence of sympathetic workers in the social agency, who work in close co-operation with such groups and actively encourage referrals.

Some individuals never go through this process of locating militant groups. Rather, they are involved from the beginning in their creation. A citizen's group more often initially resembles a service group rather than a militant one. The typical process of group formation involves a small number of citizens getting together to provide information for their mutual benefit or to publicize to the larger society some difficulty they cannot overcome. The following account is not unusual:

> There were four or five of us living in the building. The landlord never did anything. I remember it was in February when the furnace quit. We [the people in the building] weren't friends or anything but we all had this problem because we lived in the same building. We tried everything any of us could think of and finally somebody thought we should call the newspaper and try to hold a press conference to show people our problem. Somebody said they'd heard that had once worked for somebody else. You know, we'd tell everybody about who the landlord was and maybe he'd fix things.

At this stage, those involved usually do not think of themselves as a group or organization. In many cases, the idea of a group is suggested by the media. The man quoted above, for example, recalled that his first recognition that the individuals in the building might constitute a group was when the reporter from the press asked what the name of his "group" was! A good many community groups have been born under similar conditions.

Not all groups emerge through the exclusive efforts of low income citizens. "Animators" or community organizers sometimes assist individuals in the founding and particularly in the development of an organization. Once citizens see themselves as a group, members usually wish to extend the horizons of the group. This is especially true if the difficulty for which the group was formed is resolved. Animators and community organizers are then sought out to assist them. As one individual described it:

> . . . we'd organized and won. I guess we knew that we'd won a battle through working together, but nobody knew what to do next.

Losing a battle may also serve as a catalyst to seek assistance from a community organizer. People often see themselves as needing more information and a greater knowledge of strategies in order to resolve a difficulty. New groups use a variety of means to secure the services of an organizer. Newspaper accounts, reporters, established groups, gossip networks, and social agencies are all tried.

The same reluctance displayed by those making first contact with established groups is also present among group founders. Such individuals seldom see themselves as militants. They see their activities as rational and informative, rather than disruptive and confronting. They are highly sensitive to being labelled irresponsible and even being known as poor to the society at large. In extreme cases, individuals ask reporters covering a story on them to delete the fact that they receive welfare or have only $100 a month to live on. While this reaction is unusual, a certain uneasiness is normally displayed because of their understanding and partial acceptance of the larger society's image of poor people as lacking incentive and being responsible for their own misfortunes.

3. Participation in the group without identification with it

To contact a group or to be present at its inception does not ensure that an individual will participate in subsequent group activities. What factors, then, explain continued participation in an on-going or emergent militant group?

In the case of an already established group, a variety of social processes operate to promote continued participation. The development of friendship ties often ensures that new-comers will at least attend meetings for a period of time. Mrs. D. recalled her reasons for attending one group's meetings:

> I guess I was curious even though I was uneasy about it too. I kept going to the general meetings because B＿＿ and M＿＿ [friends she had met who told her about the group] keep encouraging me to come.

An elderly man who had originally been referred to a group to solve a problem now looked forward to the card games and small talk that occurred after each meeting. This opportunity to develop friendships and to engage in social activities should not be underestimated.

Very frequently individuals who come to a group for assistance are encouraged to join. Since such groups often attempt to organize and mobilize as large a number of low income people as possible, attempts at proselytism are numerous. While many do not join as a result, a significant number do. It is not unusual for people who have been assisted to feel some obligation to the group – despite whatever uneasiness they may feel about it. Attendance at general meetings where they can learn something about the group without having to "protest" seems to them a reasonable way to fulfill the obligation.

Continued participation is made easier for the new recruit because of the stance many respectable institutions in the larger society take toward it. In an important sense, such institutions help to legitimize the group. The media, certain social service agencies, and middle-class service and church groups may play an important part. In fact, during the late 1960s and early 1970s, a good many newspapers took rather sympathetic postures towards militant groups.

Participation at this stage is limited to attending meetings and working for what are quite clearly "service" projects," such as assisting teachers or running emergency food depots. The new participant conceives of the group as essentially service oriented. Picketing and sit-ins are not participated in. Friendship ties, obligations felt toward the group, and the legitimacy conferred upon the group by reputable institutions allow the new-comer to continue participating without threatening his identity. As a matter of fact, the "blameless" conception begins to receive support because the group's ideology focuses on the social system, rather than on the individual, as the cause of the members' problems.

One important fear does remain in the minds of many new participants, however. This is the fear, particularly among younger individuals, that all of this activity will not help them personally to gain respectable livelihoods. Repeatedly the comments What will all this lead to? What's going to happen in four or five years? are uttered. If one were to describe the participant at this stage, he would be an individual grateful for the opportunity to do something, different, happy with new found friends, slightly wary of the group despite the legitimacy conveyed to it by reputable institutions, and, in some cases, concerned that his participation might not be directly related to improving economically his own life.

Individuals continue to participate in groups which they help to create for similar reasons. A set of social ties develops which the participants value and desire to maintain:

> The idea of getting together and planning something was really good for us. We got to know each other and like one another ... When we finished the first project I think all of us really wanted to do something more too.

The failure to resolve successfully the original problem that generated the group action often has little impact on whether people continue to participate. When asked why the group remained together after an attempt to get housing inspectors to visit their building failed, one person said,

> Getting the inspectors out here was important but it was also good that we got to know each other too.

In many cases favourable media coverage is a factor promoting continuation of a newly formed group by extending the horizons of the participants:

> I never really thought we might be doing something important that could help anybody except us. Then I read the story they [the newspaper] did on us and they said that if we were successful we would help lots of other people too because we would show what people could do.

4. Participation and identification with a militant poor group

In the final stage of the career of the militant poor person, he (or she) comes to conceive of himself as both a "militant" and a "poor person" without any feelings of guilt. As with the preceding stages, the process of identification with an on-going group is presented separately from the process transforming an emergent group into a militant one.

Before a new member becomes a militant, he must come to see the need for militancy in securing better treatment from the institutions and individuals with whom he interacts as a low income citizen. "Militancy" is a belief that it is often necessary and legitimate to confront institutions and individuals with media exposés and such socially obtrusive tactics as picketing, sit-ins, and boycotts to secure their assistance. To be convinced of the need for militancy, the individual must personally experience additional difficulties which apparently demand militancy in order to be overcome. One woman described how she came to see the necessity of militancy:

> My youngest daughter had been sick and the doctor said she had to have a special high protein supplement. I was also told [by the pharmacist] that needy mothers [social welfare] would cover it. I went down and asked them. They said it would be covered and then two days later they changed their mind and said no. I asked them over and over why and they wouldn't tell me. I called the doctor and he said there was nothing he could do. I told some of the people I knew here [in the group]. They went down to the office with the press and some picket signs and I got the protein a day and a half later.

Accepting the necessity to act militantly propels the individual into greater group participation and disarms him of some of his earlier uneasiness. An elderly pensioner commented:

> I had always thought of people like this [group members] as rowdies. I came to see that I was more like them and they more like me. What they did they had a purpose for.

The social distance between individual and group is reduced. This sense that the group is really "more like me" is the base upon which full participation and identification are constructed. The result is that the individual is likely to attend a much larger number of group activities – including perhaps a few militant actions – then previously.

This extended participation introduces the individual to the particular beliefs and rules guiding the group. Much of this subculture is known previously, but it now takes on an added relevance for the participant. Most of the general beliefs are not new. They are usually ones the new participant has always wanted to believe, but has lacked the social support to do so. Most important is the belief that difficulties an individual may have in supporting self or family are not his or her fault, but rather are due to the lack of assistance available from help-oriented institutions. Such a belief now has strong support. Not only does the new participant see many other people echo that belief, but his (her) own experiences as well confirm it. The belief that collective rather than individual initiative is needed is confirmed in the same way.

While the developing militant learns most of the group's general beliefs in an informal manner, other dimensions of the subculture, particularly organizational skills and the norms of confrontation, are learned in a much more structured context in the more "mature" citizen's groups. The two most common devices for learning such things are leadership and confrontation classes. Leadership classes are regularly scheduled meetings in which new members learn what the purposes of the group are, why the general meetings are conducted along parliamentary rules of order, and why committees are created, and in which verbal and behavioural skills for building and maintaining an organization are demonstrated. Confrontation classes are rehearsals for militant actions where tactics are discussed, spokesmen are chosen, and various reactions by the institution to be confronted are considered. Role playing is frequently used in such meetings. The teachers are professionally trained community organizers and local group leaders who have previously developed such skills.

While it is possible for the new participant to acquire empathy for the group, it is only through participation in an action that he/she can come to be recognized as a fellow member by the other participants. The "action" is the organized act of collective protest which is directed against some individual or institution to secure a demand. It is the practical test of the beliefs upon which the group is based. An action is many things: a gala party, a serious pragmatic struggle with power, a gallant crusade against the forces of evil – or all simultaneously. Many emotions are mixed together: fear, excitement, happiness, sorrow. All the rehearsals, which stress the need for solidarity, patience, and co-operation, never prepare one for the first effort. A veteran militant described her experience of an action in this way:

Of course, you always remember your first action. I had been hanging around for a couple of months helping with some of the projects. People had asked me to go on a couple of actions, but I had declined, even though I was curious. Maybe I was a little uneasy too. Everyone is. . . . Anyway I finally decided to go to one. We were at an unemployment insurance office. There were about fifty of us to demand that a poor, disabled man get some back checks which were clearly his due. We were all in this one big room. They called the police and maybe fifteen or twenty showed up. I was really tense and scared. I wanted to leave but the police were standing in the only exit. Muriel [a veteran] gave me a reassuring glance. After an hour, the police left and told us we could stay there for the rest of the day. We started hugging and shaking hands. Some people got up and did a dance. Somebody went out to get some food and soft drinks and we had a party in the room. We had already elected a negotiation committee and they went in to talk while we stayed in the room. It took two days, but we won . . . it was such a beautiful feeling to see everybody acting together. We had been told by the organizers and the veterans that that was how it worked, but you really had to sense it to understand it. . . . It was fun and we won.

As an individual begins to lose his (or her) rookie status by participating in more actions, he sees clear indicators of group acceptance; for example, he may be nominated for committees, have opinions asked on matters of importance to the group, be invited to parties by people other than his initial friends, and even be asked to watch out for a fledgling participant at his first action. Although from time to time the individual may still be tempted to leave the group, the realization of the social costs of doing so practically prevents it. All of his friends and most of his energies are focused on the group. What meaning in life he has is now defined through participation in the group.

The acceptance accorded militant behaviour by institutions of the larger society plays a supportive function in the continuing activities of the group in the same ways indicated in stage 3: for example, media sympathy, service agency assistance and referral, and government funding both to undertake service projects (funds from OFY LIP, and Horizons) and to develop action workshops for refining techniques of protest (CYC funding).

Once one has come to see oneself as a militant (and has this perception supported by other militants), there is no longer great difficulty in accepting the label "poor person" both privately and publicly. The reason for this is simply that the guilt formally associated with the label no longer exists for the individual. Support exists for a very different connotation of "poor person." If someone calls one a "poor person," it reflects pride, not guilt. As one elderly man said:

I guess I never really thought very much about it. The main reason I never wanted to be known as a poor person is because people are always implying, no matter how much better they mean, that it's somehow a little bit your fault. Nobody believes that in our group. I remember in one of the leadership courses we talked about terms that people called others which meant they were bad, even though they weren't and how some people took these terms as a sign of pride. Like the blacks in the South in the U.S. That's like us. We're poor and we're angry and trying to do something about it. That isn't any reason to feel guilty. It's a reason to feel proud.

The Orientation of the Typical Militant to the Larger Society

What values does the militant poor person share with the larger society? What changes would he (or she) make in the organization of society? What are his (her) hopes and desires for the future? The answers to these questions are of more than passing interest. They will allow us to understand the direction(s) militants take in subsequent years.

Thus far I have presented only two general beliefs guiding such people – the perception that institutions must be confronted to be made receptive to the wishes of their clients and the feeling that co-operation is important for the successful resolution of problems that affect individuals. Beyond these beliefs and their behavioural consequences, there is actually little that would distinguish militant from other low income people – or from the society at large, for that matter. They desire a job with sufficient income and, more importantly, an opportunity to do something important, a good education for their children, close and trusting friends, a vacation, and some control over their future. Insofar as there are differences it would be that they attach rather less importance to material gain and greater priority to doing something worthwhile and important. There is no indication that they are, to use a word fashionable today, "radical." Few desire to restructure fundamentally the society in which they live. Rather, they say they want it to work more humanely by providing adequate financial resources and decent treatment. Few possess any blueprint for what a future society should look like, let along how to achieve such a society. Rather, they see themselves performing modest day-to-day assistance to people in need, while periodically calling for a larger amount of society's wealth being directed towards those who need it.

This orientation should help us to understand the major direction that large numbers of militants are taking once they have become well known for their militancy. This direction is called, by members of groups, "militant service." By "militant service" is meant the development of extensive and permanent service projects, such as welfare information offices and emergency twenty-four hour switchboard centres, backed up by the threat of militant action towards the institutions formally responsible for solving these individual problems. Such programs are entirely consistent with what we have seen so far in militant groups. Providing assistance was an important incentive for joining. To many members, a group may reach a threshold where its reputation as militant is well enough known that greater and greater amounts of effort can be allocated to the provision of services. As one person put it:

> Although I admit there were some times when we looked forward to actions as a kind of party and maybe as the most important thing to the group, we knew all the time that there was a bigger reason for the action. It was to get assistance for someone. Demonstrating had to be done because those offices just wouldn't act as quickly and fairly as they should without the prodding. After a while, everyone knows that you'll demonstrate if you have to. You don't prove anything by it anymore. Most of us recognized that that was the time when we should really be doing things which needed to be done and which nobody else was doing – or weren't doing as well as we could. People had to have help and we could give it to them better . . . actions were unproductive after this, so we had fewer, only when our credibility was challenged.

It is not unusual now for groups to become intensely involved in one or more service projects. Hundreds of hours are often expended on setting up and securing funds to operate them. Organizations petition local service agencies and various levels of government for funding to start such projects. This solicitation may be done quite politely – or, particularly if the agency or level of government refuses, not so politely. To date, funds have been readily available from these sources, and, given the general attitude of the federal government, it appears reasonable to suppose that some such funding will be available indefinitely.

A high demand for these kinds of services exists in most low income communities. Once word gets around, most projects are likely to be able to operate at a brisk place. It is not long before the staff of such projects begin to see them as a permanent part of the local social structure. The recognition that such activity might actually be permanent is very welcome to participants. It is the opportunity to do something important on a permanent basis – in the lexicon of both the militant group and the larger society, a "job." As such, it fills a great void with a predictable, responsible, and secure future, a need that has troubled participants of the group since their early days of association with it. (See discussion of Stage 3.)

Untypical-Militants: Two Variations

There are two types of individuals who are frequently found in militant poor people's groups who do not follow the "typical" career presented.

The first type is the former convict. These are younger men who have little opportunity for employment because of their previous criminal records. In two Canadian metropolitan areas at least, professional social workers dealing with the John Howard Society (a rehabilitation service for former prisoners) are also active as advisors to militant groups and encourage these young men to participate in the activities of the groups. Former prisoners appear much more willing to identify themselves as militant after a short amount of participation. Moreover, they display little uneasiness at accepting the label "poor" as well. Few labels are more damaging than that of being a former "con," and if one has learned to live with that label, to be identified as a poor person or even a militant one is not disturbing. Not infrequently, the leadership of groups is heavily composed of former convicts. One militant offered this reason:

> ... like J____. He's tough and doesn't flinch. He sometimes scares me. I guess that's what you learn if you are going to survive in prison. He's one of the best negotiators we have. Doesn't let them get away with anything, but he can also control himself, even when he might want to hit one. It's really hard. Sometimes you want to cry and others you want to hit them, but you can't really do either if you want to win.

The possibility of involvement in worthwhile service projects is particularly appreciated by such people since their record usually prevents their getting a job in which they can find any sense of pride.

The second untypical militant person is the part-time student. Some groups come to have a majority of their members comprised of students. My evidence suggests that students self-select themselves into such groups after they already consider themselves to be militant. Seldom does a student need to progress through the stages of the typical career. In addition to being militant, students are also likely to be, at least vocally, radical. Insofar as there is any attempt to provide explanations for the way society is constructed and any incitement to fundamentally restructure the social order, students tend to provide it. These students do have low incomes; many receive unemployment or welfare payments. Nevertheless, most other group members who are not students look upon them with mixed feelings of sympathy and skepticism, and sometimes with resentment. This attitude is conveyed by this not unusual comment:

Sometimes I think they're [students] playing a big game. All this talk about destroying capitalism. Maybe they're poor, but they won't always be. They're always talking about these grand things, nothing practical. Sometimes you also feel like a fool when you try to argue with them. I don't know whether it's on purpose or not but they . . . always wind up talking down to you in front of everybody. . . . But then they always turn out at the actions and there have been a few where we wouldn't have come out very well without them.

Militant Poor People and Social Change

Some observers as well as participants in militant groups have expressed displeasure with what they claim is the lack of fundamental change initiated by such groups. In the words of the harshest critics, these groups have "sold out" and become victims of "co-optation." It is puzzling that these critics ever held a view of militant poor people as some inevitable vanguard of fundamental institutional change (admittedly, part of the problem is the failure of these commentators to specify "fundamental" in clearer terms).

I have argued that the initial concerns of militants were much more modest. As groups formed and became militant, little encouragement was given to understanding the necessity for fundamental change let alone some strategies for achieving it. Any review of the literature on community action and *animation sociale*,[13] which provided the philosophical foundation and the storehouse of practical techniques that produced militancy, shows that there is a tremendous preoccupation with tactics and only an abstract reference to the ends toward which the tactics are applied. Is it surprising, then, that such militancy would be used to achieve immediate goals that a majority of the participants desired – relief from some immediate difficulty, an opportunity to do something important, or a predictable future. The availability of private and public funding was the final ingredient allowing militant activity to evolve into militant service.

A comment is also in order with respect to the charge of "co-optation." The term is meant pejoratively; it means the process whereby an institution or social system takes in elements which desire to alter it. It is said to be one-directional; that is, the "change elements" are subsumed by the organization without any impact on it. As a technical term in social science, however, "co-optation" is two-directional; it focuses not only on the drawing in of the sources of change, but also the impact this action has on the organization. In this latter sense, militant groups have indeed become co-opted into a system of organizational services directed toward low income citizens and neighbourhoods. In becoming part of this system they have also changed it in significant ways. More services are accessible to low income people; the quality of services has improved in many respects, and accountability is present where it never existed before. Whether one wants to call such changes fundamental is moot; no one would deny they have significance.

I would like to respond to the idea that the fragmentation of many militant groups is an indication of their failure to accomplish fundamental changes and the beginning of their demise. It is true that many individuals are leaving these groups. What appears to be happening, however, is that sub-groups, usually working on the same service project, are pulling out of the larger group because it has become too large, impersonal, and even bureaucratic. This response from a person who dropped out of a militant group with a membership of over two hundred illustrates the dilemmas many find in continuing to belong:

> It's so big now. There were only ten, fifteen when we started. I don't know very many people. It's hard to think of it as your group. . . . It's really impossible to get things done. We have to go through three committees to get checks to pay our rent [for a store front] where we help people with housing.

What of the future? Unless the demand for such services diminishes, through saturation of neighbourhoods or drastic reform on the part of the large institutions, or money to build and maintain services is discontinued, or some long-run, articulated vision is developed which would provide a comprehensive strategy of wide-spread change, the present pattern can be expected to continue. Becoming militant has provided a class of people with the best opportunity for acquiring a sense of responsibility and importance which has been denied them in so many traditional ways.

Notes

[1] Federal and Provincial inquiries into the problems of the "needy" are recorded in public records as far back as 1763 in various archival sites.

[2] For a theoretical overview see: G. H. Mead, *Mind, Self and Society* (Chicago: University of Chicago Press, 1934); G. H. Mead, *The Philosophy of the Act* (Chicago: University of Chicago Press, 1938); E. Hughes, *Men and Their Work* (Glencoe: Free Press, 1958).

For an illustration using empirical information see H. S. Becker, *Outsiders: Studies in the Sociology of Deviance* (Glencoe: Free Press, 1963).

[3] The term is derived from the notion of an "occupational career." See H. S. Becker, ibid.

[4] *Poverty in Canada* (Ottawa: Information Canada, 1972), Section I. "The meaning of poverty."

[5] I. Adams, et al. *The Real Poverty Report* (Edmonton: Hurtig, 1972), Chapter I, "Counting the Poor."

[6] Ibid.

⁷ Gallup Polls results, as reported in various media, vary from 70 to 80 per cent.
⁸ For a review of this general position, see R. Hamilton, *Class and Politics in the United States* (New York: Wiley, 1973).
⁹ L. Draper, ed. *Citizen Participation: Canada* (Toronto: New Press, 1971).
¹⁰ F. Lesemann, *Animations Sociales au Québec* (Montreal: Les Presses de l'Université de Montréal, 1973).
¹¹ This is part of the "sub-cultural" perspective often associated with anthropological studies of poverty. See O. Lewis *La Vida* (New York: Random House, 1965).
¹² Numerous profiles of activists have appeared in newspapers across Canada as well as popular magazines such as *Chatelaine*.
¹³ See Saul Alinsky, *Reveille for Radicals* (New York: Random House, 1969) or *Rules for Radicals*, by the same author (New York: Random House, 1969). Other literature frequently cited is: W. Hagstrom, "The power of the poor" in I. Howe, ed., *Poverty: Views from the Left* (New York: New American, 1970); M. Bondin, "Animation sociale at the Conseil de Développement Social in Montreal" in J. Harp and J. Hofley, eds. *Poverty in Canada* (Toronto: Prentice-Hall, 1971); and F. Lesemann, *op. cit.*

Bibliography

Adams, Ian, *The Poverty Wall* (Edmonton: Hurtig, 1969).

———— et al. *The Real Poverty Report* Edmonton: Hurtig, 1972).

Alinsky, Saul, *Reveille for Radicals* (New York: Random House, 1969).

————, *Rules for Radicals* (New York: Random House, 1969).

Becker, Howard S. *Outsiders: Studies in the Sociology of Deviance* (Glencoe: Free Press, 1963).

Blondin, Michel, "Animation Sociale at the Conseil de Developpement Social in Montreal" in J. Harp and J. Hofley, eds., *Poverty in Canada* (Toronto: Prentice-Hall, 1971).

Draper, L., ed. *Citizen Participation: Canada* (Toronto: New Press, 1969).

Felt, Lawrence F. "Some problems in organizing welfare activist groups in Montreal: the case of the welfare broker," Paper given at the annual meeting of the *Canadian Association of Sociologists and Anthropologists*, St. Johns, Newfoundland, June, 1971.

Hughes, Everett. *Men and Their Work* (Glencoe: Free Press, 1958).

Hagstrom, Warren. "The power of the poor" in I. Howe, ed. *Poverty: Views from the Left* (New York: New American, 1970).

Harp, John and John Hofley, *Poverty in Canada* (Toronto: Prentice-Hall, 1971).

Lesemann, Frederic, *Animations Sociales au Québec* (Montreal: Les Presses de l'Université de Montreal, 1973).

Mead, George Herbert, *Mind, Self and Society* (Chicago: University of Chicago Press, 1934).

————, *The Philosophy of the Act* (Chicago: University of Chicago Press, 1938).

ACKNOWLEDGEMENTS

"On the Politics and Sociology of Stupidity in Our Society" – Reprinted with permission of Macmillan Publishing Co., Inc. from *The Other Side: Perspectives on Deviance* by Howard Becker. Copyright © The Free Press of Glencoe, a Division of Macmillan Publishing Co., Inc. 1964.

"On Being Sane in Insane Places" – Copyright 1973 by the American Association for the Advancement of Science. Reprinted by permission of the publisher and the author.

"White Collar Crime" – Reproduced by arrangement with Holt, Rinehart & Winston, Inc., New York, from *White Collar Crime*, by E. H. Sutherland, © 1961.

"Some of the Best People Smoke Pot" – Reprinted from *Maclean's*, January 1969, by permission of the publisher.

"My Case Against the RCMP" – Reprinted from *Maclean's*, July 1972, by permission of the publisher.

"Paranoia and the Dynamics of Exclusion" – Reprinted from *Sociometry*, Vol 25, by permission of the publisher, The American Sociological Association, and the author.

"Tim Crawford Meets the Mind Police" – Reprinted from *Saturday Night*, November 1972, by permission of the author.

"Memoirs of an Intermittent Madman" – Originally appeared in *Playboy Magazine*. Copyright 1972 by Carlton Brown. Reprinted by permission of the Harold Matson Company, Inc.

We are indebted to our colleagues, Berkeley Fleming and Richard Brymer, for their helpful suggestions and to Peter Pineo and Dean Saul Frankel for their generous support.